P9-BZK-869

The Power of Culture
Teaching Across Language Difference

edited by

ZEYNEP F. BEYKONT

Harvard Education Publishing Group

© 2002

Library of Congress Control Number 2002102113
ISBN 1-891792-03-2

Harvard Education Publishing Group
Harvard Graduate School of Education
8 Story Street, 5th Floor
Cambridge, MA 02138

Cover Art and Design: blondèl joseph
Editorial Production: Dody Riggs
Typography: Sheila Walsh

Dedication

I dedicate my work on this book to

Mel King

*and to all those who care and dare
to teach for social justice every day.*

Contents

Introduction

S ince 1965, the cultural fabric of the United States has been enriched by immigrants from Latin America, Asia, Africa, Eastern Europe, and the Middle East.[1] Classrooms are filled with students who represent varied cultural, ethnic, and national origins, speak 129 different languages at home, and have diverse religious, socioeconomic, and academic backgrounds. U.S. Census 2000 data show increasing linguistic diversity, particularly among school-age populations. About one in five students throughout the nation comes from a home in which a language other than English is spoken (Crawford, 2001a). By 2030, White native English speakers will constitute less than half of the U.S. student population (Macias, 2000).[2] While demographic shifts have altered the student population, the overwhelming majority of teachers in the United States are monolingual English speakers of European American heritage (Maxwell-Jolly & Gándara, this volume; McLeod, 1994; National Center for Education Statistics [NCES], 1995b). Teachers increasingly face the challenge of teaching students whose cultural and linguistic backgrounds are different from their own.

Commonly used demographic terms that lump students into broad groups, such as Latino, Asian, and Limited English Proficient (LEP), obscure the diversity within each language minority group. Some language minority students are born in the United States, and although they appear to be fluent in English they often do not do well in school and drop out at higher rates than their foreign-born peers (NCES, 1995a).[3] Others come to the United States and enter school when they are relatively young and have limited English skills. They are forced to use English to learn academic content and must acquire English fluency quickly in order to perform at grade level and participate in classroom activities (Fillmore, 1982). Language minority students who enter U.S. schools as teenagers after many years of rigorous education in their home country may have limited or no English proficiency, but they often have an easier time adjusting to school academically. Among their biggest challenges is learning English quickly and well in order to gain access to age-appropriate, rigorous classroom content (Kwong, 2000; Ruiz-de-Velasco & Fix, 2000). A growing number of teenagers arrive in U.S. schools having had only interrupted schooling in their home countries. These students must learn English and catch up academically within the few years remaining until their expected high school graduation (Farah, 2000; Friedman, this volume, ch. 6). Language minority students vary in the type of educational supports they need in school, depending on background factors including age, English fluency, and academic history.

Despite their diversity, language minority students encounter similar systemic obstacles that constrain their access to educational opportunities and inhibit their academic development in U.S. schools. They frequently attend segregated, crowded, underfunded urban schools that lack adequate educational resources and materials (NCES, 1997; Ruiz-de-Velasco & Fix, 2000; Uriarte, this volume). In these schools, few if any adults speak their language, represent their culture, or are prepared to teach across language difference (NCES, 1997; Macias, 1998; Maxwell-Jolly & Gándara, this volume).[4] Language minority students quickly discover that their home cultures and languages are viewed as deficient; early on, disproportionate numbers of language minority students find themselves relegated to remedial, low-track, or special education classes and excluded from the challenging courses that are required for high school graduation and eventual college enrollment (Beykont, 2000; Mehan, Villanueva, Hubbard, & Lintz, 1996; Oakes, 1985; Rice & Walsh, 1996; Stefanakis, 2000; Tomlinson, 1999; Wheelock, 1990). Generally, the curriculum does not reflect their daily experiences outside of school and classroom activities do not build on their culturally based knowledge (Berriz, 2000, this volume; Nielsen & Beykont, 1997). Designed for a homogeneous, White, middle-class, native English-speaking student population, schools rarely adjust to language minority students; these students are left on their own to understand what is expected of them, to learn the appropriate ways of thinking and expressing thought in school, and to draw connections and bridge discontinuities between their experiences at home and what they learn at school (Heath, 1983; Mehan,

1979; Tharp & Galimore, 1988). Due to these myriad systemic problems and the absence of sustained pedagogical supports, language minority students tend to underperform in U.S. schools.

The educational experiences of language minority students are
also influenced by a generally conservative and anti-immigrant political climate.[5] Demographic projections that no ethnic group will be a
numerical majority in the near future have prompted concerns about
the status of English as the dominant U.S. language and English
monolingualism as the norm. On the policy front, legislators and public opinion have embraced the English Only movement, which seeks
to have English adopted as the official language of the United States
and to curtail the use of other languages in government and public
services, including schools (Beykont, 2000; Crawford, 1992a, 1992b,
2000; Macedo, 2000). Ultimately, the movement aims to institutional-
ize the cultural, linguistic, and economic power and privileges currently enjoyed by native speakers of English. Leaders of the movement
argue that bilingual services and schooling are communicating the
wrong message — that is, that people can survive without English language skills. In order to give immigrants the incentive to learn English
quickly, the movement urges that the use of other languages in government and education be banned. They maintain that public funds
should not be spent on bilingual programs that are not efficient in
teaching English because these programs are sidetracked by the "competing" goal of teaching students in their native languages.[6] In short,
political currents have eliminated educational programs and services
designed to address language minority students' particular linguistic
and academic needs.

In the past two decades, twenty-three states across the country
passed laws in support of the English Only movement.[7] Most recently,
Arizona voted for a restrictive English Only law (Proposition 203) that
bans bilingual instruction (Crawford, 2001b). This new law limits
school services for language minority students to a one-year structured
immersion program that includes English as a Second Language (reading, writing, speaking, and grammar) and content-based English instruction. While mixing students from different language groups and
age levels for English instruction is allowed, using students' native languages for educational purposes is strictly prohibited.[8] The net impact
of the English Only movement is that it puts pressure on schools and
teachers to rush language minority students into mainstream class-

rooms before they have a chance to develop English proficiency or grade-level competencies. Thus, along with the demographic shifts, the student composition of mainstream classrooms has been altered by changes in language policies and social attitudes. Mainstream teachers are responsible for language minority students who used to be the responsibility of language specialists.

Language minority students find themselves rushed into mainstream classes at a time when nationwide reform efforts are aiming to meet rigorous academic standards. Widescale assessment, accountability for student performance, teacher preparation, and instructional quality are key to the success of standards-based educational reforms (DiCerbo, 2000; Menken, 2000; Rice & Walsh, 1996). Federal laws require that states articulate curricular and performance standards that strictly define what students graduating from each grade should know and be able to do. States are mandated to adopt standardized tests that are aligned with their curriculum standards and to use test results to determine decisions on grade retention and high school graduation. The high-stakes nature of test outcomes are designed to motivate school districts, schools, and teachers to teach all students to the statewide standards and provide extra assistance to low-achieving students. Unfortunately, only a small percentage of teachers are prepared to teach across language difference, and the overwhelming majority of teachers do not have certification or any relevant training in working with language minority students (Macias, 1998; Menken & Antunez, 2001).[9] Within a high-stakes educational context, mainstream teachers are accountable for the performance of language minority students whom they are not prepared to teach.

The Power of Culture: Teaching Across Language Difference brings together studies on the education of language minority students in mainstream classrooms. The book focuses particularly on three key issues of educational reform — high-stakes assessment, classroom instruction, and teacher preparation — as they relate to teaching a diverse student body to challenging academic standards. *The Power of Culture* starts with the premise that it is unrealistic to expect language minority students to succeed with no extra supports in an educational system that was designed for a homogeneous, native English-speaking student population. Educational policies, public schools, and teacher preparation programs should be remodeled to respond to the needs of language minority students and provide teachers with the professional supports they need to help these students succeed. *The Power of Culture* does not directly address whether mainstream classrooms offer the best educational option for language minority students, because the fact is that large numbers of these students *are* in mainstream classrooms. This volume instead examines the pedagogical and political supports necessary to provide a high-quality education to language minority students in mainstream classrooms.

As an experienced researcher in the field of language minority education, I compiled this book based on my view that an essential principle of successful teaching across language difference lies in recognizing and utilizing the power of culture: the power of students' home cultures and the power of the mainstream school culture. Schools currently neither teach the mainstream school culture nor capitalize on students' home cultures, thereby doubly limiting the academic development of language minority students (Baratz & Baratz, 1970; Delpit, 1995; Heath, 1983). Students' home cultures, native languages, and ways of thinking and communicating thoughts are often treated as obstacles to their learning the mainstream culture and impediments to their academic development (Cazden, 1988; Gonzalez, 1975; Ruiz, 1984; Sue & Padilla, 1992). Native English-speaking students enjoy power and privileges that language minorities do not, and, in an education system that was designed by and for them, they constitute the invisible norm to which all students are expected to measure up (Delpit, 1988, 1995; Giroux, 1988, 1992). To succeed in school and later in society, language minority students are pressured to abandon their home cultures and adopt the mainstream culture. Yet, schools do not systematically teach students the norms, beliefs, and expectations of the mainstream culture, such as patterns of academic language communication and rules of participation that are typical of U.S. classrooms (Baratz-Baratz, 1970; Delpit, 1986, 1988, 1995; Heath, 1983; Mehan, 1979). Consequently, language minority students are being stripped of their cultures, languages, and funds of knowledge, yet are not gaining access to the mainstream school culture. Success in teaching across language difference lies in capitalizing on students' home cultures and explicitly teaching the mainstream culture.

The Power of Culture offers a comprehensive analysis of challenges faced by language minority students and their teachers in the current educational reform context and presents concrete examples of how the principle of utilizing the power of culture has been adopted successfully in some mainstream classrooms and teacher education programs. The book is organized into three parts. Part One sets the policy context in which language minority students and their teachers are working. The authors in Part One focus on current standards-based reforms and policy changes as they relate to the education of language minority students. Specifically, they discuss research conducted in Massachusetts, Texas, and California that reveals the disproportionately negative impact on language minority students of the narrow reform focus on high-stakes tests and the inadequate preparation of teachers to teach across language difference.

In Part Two, researchers report on studies of effective pedagogy conducted in K–12 mainstream classrooms that serve students from a variety of cultural, educational, and immigrant backgrounds. Included are vivid descriptions of classrooms that exemplify the art and science of teaching language minority students to high standards using the power of culture. The first three chapters profile the teaching of English literacy and the academic skills that are highly valued in the mainstream culture. They focus on seventh-grade Somali literacy students developing academic writing skills; on first- through fourth-grade elementary school students from Spanish-speaking homes who are developing reading skills; and on third-grade Cambodian students learning to read. The final chapter in Part Two reports on observations of mainstream teachers who recognize the power of students' home cultures and make a conscious effort to link academic knowledge, community knowledge, a standards-based curriculum, and student experiences outside of school. The examples are drawn from several classroom settings, including an elementary social studies classroom in which students of Cape Verdean, African, Puerto Rican, and Chinese heritage are gaining academic English skills; a middle school English writing classroom serving literacy students from Guatemala, the Dominican Republic, and El Salvador who arrived in the United States with no literacy skills in either English or Spanish; and a high school classroom in which students from Spanish- and English-speaking homes are studying health science.

Part Three of the book addresses issues and challenges involved in preparing teachers to teach successfully across language difference. Authors' descriptions of program development efforts and interviews they conducted with preservice and practicing teachers reveal the goals, fundamental program elements, and professional supports that teacher preparation programs can provide. The first chapter identifies qualities of successful teachers of language minority students that inform the design of teacher preparation programs. The final two chapters focus on the promises and challenges of developing two specific teacher education programs.

Educational Reforms and Language Minority Students

Nationwide standards-based reform efforts have sought to improve academic standards, increase accountability for student achievement, and enhance teacher quality (H. Res. 1804, 1994; H. Res. 1, 2001). Placing rhetorical emphasis on equity and excellence, standards-based reforms aim to enhance the quality of education for all students and reduce the achievement disparities among ethnic, linguistic, and socioeconomic groups (DiCerbo, 2000; Menken, 2000; Menken & Holmes, 2000). Many states have adopted challenging curricular and performance standards, and standardized assessments are used to verify that students are reaching these learning goals — including language minority students. School districts, schools, and teachers are held accountable for the measurable progress of all students on standardized tests. Accountability for student progress is reinforced by sanctions and rewards. Schools face monetary sanctions and possible closure if student performance goals are not met and if low-achieving students fail to show measurable progress. Students also face sanctions in that low test scores result in grade retention and denial of a high school diploma.

Federal legislation has also prioritized improving teacher quality and provided funds for states to enhance preservice teacher preparation, increase accreditation standards, and focus in-service professional development activities on effective research-based teaching approaches (H. Res. 1, 2001). High-quality preservice teacher preparation and ongoing professional development activities are expected to help teachers incorporate the statewide curricular frameworks, align their curriculum and instruction with the standardized tests, and gain the "knowledge and skills needed to teach an increasingly diverse student population with a variety of educational, social, and health needs" (H. Res. 1804, 1994, p. 2). Thus, in theory, the standards-based reform efforts place equal emphasis on the principles of equity and excellence in public education and propose comprehensive measures to educate all students, including language minority students, to high standards. This vision, however, remains more a promise than a reality.

In implementation, reforms focus narrowly on high-stakes tests prior to addressing the broad range of constraints to language minority students' academic progress, such as inadequate teacher preparation and lack of student access to challenging academic content. The authors in Part One document a grim reality: language minority students are adversely affected by the narrow focus on high-stakes tests. Drawing from their research in Massachusetts, Texas, and California, these authors demonstrate that in the rush to reach educational excellence, the equity goal is being undermined. While there has been improvement in student test scores on average, a large percentage of language minority students are failing high-stakes tests, being retained in grade, and dropping out of school. If current policies stay in effect, most of these students will leave high school without a diploma.

Miren Uriarte addresses the history of inequitable treatment of Latino students in substandard urban schools and the current standards-based reform efforts in Massachusetts. These reform efforts were originally intended to improve learning standards and alter the disproportionate failure of minority students by taking measures such as redistributing funding across urban and suburban schools, establishing higher standards for teacher certification, providing professional development for teachers already in the system, instituting accountability based on multiple measures of student performance over time, and encouraging school-based decisionmaking and parent participation. Yet leadership changes in the state government and the state board of education led to a shift in reform focus. The most notable shift was the board's decision to require that all public school students pass a tenth-grade test in math, science, and English-language arts in order to graduate from high school; failing any section of the test means that a student cannot graduate.

The first three rounds of high-stakes testing in Massachusetts resulted in low scores for all students. Language minority students and students of color scored particularly poorly. For example, in 2000, 45 percent of all tenth graders, 79 percent of Latino students, 78 percent of LEP students, and 77 percent of African American students failed the math portion of the tenth-grade test (these results actually reflected an *improvement* over the previous two years). Based on analyses of scores and dropout rates over time, Uriarte estimates that under current conditions 75 to 80 percent of racial minority and language minority students in Massachusetts will not be able to graduate from high school in 2003. She concludes by recommending that reform efforts focus on providing the necessary supports and resources to educate language minority students to high standards. Uriarte asserts that penalizing the students for the system's persistent failure to respond to their academic needs is unacceptable, a critique that has relevance far beyond the borders of Massachusetts.

Texas has received national attention as a model of standards-based education reform based on claims that the state's school districts had raised scores, reduced the achievement gap between Whites and minorities on statewide standardized tests, lowered dropout rates, and improved student performance on the National Assessment of Educational Progress (NAEP). Walt Haney shows that the Texas success story is mostly an illusion when closer attention is paid to minority student achievement and enrollment data. He argues that the so-called improvements are due to a systematic exclusion of low-achieving students from taking the tenth-grade high-stakes test, the Texas Assessment of Academic Skills (TAAS), which students need to pass in order to leave high school with a diploma. His longitudinal analyses of TAAS scores, dropout rates, retention data, and special education placement rates demonstrate that, since the onset of educational reforms in Texas, more minority students have been retained, more have been placed in special education classes, and more have dropped out of school. Ninth-grade retention rates in Texas are well beyond the national average, and dropout rates today are actually higher than the dropout rates before education reform was implemented: 30 percent of all students and 40 percent of minority students do not graduate from high school.

Haney concludes that it is deceptive to base the evaluation of educational reform efforts on only one form of evidence, such as standardized test scores. While there has been an apparent increase in student scores on the TAAS over the past decade, it is not clear that this increase reflects improved student learning. If rising scores on statewide standardized tests were a true reflection of improved student learning, then that improvement would be duplicated on national tests such as the SAT or Texas college readiness tests, but this has not occurred. He cautions that in high-stakes contexts school districts may attempt to influence average test scores by changing student grade-promotion and placement procedures to exclude low-achieving students from taking the test. Haney recommends using standardized assessment as only one tool among many in establishing accountability, informing instruction, and improving the quality of education.

Julie Maxwell-Jolly and Patricia Gándara discuss recent reform efforts and policy changes in California that have exacerbated two long-standing problems — the lack of qualified teachers for language minority students, and achievement disparities between native English speakers and language minority students. Several statewide policy decisions have contributed to the current situation. First, Proposition 227 eliminated most bilingual programs and pushed language minority students into mainstream classrooms. Second, well-intentioned class-size-reduction reforms resulted in a teacher shortage and brought large numbers of inexperienced teachers into California's classrooms. Third, like Texas and Massachusetts, California has sought to promote the accountability of schools, teachers, and students by establishing a plan to implement statewide curriculum standards and to test students based on these standards. The authors point to the fact that, in implementation, the high-stakes test that is used (SAT 9) has little in common with the statewide curricular frameworks. Teacher interviews and systematic classroom observations in sixteen California school districts revealed that teachers were hard pressed to adopt the new statewide curriculum and at the same time prepare students to pass a test not aligned with that curriculum. While there has been an overall increase in student test scores, the authors show that there is a dramatically widening achievement gap between native English speakers and language minority students after second grade, when the test becomes more difficult.

California has not fulfilled the promise to improve teacher quality and promote academic excellence for all students. Based on an extensive literature review, Maxwell-Jolly and Gándara propose several strategies to select, recruit, and prepare teachers in order to build a cadre of teachers qualified to teach language minority students to high standards. They maintain that the selection and recruitment of potential teachers should target those who are most likely to have the desire, interest, and experience to work with language minority students. Minority individuals from varied cultural backgrounds would provide role models for diverse students and a bridge between schools and students' communities, and would be most likely to persist in teaching language minority students. To help diversify the teaching force, the authors suggest that minority individuals be encouraged to pursue teaching credentials by expanding the funding to forgive student loans and offer sign-up bonuses. They further suggest that teacher preparation and ongoing professional development be reorganized to give prospective and practicing European American teachers the skills to teach and assess language minority students and promote reflection on the political nature of their work.

The studies presented in Part One provide compelling evidence of the disproportionately negative impact on language minority students of the recent policy focus on high-stakes tests coupled with a lack of well-prepared teachers. School systems that have not previously held themselves accountable for language minority students' learning and performing to grade-level standards are now using test results to make decisions on high school graduation, but have not changed the conditions that have historically caused language minority student failure. Education reform began with the goal of academic excellence for all students, but the principle of equity has been compromised in the rush to high-stakes testing. Research from three states that are heavily populated by language minority students illustrates the need for re-evaluation and adjustment of many aspects of our national efforts at education reform. One aspect of reform involves teaching all students, including language minority students, to high standards. The authors in Part Two turn our attention to research on classroom pedagogy and help to demystify good teaching across language difference.

Successful Teaching Across Language Difference

There is no blueprint for teaching across language difference. In order to respond to the widely varying educational and linguistic needs and histories of language minority students, teachers use a variety of pedagogical approaches and strategies. There is, however, a fundamental principle: language minority students succeed in classrooms that recognize and utilize the power of the mainstream culture *and* the power of students' home cultures. Recognizing that the values, beliefs, communication patterns, and language use that language minority students experience at home are different from those that are valued in the mainstream, effective teachers assume the role of cultural interpreter and make a concerted effort to deliberately teach language minority students the mainstream academic expectations and skills. In addition, successful teachers harness the power of students' diverse cultural knowledge by using parents and community members as an important resource for academic learning. Informed by the well-established pedagogical postulate that students learn best when new knowledge is added to existing knowledge, effective teachers create continuity and connection among learning experiences, and offer content and learning activities that are interesting and pertinent to students' lives beyond school.

Convincing empirical evidence indicates that one aspect of the mainstream school culture — namely, the value placed on academic uses of English — is key to language minority students' long-term school progress in the United States (see, e.g., Beykont, 1994, 1997a, 1997b; Cummins, 1981, 1984, 1986; Fillmore & Snow, 2000; Garcia, 1998; Snow, 1987, 1990). Formal, academic uses of language do not assume shared information, familiarity, or background knowledge. Rather, they rely almost exclusively on linguistic cues, and therefore constitute a more challenging communication task for language minority students when compared to the contextualized everyday uses of English. Context-reduced language skills do not develop by simple exposure but by teachers focusing consciously on formal language use across the curriculum and on integrating the teaching of English and academic content (Faltis, 2001; Garcia, 1998). Nancy Hornberger illuminates this point in her ethnographic study of a mainstream classroom in which third-grade Cambodian students are effectively taught English literacy skills. She delineates the specific instructional strategies and language accommodations used by a European American mainstream teacher that were helpful in teaching language minority students the formal uses of English and academic expectations.

Hornberger describes the teacher's explicit focus on decontextualized language-skill development across the curriculum by, for example, giving students ample practice in word definitions and insisting that they produce full sentences in writing and speech. In this language-rich classroom, mandated basal readers were supplemented with interesting children's books and readings in a wide variety of genres so that students were exposed to material they would be tested on while being encouraged to love reading and books. The teacher had high academic expectations and provided students with the appropriate pedagogical supports to achieve those standards. For example, students were expected not only to read, but also to infer, predict from text, and explore alternative explanations, and were given extensive practice in these skills. Hornberger recognizes that mainstream teachers face a great challenge in teaching across language and cultural difference. Her chapter documents how one teacher overcame her lack of a common cultural and linguistic heritage with her students, created a classroom environment that motivated students to learn, clearly communicated the purposes of literacy activities, and promoted deep engagement with and a love of texts.

María Estela Brisk, Mary Dawson, Millicent Hartgering, Elizabeth MacDonald, and Lucinda Zehr continue the discussion on teaching the academic uses of English and expand the literature on effective teaching strategies for bilingual learners (for reviews, see Brisk & Harrington, 2000; Carrasquillo & Rodriguez, 1996; Faltis, 2001). Dawson, Hartgering, MacDonald, and Zehr recorded detailed accounts of teaching early English literacy skills to a selected student in each of their respective classrooms. The selected students lived in Spanish-speaking homes, represented a variety of ethnic backgrounds, and exhibited a range of skills in Spanish and English. Having taken relevant classes on second language and literacy skills in school settings and developed a repertoire of teaching strategies and approaches, these teachers felt more confident to take on the challenge and responsibility of teaching across language difference. Based on the careful assessment of students' needs, they experimented with strategies — such as dialogue journals, reader generated questions, shared reading, and word cards — that the literature identifies as effective in teaching language minority students (see Brisk & Harrington, 2000, for a review).

The authors draw several lessons from these teaching experiences. Discerning the academic strengths and weaknesses of each student was essential in order to identify the necessary pedagogical supports, as teaching strategies were most effective when adapted to the classroom context and students' individual needs. In the absence of a common language or cultural background with their students, it was helpful for these teachers to turn to outside resources, such as bilingual relatives or adult members of the students' communities to help assess students' academic strengths and weaknesses. The authors observe that instructional strategies that were particularly helpful for language minority students were often helpful to all students, such as presenting unfamiliar vocabulary before introducing a new reading. Brisk and her colleagues conclude by emphasizing the importance of teachers having high expectations for themselves and their students. Language minority students need the appropriate pedagogical supports to achieve to rigorous academic standards, and teachers need professional development that focuses on addressing these students' specific academic and linguistic needs.

In the United States, success in the mainstream culture often relies on the ability to express thought in a linear fashion in writing. Audrey Friedman examines teaching English academic writing skills to Somali students and contributes to the literature that conceptualizes writing as a social process (Calkins, 1985; Cummins & Sayers, 2000; Graves, 1983; McLane, 1990; Moll, 1989; Vygotsky, 1978). Working as a literacy specialist and researcher, Friedman collaborated with a European American classroom teacher as she engaged a group of Somali middle school students who had limited and/or interrupted schooling. Displaced by social upheaval in Somalia and sent to refugee camps in neighboring countries before emigrating to Boston, these students had studied in U.S. schools for varied lengths of time and exhibited a wide range of oral, written, and reading skills in both Somali and English. Their teacher employed a rigorous iterative process, clearly communicating standards-based criteria for good writing. She provided examples of organization, content, style, and mechanics; required multiple rounds of editing and revising; frequently assessed students' writing; and altered classroom instruction based on the results of her assessments and individual student needs. The students made impressive progress, as exemplified by their grade-level performance on a schoolwide end-of-the-year writing assessment.

Friedman describes how many individuals in the school acted as change agents, thus contributing to the Somali students' writing development. As a primary agent of literacy change, the classroom teacher held her students to high academic standards and helped them achieve those standards by practicing the steps that expert writers use — first writing, then editing and revising, and finally rewriting. The teacher and Friedman collaborated as change agents as they repeatedly assessed students' writing and identified strengths and weaknesses. This in turn informed classroom instruction and allowed the teacher and the literacy specialist to intervene and address areas of weakness in student writing. The students themselves acted as agents of literacy change, assuming responsibility for their own and their peers' writing improvement in a safe, respectful, and interactive classroom context that encouraged them to take risks in using English and negotiating meaning. They were taught skills of self-criticism, self-correction, and giving and receiving peer feedback. Other grade-level teachers and specialists also acted as change agents as they met on a weekly basis, established writing rubrics aligned with systemwide standards, discussed students' writing development based on school-wide assessments, and offered one another professional support while sharing good teaching practices. Finally, administrators acted as change agents by creating the organizational structures that allowed a common planning time for all grade-level teachers and specialists to come together in weekly meetings where they could contribute to one another's professional development. Friedman argues that, given the correct pedagogical supports, all children can learn. The challenge is to identify and use all resources available within and beyond the classroom for successful teaching across language difference.

A growing body of research reveals that students' families and communities offer untapped intellectual and curricular resources for teaching language minority students to high standards (Berriz, 2000, this volume; Diaz, Moll, & Mehan, 1992; Moll, 1988, 1992; Moll, Diaz, Estrada, & Lopes, 1992; Moll & Greenberg, 1990; Moll & Vellez-Ibanez, 1992; Phillips, 1993; Torres-Guzman, 1992). In the final chapter of Part Two, Berta Berriz reports on her observations in three mainstream classrooms — at the elementary, middle school, and high school level — where teachers found authentic ways of successfully tapping into students' cultural stores of knowledge and connecting them to rigorous classroom content. Berriz identifies specific instructional strategies and learning activities that link academic knowledge to students' lives beyond school and expands the literature on teaching students to high standards in culturally responsive ways (Boggs, 1972; Heath, 1983; Jordan, Tharp, & Baird-Vogt, 1992; Saravia-Shore & Arvizu, 1992).

The linguistically and ethnically mixed elementary classroom that Berriz discusses adopted a project-based approach to teaching literacy and social studies. Cape Verdean, African American, Puerto Rican, Chinese, and Dominican students in this classroom learned reading, writing, and geography through intrinsically motivating activities and research projects that incorporated community arts and oral narratives. The European American teacher brought the children's worlds into the classroom by creating projects that required each student to collect stories, photos, and drawings related to their family's country of origin, history, and immigration routes. In addition to fostering students' peer relationships, Berriz found that the academic learning of all students was enhanced because every child learned from their peers and their peers' communities.

The second classroom that Berriz describes is a middle school classroom that capitalized on the parents' role in teaching children reading and writing. The teacher recruited and brought parents into the school to provide extra support to literacy students from Guatemala, the Dominican Republic, and El Salvador. These students had received limited formal education prior to entering U.S. schools and were not proficient readers and writers in either Spanish or English. Berriz observed a series of literacy workshops that this Guatemalan teacher offered to her students and their parents. Family members read aloud together; practiced strategies to improve reading comprehension; wrote books based on cultural stories, poems, songs, and rhymes; and simultaneously learned the qualities of good writing in English. Learning mainstream strategies for reading a book or writing a story seemed easier for students because the content of school activities was familiar, their families were welcome to contribute to academic discussions, and reading and writing were taught within the context of a larger authentic project.

Berriz also conducted observations in a high school health career program in which students from Spanish- and English-speaking homes were learning Spanish while studying health issues. The Puerto Rican classroom teacher designed a meaningful community research project in which students investigated health-related issues affecting their communities. Students interviewed family and community members about their definitions of a healthy community and their views on major obstacles to quality health care in the United States. Family and community knowledge and experiences were brought into the class, which was intended to integrate content learning and Spanish-language learning. The community health data collected was then analyzed and presented through dramatic skits in Spanish. The project engaged students in issues in their own and one another's communities, and helped them develop a critical perspective on inequities in the larger society, such as low-income people's lack of access to quality health care.

Based on her observations in these three classrooms, Berriz argues that culturally inclusive instruction contributes to equal access to learning and greater school success for culturally and linguistically diverse students. While teaching strategies and approaches in these classrooms varied widely, she notes that in each case cultural arts were an important vehicle for academic learning. She urges educators to find innovative ways to acknowledge and connect the experiences and knowledge of children, families, and communities to classroom curricula, and thereby promote academic progress, teach students respect for peers of varied cultural backgrounds, and help them see one another as resources.

The studies presented in Part Two illuminate a variety of approaches though which mainstream teachers use the power of culture to teach language minority students to challenging academic standards. The authors offer rich and varied examples of good teaching across language difference in K–12 mainstream classrooms that serve diverse groups of students. What type of preparation is necessary to nurture the awareness, knowledge, and skills that prospective teachers need in order to provide such high-quality education to language minority students? Part Three of *The Power of Culture* focuses our attention on this important question.

Preparing Teachers to Teach Across Language Difference

Recognizing the power of culture as an essential tenet of effective teaching across language difference has implications for the design of teacher education programs. In addition to the content knowledge in the various subject areas, teachers today need to be well equipped with a large repertoire of instructional strategies to socialize language minority students to the mainstream school culture, teach them academic skills, and develop culturally responsive and respectful classrooms that connect what students already know to what they need to learn (Delpit, 1995; Fillmore & Snow, 2000; Garcia, 1996; González & Darling-Hammond, 1997; Moll, 1992; Zeichner, 1996). Theories on second language and literacy development and a growing body of classroom research have identified pedagogical approaches, teaching strategies, classroom organization, and language accommodations that are responsive to the specific linguistic and academic needs of language minority students (Beykont, 1994, 1997a, 1997b; Beykont & Johnson-Beykont, in press; Cummins, 1981, 1984, 1986; Faltis, 2001; Fillmore & Snow, 2000). In response to the increasing number of students whose home languages and cultures are different from the one valued in school, this knowledge base must become a central component of all teacher preparation programs and ongoing professional development.

A major but often overlooked challenge of U.S. teacher education programs concerns the preparation of predominantly White, middle-class, English monolingual preservice teachers to teach a student body whose home cultures are not only different from the school culture but also low in status in the wider society. Teaching across language difference also means teaching across power difference (Delpit, 1988, 1995; Giroux, 1988, 1992). Teachers need to have a clear understanding of the many ways that the hierarchy of cultures and languages in the larger society is reinforced in schools, and the disadvantages, stigmas, and pressures that language minority students experience by virtue of coming from cultures that are devalued and not supported in schools (Bartolomé, 2000, this volume; Bourdieu & Passeron, 1977; Cochran-Smith, 1995; Delpit, 1995; Ladson-Billings, 2000; Mehan et al., 1996; Nieto, 2000). The development of teachers' critical understanding requires analysis at both the individual and societal level. Teacher preparation programs and ongoing professional development can assist teachers who are themselves products of and contributors to the mainstream culture by offering structured and sustained support in questioning their own biases and prejudices about other languages and cultures, the existing power hierarchy, the privileges accrued to White middle-class students, and the inequities in the learning opportunities available for language minority students (Bartolomé, 2000, this volume; Cochran-Smith, 2000; Friedman, this volume, ch. 9; Garcia, 1996; Gebhard et al., this volume; Giroux, 1988, 1992; Ladson-Billings, 2000; Maxwell-Jolly & Gándara, this volume; Nieto, 2000).

In the first chapter in Part Three, Lilia Bartolomé draws on teacher interviews to address an often neglected aspect of teacher preparation — teacher political clarity — that enables teachers to examine the link between the subordination of minority groups in the larger society and the academic failure of these groups in schools. Four educators — in-

cluding a White female principal, a Chicano history teacher, a White female English teacher, and a White male math teacher — identified as
exemplary by colleagues and administrators were interviewed concerning their views on effective instruction of language minority students,
in particular low-income Mexicano/Latino students. These teachers
worked at a high school with a good record of providing a high-quality
education to its predominantly low-income and Latino student body,
many of whom have gone on to college. In her analysis, Bartolomé delineates the qualities that distinguish these teachers. Going beyond
their pedagogical skills, she discusses their critical views of the cultural
hierarchy in the United States, the prevalent mainstream myths and beliefs that justify this hierarchy, and their own role in altering the inequities that it creates for language minority students.

Bartolomé notes that these educators understood teaching as a political endeavor. They identified strongly with their students, had high
expectations for their academic performance, defined themselves as
student advocates, and saw it as their professional responsibility to facilitate their students' access to the mainstream culture and teach to
its academic expectations. Despite their various political views, they
all rejected prevalent dominant-culture myths, including merit-based
explanations of the existing hierarchy of groups, views of low-income
Mexicano/Latino students as intellectually and culturally inferior, and
uncritical acceptance of White, middle-class, mainstream culture as
superior. Bartolomé suggests that, in order to prepare teachers to teach
in diverse classrooms, teacher preparation coursework and practicum
experiences should focus on promoting political clarity and an understanding of the myriad ways in which the prevailing power hierarchy
in U.S. society is reinforced in schools and perpetuates the underachievement of minority students. She recommends redesigning
teacher preparation with a focus on culture, ideology, power, and
group relations so that teachers develop the critical posture and ideological clarity to transform, rather than reproduce, the inequities in
the larger society and create a just and equal playing field for all students in their classrooms.

Audrey Friedman describes the teacher preparation program at the
Lynch School of Education at Boston College, which aims to prepare
White, middle-class preservice teachers to work in a variety of secondary school settings, including urban schools. In addition to a major in a
particular content area, preservice teachers in this program are expected

to take a range of courses on assessment, instruction, curriculum, social policy, theory, and practice in teaching diverse learners. Prospective mainstream, bilingual, and special education teachers are integrated in these classes, giving them the benefit of interacting with colleagues and the opportunity to develop an interdisciplinary perspective and sensitivity toward a wide variety of learning issues. Through a combination of coursework, abundant school-based experiences, on-site supervision, and training as teacher researchers, the program aims to endow teachers with the skills to accommodate a diverse student body, implement a student-centered approach to teaching, become reflective practitioners, teach with the goal of social justice, and collaborate effectively with all stakeholders in the school community.

Friedman also discusses interviews with eight program participants that generated reflections on the program's effectiveness in preparing preservice teachers to teach across difference. These teachers (seven White, one Latina) shared thoughts on their experiences at their urban practicum site and identified areas of weakness in their preparation. Three main supports emerged as being necessary to improve their work in urban schools. First, they saw a need for more support in reflecting on their personal beliefs and biases about students whose racial, ethnic, class, and linguistic backgrounds are different from their own, and in learning to teach in culturally and linguistically responsive ways. Comments also focused on the connection between theory and practice: these preservice teachers wanted greater familiarity with the standards-based curriculum that they would soon be teaching and more focus on the pedagogical skills needed to teach students to these standards. Finally, they felt a need to learn more about when and how to negotiate their way within school hierarchies in order to advocate effectively for their students.

Friedman concludes by discussing a number of programmatic changes instituted at the Lynch School in response to concerns raised in interviews. One change was to initiate a bilingual education and English as a Second Language minor that will enable preservice teachers to benefit from a larger variety of coursework focused on language issues. Another change involved encouraging closer collaboration between the arts and sciences faculty and the education faculty in designing classes that address more directly the teaching of standards-based curriculum content in culturally and linguistically inclusive ways. The faculty is currently considering whether to require prospective teachers to learn a second language and is piloting a program that provides more systematic support to first-year preservice teachers as they reflect on issues of culture, values, bias, and privilege.

In the final chapter of this volume, Meg Gebhard, Theresa Austin, Sonia Nieto, and Jerri Willett describe their teacher education program at the University of Massachusetts in Amherst. The program aims to graduate teachers who are able to serve as cultural mediators and leaders in creating democratic, cognitively challenging, and culturally inclusive classrooms. A social justice perspective, a dialogic stance, and a praxis orientation are key concepts that permeate all aspects of the program. A social justice perspective, for example, guides the program's recruitment policy to bring together U.S.- and foreign-born students who have experienced various types of oppression, such as racism, sexism, and classism, and who demonstrate a willingness to question the status quo. In leadership projects outside the university, preservice teachers gain experience in organizing for justice in schools and communities. Overall, the program attempts to create a safe environment to communicate across differences, to examine personal prejudices, identities, privileges, and the power hierarchy, and to raise awareness on diversity issues.

The authors also discuss five interviews that Gebhard conducted with recent graduates and current students (all White teachers) about their experiences in the program and their reflections on the principles that guide their work. The interviews revealed that these teachers were aware that culture, race, social class, and personal histories shape their views of students. Their role definition went beyond the walls of their classrooms to include work with students' parents and communities. They saw themselves as cultural mediators between students' homes and communities and the school, and realized that teachers need to help parents understand the school system and help colleagues reflect on their own prejudices about students and their families. These interview findings guided programmatic changes; for example, the faculty decided to require a course that directly addresses the connections among language, culture, and social justice. They also recognized the need to help graduates develop a political base and create ongoing support systems for their work with diverse students.

The authors in Part Three offer cogent analyses of the skills and characteristics that teachers need to teach successfully across language difference. They also draw lessons learned from two teacher preparation programs engaged in bringing the vision of critical teacher education from theory into practice.

Concluding Thoughts

The United States is at a watershed moment in history vis-à-vis its commitment to the principle of providing equal educational opportunity to all its children, native English speakers and language minority students alike. The student population is increasingly diverse, while the teaching force is predominantly White and unprepared to teach across language difference. The U.S. education system and teacher preparation institutions have for too long neglected demographic changes in the student population and tolerated the persistent academic failure of language minority students. Within the current political context, programs tailored to the linguistic and academic needs of language minority students are being eliminated, and language minority students are being rushed into mainstream classrooms without sufficient time to develop grade-level English and academic skills. Furthermore, mainstream teachers are expected to teach language minority students to high standards before receiving proper training to teach across language difference. The research studies compiled in *The Power of Culture* shed light on mainstream teachers and teacher preparation programs that are taking the diversity challenge seriously and responding to the complexities of teaching language minority students in constructive and innovative ways.

There is currently a troubling gap between the stated goals and promises of standards-based reforms and the implementation of policies designed to achieve these goals. Reform efforts have narrowly focused on high-stakes tests. School systems that have not held themselves accountable for language minority students' learning are now using student performance on these tests to make decisions about high school graduation, yet the myriad systemic obstacles that have caused language minority failure in schools prevail. Originally intended to provide a high-quality education for all students, educational reform has, in implementation, drifted away from the principle of equity. The research presented in *The Power of Culture* starkly illustrates that, in order to reach the reform promise of equity and excellence, U.S. schools must do a far better job of educating language minority students to high standards. We can no longer tolerate the abysmal academic performance, high retention and dropout trends, and low high school graduation and college attendance rates of language minority students. Nor can we afford to have a predominantly monocultural and monolingual teaching force that is unprepared to teach effectively across language difference. Within the current high- stakes environment, failing to educate language minority students to high standards will soon mean forcing an overwhelming percentage of these young people to leave high school without a diploma. Failing to prepare teachers to teach across language difference will mean that the majority of teachers are not equipped for the daily challenges of their jobs.

One of the persistent educational obstacles to language minority student achievement has been the lack of access to quality instruction. The classroom studies presented in *The Power of Culture* provide concrete examples of successful teaching across language difference. In these classrooms, teachers demonstrated a keen understanding of their students' academic strengths and weaknesses, had high expectations for students' academic performance, provided the necessary pedagogical supports so each student could meet those expectations, experimented with new strategies, reflected on their own practice, and adapted their teaching to the classroom context and the particular needs of students. Teachers recognized and utilized the power of the mainstream culture and used varied instructional techniques to explicitly teach the academic expectations, literacy skills, valued language use, and thinking and communication patterns necessary for success in school. Some teachers also recognized the power of the students' home cultures and took the extra step of tapping into students' extensive personal and community resources to enrich and motivate their learning. They brought students' cultures into the classroom, took the classroom into their communities, connected the curriculum to students' lives, and taught mainstream academic skills using familiar content. These classrooms enhanced language minority students' learning by building on what they already knew and drawing links between two socializing contexts — home and school — and the knowledge valued in each. Furthermore, the studies gathered in *The Power of Culture* demonstrate the importance of teachers' breaking through their professional isolation to reach out to colleagues, to seek language, cultural, and academic resources within and beyond the classroom walls, and to join with other teachers to create networks of professional and political support for the work that they do.

Teachers are often language minority students' most important point of contact with the dominant culture and institutions. They can play a pivotal role as cultural interpreters, providing full access to the academic skills and expectations valued in the mainstream school culture so that each child has a more equal opportunity to succeed. The studies on teacher preparation collected in *The Power of Culture* underscore the need to redesign teacher preparation to place an equal emphasis on the pedagogical and political dimensions of teaching across language difference. Teachers certainly need to know the theory and research on second language literacy and academic development of language minority students in school settings and have the pedagogical skills and field experience to teach to challenging content standards in culturally responsive ways. However, political clarity is also vitally important when teaching across language difference. Teachers' critical analysis of the hierarchy of languages and cultures in the larger society and the many ways that the hierarchy is reinforced in schools will help them problematize the unrealistic expectation that students from diverse backgrounds should succeed with no extra supports in an education system that was designed for a homogenous White, middle-class student population.

Teachers who do not understand the systemic obstacles faced by language minority students and lack the skills to respond to second language development challenges generally fail to meet the reform goals of equity and excellence for all. Some set high standards but do not give students the needed pedagogical supports, while others set low academic expectations and thereby reproduce in their own classrooms the learning conditions that have historically sentenced language minority students to low academic achievement. Evidence gathered in *The Power of Culture* illustrates that well-developed pedagogical skills are necessary, but alone they are not sufficient for creating excellent classrooms. Political clarity by itself is also not enough. Excellent teaching across language difference in mainstream classrooms requires the moral resolve to hold all students to high academic standards, the political clarity to understand the sociohistorical factors that have inhibited language minority student success, and the pedagogical expertise to use the power of culture as a means of offering the educational supports language minority students need to succeed in U.S. schools.

Zeynep F. Beykont
Editor

Notes

1. Before 1965 most immigrants came from European countries.
2. These U.S. Census Bureau projections are conservative and it is highly likely that minority school-age children will be in the majority even sooner. Census 2000 results show that the White population in the United States is 69 percent. This is below the previously projected drop to 75 percent that had been anticipated for the year 2000 (see Macias, 2000, for detailed discussion).
3. National comparisons of dropout rates of foreign- and U.S.-born Hispanics show, for example, that foreign-born students are much less likely to drop out of school. The longer immigrants stay in the United States, the worse they perform in school (see, e.g., NCES, 1995a). Contrary to popular beliefs, English fluency is not the most important predictor of student performance in U.S. schools.
4. Teaching across language difference means teaching students who are unfamiliar with the standard/formal/academic uses of English language for various reasons, including their family's language background and formal educational background.
5. We have yet to see the long-term effects of the September 11, 2001, terrorist attacks on attitudes toward immigrants, particularly immigrants from Islamic countries, including those who have lived in the United States for several generations.
6. There is abundant research showing that language minority students in well-designed bilingual programs receive the necessary academic, linguistic, and emotional support, stay in school, develop grade-level academic competencies and English literacy skills, and graduate with a positive sense of themselves, their home culture, and their native language (see Beykont, 1997a, Collier, 1992, Crawford, 1995, and Cummins, 1981, for reviews of this literature, and Beykont, 2000, for a collection of studies on high-quality education of language minority students in bilingual programs).
7. The twenty-three states that have adopted English Only laws include Alabama (1990), Alaska (1998), Arizona (1988), Arkansas (1987), California (1986), Colorado (1988), Florida (1988), Georgia (1996), Indiana (1984), Iowa (2002), Kentucky (1984), Mississippi (1987), Missouri (1998), Montana (1995), New Hampshire (1995), North Carolina (1987), North Dakota (1987), South Carolina (1987), South Dakota (1995), Tennessee, (1984), Utah, (2000), Virginia (1981), and Wyoming (1996).
8. The Arizona initiative was modeled after California's English Only law (Proposition 227) that was approved in 1998, but is more restrictive. In Arizona, even when parents request waivers, school officials can refuse to offer bilingual services without providing any reason (see Crawford, 2001b, for detailed analysis of English Only initiatives in California and Arizona).
9. The 1994 Nationwide Staffing Survey results indicated that 97 percent of teachers do not have certification and 70 percent have no training to work with language minority students (Macias, 1998).

References

Baratz, S., & Baratz, J. (1970). Early childhood intervention: The social science base for institutional racism. *Harvard Educational Review, 40,* 29–50.

Bartolomé, L. I. (2000). Democratizing bilingualism: The role of critical teacher education. In Z. F. Beykont (Ed.), *Lifting every voice: Politics and pedagogy of bilingualism* (pp. 167–186). Cambridge, MA: Harvard Education Publishing Group.

Berriz, B. R. (2000). Raising children's cultural voices: Strategies for developing literacy in two languages. In Z. F. Beykont (Ed.), *Lifting every voice: Politics and pedagogy of bilingualism* (pp. 71–94) Cambridge, MA: Harvard Education Publishing Group.

Beykont, Z. (1994). *Academic progress of a nondominant group: A longitudinal study of Puerto Ricans in New York City's late-exit programs.* Unpublished doctoral dissertation, Harvard Graduate School of Education, Cambridge, MA.

Beykont, Z. (1997a). Refocusing school language policy discussions. In W. K. Cummings & N. F. McGinn (Eds.), *International handbook of education and development: Preparing schools, students, and nations for the twenty-first century* (pp. 263–282). New York: Pergamon.

Beykont, Z. (1997b). School-language policy decisions for nondominant language groups. In H. D. Nielsen & W. K. Cummings (Eds.), *Quality education for all: Community-oriented approaches* (pp. 79–122). New York: Garland.

Beykont, Z. F. (Ed.). (2000). Introduction. In Z. F. Beykont (Ed.), *Lifting every voice: Politics and pedagogy of bilingualism* (pp. vii–xix). Cambridge, MA: Harvard Education Publishing Group.

Beykont, Z. F., & Johnson-Beykont, B. (in press). Against the assimilationist tide. In J. Cummins, D. Dragonas, A. Frangoudaki, & H. Smith (Eds.), *History lessons: Transforming social relations of power in the classroom.* Clevedon, Eng.: Multilingual Matters.

Boggs, S. T. (1972). The meaning of narratives and questions to Hawaiian children. In C. B. Cazden, V. P. John, & D. Hymes (Eds.), *Functions of language in the classroom* (pp. 299–300). New York: Teachers College Press.

Bourdieu, P., & Passeron, C. (1977). *Reproduction in education, society, and culture.* London: Sage.

Brisk, M. E., & Harrington, M. M. (2000). *Literacy and bilingualism.* Mahwah, NJ: Lawrence Erlbaum Associates.

Calkins, L. (1985). *The art of teaching writing.* Exeter, NH: Heinemann.

Carasquillo, A., & Rodriguez, V. (1996). *Bilingual students in mainstream classrooms.* Clevedon, Eng.: Multilingual Matters.

Cazden, B. C. (1988). *Classroom discourse: The language of teaching and learning.* Portsmouth, NH: Heinemann Press.

Cochran-Smith, M. (1995). Color blindness and basket making are not the answers: Confronting the dilemmas of race, culture, and language diversity in teacher education. *American Educational Research Journal, 32,* 493–522.

Cochran-Smith, M. (2000). Blind vision: Unlearning racism in teacher education. *Harvard Educational Review, 70,* 157–190.

Collier, V. P. (1992). A synthesis of studies examining long-term language minority student data on academic achievement. *Bilingual Research Journal, 16,* 187–212.

Crawford, J. (1992a). *Hold your tongue: Bilingualism and the politics of English Only.* Reading, MA: Addison-Wesley.

Crawford, J. (Ed.). (1992b). *Language loyalties: A source book on the official English controversy.* Chicago: University of Chicago Press.

Crawford, J. (1995). *Bilingual education: History, politics, theory, and practice* (3rd ed.). Los Angeles: Bilingual Education Services.

Crawford, J. (2000). *At war with diversity: U.S. language policy in an age of anxiety.* Clevedon, Eng.: Multilingual Matters.

Crawford, J. (2001a). Demographic Change and Language [On-line]. Available: http://ourworld.compuserve.com/homepages/JWCRAWFORD/can-pop.htm

Crawford, J. (2001b). Bilingual education: Strike two. *Rethinking Schools Online: An Urban Educational Journal* [On-line], *15*(2). Available: http://ourworld. compuserve.com/homepages/jwcrawford/RS-az.htm)

Cummins, J. (1981). The role of primary language development in promoting educational success for language minority students. In California State Department of Education (Ed.), *Schooling and language minority students: A theoretical framework* (pp. 3–50). Los Angeles: California State University, Evaluation, Dissemination, and Assessment Center.

Cummins, J. (1984). *Bilingualism and special education: Issues in assessment and pedagogy.* Clevedon, Eng.: Multilingual Matters.

Cummins, J. (1986). Empowering minority students: A framework for intervention. *Harvard Educational Review, 56,* 18–36.

Cummins, J., & Sayers, D. (2000). Families and communities learning together: Becoming literate, confronting prejudice. In Z. F. Beykont (Ed.), *Lifting every voice: Pedagogy and politics of bilingualism* (pp. 113–138). Cambridge, MA: Harvard Education Publishing Group.

Delpit, L. (1986). Skills and other dilemmas of a progressive Black educator. *Harvard Educational Review, 56,* 379–385.

Delpit, L. (1988). The silenced dialogue: Power and pedagogy in educating other people's children. *Harvard Educational Review, 58,* 280–298.

Delpit, L. (1995). *Other people's children: Cultural conflict in the classroom.* New York: New Press.

Diaz, S., Moll, L. C., & Mehan, H. (1992). Sociocultural resources in instruction: A context-specific approach. In *Beyond language: Social and cultural factors in schooling language minority students* (5th ed., pp. 187–230). Los Angeles: California State University, Evaluation, Dissemination, and Assessment Center.

DiCerbo, P. A. (2000). *Framing effective practice: Topics and issues in education of English language learners* (NCBE Issue Brief No. 6). Washington, DC: National Clearinghouse for Bilingual Education.

Faltis, C. J. (2001). *Joinfostering: Teaching and learning in multilingual classrooms.* Upper Saddle River, NJ: Merrill Prentice-Hall.

Farah, M. (2000). Reaping the benefits of bilingualism: The case of Somali refugee students. In Z. F. Beykont (Ed.), *Lifting every voice: Pedagogy and politics of bilingualism* (pp. 59–70) Cambridge, MA: Harvard Education Publishing Group.

Fillmore, L. W. (1982). Language minority students and school participation: What kind of English is needed? *Journal of Education, 164,* 143–156.

Fillmore, L. W., & Snow, C. E. (2000). *What teachers need to know about language.* Washington, DC: Center of Applied Linguistics.

Garcia, E. E. (1996). Preparing instructional professionals for linguistically and culturally diverse students. In J. Sikula (Ed.), *Handbook of research on teacher education* (pp. 802–813). New York: Simon & Schuster Macmillan.

Garcia, E. E. (1998). *Multilingualism in U.S. schools: From research to practice.* Paper presented at the Reading and English Language Learner Forum, Sacramento, CA.

Giroux, H. A. (1988). *Teachers as intellectuals: Toward a critical pedagogy of learning.* Westport, CT: Bergin & Garvey.

Giroux, H. A. (1992). *Border crossings: Cultural workers and the politics of education.* New York: Routledge.

González, J. M. (1975). Coming of age in bilingual/bicultural education: A historical perspective. *Inequality in Education, 19,* 5–17.

González, J. M., & Darling-Hammond, L. (1997). *New concepts for new challenges: Professional development for immigrant youth.* McHenry, IL: Delta Systems.

Graves, D. (1983). *Writing: Teachers and children at work.* Exeter, NH: Heinemann.

Heath, S. B. (1983). *Ways with words: Language, life, and work in communities and classrooms.* Cambridge, Eng.: Cambridge University Press.

H. R. 1804. (1994). Goals 2000: Educate America Act. 103rd Congress of the United States of America.

H. R. 1 (2001). No Child Left Behind Act. 107th Congress of the United States of America.

Jordan, C., Tharp, R. G., & Baird-Vogt, L. (1992). "Just open the door": Cultural compatibility and classroom rapport. In M. Saravia-Shore & S. F. Arvizu (Eds.), *Cross-cultural literacy: Ethnographies of communication in multiethnic classrooms* (pp. 3–18). New York: Garland.

Kwong, K. M. (2000). Bilingualism equals access: The case of Chinese high school students. In Z. F. Beykont (Ed.), *Lifting every voice: Pedagogy and politics of bilingualism* (pp. 43–52). Cambridge, MA: Harvard Education Publishing Group.

Ladson-Billings, G. J. (2000). Fighting for our lives: Preparing teachers to teach African American students. *Journal of Teacher Education, 51,* 206–214.

Macedo, D. (2000). Decolonizing English only: The democratic power of bilingualism. In Z. F. Beykont (Ed.), *Lifting every voice: Pedagogy and politics of bilingualism* (pp. 21–43). Cambridge, MA: Harvard Education Publishing Group.

Macias, R. F. (1998). *Summary report of the survey of the states' limited English proficient students and available educational programs and services, 1996–1997.* Washington, DC: National Clearinghouse for Bilingual Education.

Macias, R. F. (2000). The flowering of America: Linguistic diversity in the United States. In S. L. McKay & S. C. Wong (Eds.), *New immigrants in the United States: Readings for second language educators* (pp. 11–57). Cambridge, Eng.: Cambridge University Press.

McLane, J. B. (1990). Writing as a social process. In L. C. Moll (Ed.), *Vygotsky and education* (pp. 304–318). New York: Cambridge University Press.

McLeod, B. (Ed.). (1994). *Language and learning: Educating linguistically diverse students.* Albany: State University of New York Press.

Mehan, H. (1979). *Learning lessons: The social organization of classroom instruction.* Cambridge, MA: Harvard University Press.

Mehan, H., Villanueva, I., Hubbard, L., & Lintz, A. (1996). *Constructing school success: The consequences of untracking low achieving students.* New York: Cambridge University Press.

Menken, K. (2000). *What are the critical issues in wide-scale assessment of English language learners?* (NCBE Issue Brief No. 6). Washington, DC: National Clearinghouse for Bilingual Education.

Menken, K., & Antunez, B. (2001). *An overview of the preparation and certification of teachers working with limited English proficient students.* Washington, DC: National Clearinghouse of Bilingual Education. Available on-line: ncbe.gwu.edu/ncbepubs/reports/teacherprep/teacherprep.pdf

Menken, K., & Holmes, P. (2000). *Standards-based education reform and English language learners* (NCBE Issue Brief No. 6). Washington, DC: National Clearinghouse for Bilingual Education.

Moll, L. (1988). Educating Latino students. *Language Arts, 64,* 315–324.

Moll, L. C. (1989). Teaching second language students: A Vygotskian perspective. In D. M. Johnson & D. H. Roen (Eds.), *Richness in writing: Empowering ESL students* (pp. 55–70). New York: Longman.

Moll, L. C. (1992). Bilingual classroom studies and community analysis: Some recent trends. *Educational Researcher, 21*(2), 20–24.

Moll, L. C., Diaz, S., Estrada, E., & Lopes, L. M. (1992). Making contexts: The social construction of lessons in two languages. In M. Saravia-Shore & S. F. Arvizu (Eds.), *Cross cultural literacy* (pp. 339–366). New York: Garland.

Moll, L., & Greenberg, J. (1990). Creating zones of possibilities: Combining social contexts for instruction. In L. Moll (Ed.), *Vygotsky and education: Instructional implications and applications of sociohistorical psychology* (pp. 319–348). Cambridge, Eng.: Cambridge University Press.

Moll, L., & Vellez-Ibanez, C. (1992). Funds of knowledge for teaching: Using a qualitative approach to connect homes and classrooms. *Theory Into Practice, 31,* 132–141.

National Center for Education Statistics. (1995a). *Dropout rates in the United States.* Washington, DC: U.S. Department of Education.

National Center for Education Statistics. (1995b). *Schools and staffing survey, 1993–94.* Washington, DC: U.S. Department of Education.

National Center for Education Statistics. (1997). *A profile of policies and practices for limited English proficient students: Screening methods, program support, and teacher training, 1993–94.* Washington, DC: U.S. Department of Education, Office of Educational Research and Improvement.

Nielsen, H. D., & Beykont, Z. (1997). Reaching the periphery: Toward a community-oriented education. In H. D. Nielsen & W. K. Cummings (Eds.), *Quality education for all: Community-oriented approaches* (pp. 246–266). New York: Garland.

Nieto, S. (2000). Bringing bilingual education out of the basement, and other imperatives for teacher education. In Z. F. Beykont (Ed.), *Lifting every voice: Pedagogy and politics of bilingualism* (pp. 187–208). Cambridge, MA: Harvard Education Publishing Group.

Oakes, J. (1985). *Keeping track: How schools structure inequality.* New Haven, CT: Yale University Press.

Phillips, S. U. (1993). *The invisible culture: Communication in the classroom and community on the Warm Springs Indian Reservation* (2nd ed.) New York: Free Press.

Rice, R., & Walsh, C. (1996). Equity at risk: The problem with state and federal education reform efforts. In C. E. Walsh (Ed.), *Education reform and social change* (pp. 7–20). Mahwah, NJ: Lawrence Erlbaum.

Ruiz, R. (1984). Orientations in language planning. *NABE Journal, 8*(2), 15–34.

Ruiz-de-Velasco, J., & Fix, M. (2000). *Overlooked and underserved: Immigrant students in U.S. secondary schools.* Washington, DC: Urban Institute.

Saravia-Shore, M., & Arvizu, S. F. (Eds.). (1992). Introduction. *Cross-cultural literacy: Ethnographies of communication in multiethnic classrooms* (pp. xv–xxxviii). New York: Garland.

Snow, C. E. (1987). Relevance of the notion of a critical period to language acquisition. In M. Bornstein (Ed.), *Sensitive periods in development* (pp. 183–209). Hillsdale, NJ: Erlbaum.

Snow, C. E. (1990). The development of definitional skill. *Journal of Child Language, 17,* 697–710.

Stefanakis, E. H. (2000). Teachers' judgments do count: Assessing bilingual students. In Z. F. Beykont (Ed.), *Lifting every voice: Pedagogy and politics of bilingualism* (pp. 139–160). Cambridge, MA: Harvard Education Publishing Group.

Sue, S., & Padilla, A. (1992). Ethnic minority issues in the United States. In California State University (Ed.), *Beyond language: Social and cultural factors in schooling language minority students* (5th ed., pp. 35–72). Los Angeles: California State University, Evaluation, Dissemination, and Assessment Center.

Tharp, R., & Gallimore, R. (1988). *Rousing minds to life: Teaching, learning, and schooling in a social context.* Cambridge, Eng.: Cambridge University Press.

Tomlinson, C. A. (1999). *The differentiated classroom.* Alexandria, VA: Association for Supervision and Curriculum Development.

Torres-Guzman, M. E. (1992). Stories of hope in the midst of despair: Culturally responsive education for Latino students in an alternative high school. In M. Saravia-Shore & S. F. Arvizu (Eds.), *Cross-cultural literacy: Ethnographies of communication in multiethnic classrooms* (pp. 477–490). New York: Garland.

Vygotsky, L. S. (1978). *Mind in society: The development of higher psychological processes* (M. Cole, C. John-Steiner, S. Scribner, & E. Souberman, Eds.). Cambridge, MA: Harvard University Press.

Wheelock, A. (1990). *Crossing the tracks: How untracking can save America's schools.* New York: New Press.

Zeichner, K. (1996). Educating teachers for cultural diversity. In K. Zeichner, S. Melnick, & M. L. Gómez (Eds.), *Currents of reform in preservice teacher education* (pp. 133–175). New York: Teachers College Press.

PART ONE

Educational Reforms and Language Minority Students

The High Stakes of High-Stakes Testing

MIREN URIARTE

When the Commonwealth of Massachusetts embarked on its process of educational reform in 1993, no group in the Commonwealth stood to gain more from changes in the public education system than Latinos.[1] Latino enrollment in the state's public schools, which had been growing for three decades, had skyrocketed, particularly in the urban districts. At that time, more than 66,000 Latino children were enrolled in Massachusetts schools, a 20 percent increase in just five years. Eight percent of the state's students were Latino. In some areas, Latinos were more densely present: in Boston, for example, 20 percent of enrolled students were Latinos, but in Lawrence and Holyoke, Latino children made up about 70 percent of students.[2]

Many of these children came from a well-established Puerto Rican population that had first arrived in the state in the 1960s. This group, whose numbers were constantly renewed with arrivals from the island, accounted for most of the Latino children in the state. Dominicans, who began arriving in the 1970s, were also represented in large numbers, particularly in the eastern area of the state. Besides the Puerto Ricans and Dominicans, Massachusetts had a growing and increasingly diverse contingent of immigrants from Central and South America. Most Latino students came from homes where the first language was not English; about one-third of the Latino children enrolled in school could not perform classroom work in English[3] and were designated as Limited English Proficient (LEP).[4]

3

Aside from their growing numbers and diversity, perhaps the most salient characteristic of Latino children was the fact that they were not doing well in Massachusetts schools. Since the 1970s, Latino children as a group have had the lowest levels of achievement of any group in the Commonwealth.[5] The 9.6 percent dropout rate among Latinos in 1992–1993 was three and one-half times that of White students in the state.[6] About 10 percent of Latino children are retained in grade each year, which is three times the rate of White students.[7] Language minority students attending bilingual education programs appear to be somewhat protected from both high dropout rates and high rates of retention in grade, but indicators for this group are still extraordinarily high compared with those of White students.[8]

The problem of student achievement had long elicited the attention of parents and leaders in the Latino community. Reports by Latino community agencies as far back as 1976 pointed to high rates of retention in grade and attrition from school.[9] In 1986, the Education Task Force of the Massachusetts Commission on Hispanic Affairs, a commission sponsored by the Massachusetts legislature, analyzed Latino education statewide and concluded that "the Massachusetts public education system is failing to carry out its mission and its responsibility to the Hispanic community"[10] and its children. This was due, the Task Force argued, to the underfunding of school systems where Latinos predominate and the absence of culturally sensitive curricula and classroom practices.

In 1989 and 1990, protests reached a crescendo in a series of contentious meetings with the leadership of the Boston Public Schools. Annual Latino dropout rates had reached 30 percent in some Boston high schools.[11] The newly formed Latino Parents Association forced the leadership of the city's schools to collaborate in the development of a Hispanic dropout prevention plan. For the first time, the city recognized the system's failure to address the educational needs of Latino children and proposed a set of prevention, intervention, and remediation strategies.[12]

Therefore, in 1993, when the Massachusetts legislature passed the Educational Reform Law, many Latinos supported the initiative, as did business, educators, politicians, advocacy groups, and other parents in the state. The broad initiative increased spending in education and distributed funding more equitably between urban and suburban districts, bringing new resources to the education of children of color and language minority children, who were largely concentrated in urban districts.[13] Especially significant was a large increase in funds for early childhood education and for the introduction and use of technology in schools.[14]

The initiative proposed to set higher standards for all students and schools: the state was to develop new curriculum standards and requirements in core academic areas, which were to guide the development of local curricula and classroom activities. To implement these higher standards, the reform proposed increased time-on-task for students and established tougher standards for new teacher certification and teacher education, and retraining for established teachers. The objective of the retraining was to support the development of local curricula and their implementation in classrooms. For example, teachers in districts with large populations of language minority students had to meet special training requirements in multicultural education and teaching strategies with language minority children. This was a welcome step toward alleviating the devastating results of the clash of cultural backgrounds between minority children and the mostly White teaching force. Higher expectations, equity in access to curriculum, and improved quality of instruction and school climate have been common demands on the part of Latinos and other communities of color.

The Educational Reform Law also highlighted the responsibility of all stakeholders for student learning. One aspect of this responsibility was a process of decentralization, which placed increased responsibility on school committees and superintendents and, ultimately, on principals and school councils.[15] For example, the councils, made up of the principal, parents, teachers, and community partners, as well as students at the high school level, were meant to provide a context for decisionmaking at the school level in areas that contribute to school improvement, such as professional development, student learning time, safety, and parental involvement. Schools were encouraged to seek support from their communities and develop partnerships with businesses and other institutions in their communities.

The reform also introduced measures to hold districts accountable for school performance and student achievement. The aim was to identify students, schools, and districts in need of assistance with the promise that they would get the necessary support to reach the new standards. Multiple measures of student achievement were to be integrated into the process of aligning local curricula to the statewide "frameworks" as a way of establishing student competence in those areas. The law further proposed that high school graduation be contingent on the determination of competence, but the assessment method was left to the board of education. Schools in which students underperformed and did not show improvement over time would be targeted for assistance.

Nirvana, you say? Not for long. A change in leadership of the state government led to changes in the composition of the state's board of education, and in time to strong shifts in the orientation of reform. Most notable and controversial was the board's decision to adopt a series of standardized tests administered in several grades as the primary measure of student achievement and to require that students pass the tenth-grade version of the standardized test in order to graduate. With the Massachusetts Comprehensive Assessment System (MCAS), as it is called, Massachusetts began the implementation of a high-stakes test as the sole measure for graduation.

Truthfully, Latinos paid little attention to these events. The next time many became aware of the process of educational reform was in December 1998, when their fourth, eighth, or tenth grader appeared with the results of his or her test. Most likely the child had failed, as most Latino children did. Starting from the point at which the MCAS test results were revealed, this chapter examines the outcomes for Latino students and other children of color in the assessments being carried out as part of the reform process, presents some perspectives on these dismal outcomes, and offers several thoughts on the meaning of the high stakes of high-stakes testing.

Taking the Test

Massachusetts's educational reform showcased the MCAS as the primary measure of student achievement; its use has been highly controversial. There has been a great deal of debate about the merits of standardized testing and its validity in testing student achievement. There has also been significant debate about the technical merits of the test itself and its capacity to validly reflect diversity in the range of knowledge tested. What makes the MCAS most controversial by far, however, is the use that will be made of its scores. Beginning in 2003, current state educational policy requires tenth graders to obtain a passing score in math and in English language arts in order to graduate from high school. No other single measure of achievement, not grades, portfolios, or teachers' recommendations, will determine a student's eligibility for graduation.[16]

The MCAS tests have been administered to students in grades four, eight, and ten.[17] Children from all school districts must take the tests in English language arts, mathematics, and science and technology. Eighth graders are also tested in history and social sciences. Only public school children are tested; the MCAS tests are not given to private or parochial school students. Test-takers include students in regular education, vocational education, and special education, as well as LEP students.

In 1999, 26 percent of the Latino children in the state's public schools were determined to be limited in their English proficiency,[18] accounting for 60 percent of the children in the state's bilingual education program.[19] Because of their high representation among LEP students, special attention was given to the testing of LEP students whose first language is Spanish. Native Spanish speakers who had been enrolled in schools for less than three years were required to take the Spanish version of the mathematics and the science and technology tests if they met the following requirements:

- they were enrolled in the Transitional Bilingual Education Program or received English as a Second Language support;
- they did not have reading and writing skills sufficient to take the English-language test and they were able to read and write in Spanish.[20]

The MCAS test is not available in any other language. Other language minority children are required to take all sections of the test in English if they have been in U.S. schools for more than three years or if they will be placed into mainstream classrooms the following school year, regardless of the time spent in U.S. schools.[21] This requirement relies on the expectation that (a) curricula in the bilingual program are closely aligned with the learning standards of the curriculum frameworks developed for statewide application and that (b) immigrant children can attain enough proficiency in English in three years to score successfully on the MCAS. These expectations have been the source of a great deal of controversy.

Every year since 1998, more than 200,000 children in the fourth, eighth, and tenth grades have taken the MCAS tests.[22] In 2000, test-takers accounted for about 94 percent of the children enrolled in those grades;[23] absences and lower levels of participation by special education and LEP students account for the remainder. Although most of the test-takers were White, as are most students enrolled in the state's public schools, in 2000, approximately 37 percent were children of color. Specifically, Asian, Black, Latino, and mixed-race children make up the groups of color; of these, Latinos account for the largest proportion (see Figure 1). Some 4,400 of the MCAS test-takers were LEP children.[24] Among LEP test-takers, the proportion of children of color is much larger, with Asians, Latinos, and Blacks accounting for about 85 percent of these test-takers. Among LEP students, Latinos were by far the largest group, accounting for 49 percent of all LEP test-takers in 1999.[25]

Test Results

The Department of Education categorizes student performance into one of four levels in each area of knowledge for each grade: advanced, proficient, needs improvement, and failing. The criteria for each level were the following:

- *Advanced:* The student demonstrates a comprehensive and in-depth understanding of rigorous subject matter and provides sophisticated solutions to complex problems.
- *Proficient:* The student demonstrates a solid understanding of challenging subject matter and solves a wide variety of problems.
- *Needs Improvement:* The student demonstrates partial understanding of subject matter and solves simple problems.
- *Failing:* The student demonstrates minimal understanding of subject matter and does not solve even simple problems.

The first three administrations of the MCAS test resulted in very low scores across all groups. Statewide average scaled scores for all subjects and at all grade levels only reached the level of "needs improvement," except fourth-grade science and technology in 1999 and 2000 and eighth-grade English language arts in 2000. In 2000, 45 percent of tenth graders had a failing score in math, which was in fact an improvement over the 53 percent that had failed the year before. Fewer than 15 percent of students at any level achieved an "advanced" rating in any subject (grade-10 math also had the largest percentage of advanced students).[26]

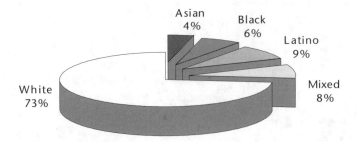

Figure 1   Racial/Ethnic Makeup of MCAS Test-Takers, 2000

Source: Massachusetts Department of Education, *Spring 2000 MCAS Tests, Report of State Results,* November 2000.

Black and Latino children did by far the worst. Figures 2, 3, and 4 show the failure rates for students from different racial groups. Across all grades and all areas tested, the rates of failure for Black and Latino children were the highest. In general, all children in the fourth grade did better than those in the higher grades, but even at this level, Black and Latino failure rates were several times higher than those of Asian and White children. In all grades, all children, including Black and Latino children, did better in English language arts than in math and in science and technology.[27] This pattern was particularly pronounced in the eighth grade. In the areas of math and science, however, the difference between the rates of Black and Latino students and those of Asian and White students was most salient. In the fourth grade, the rates of failure for Black and Latino children were three and four times those of Asian and White children, respectively. This pattern remained across the grades. In sum, across all grades and across all areas of knowledge tested, the three administrations of the MCAS have shown that the outcomes of Latino students are the worst in the state, followed closely by those of Blacks.

Because of the relevance of the MCAS outcomes to the graduation of tenth graders, it is important to look at these scores more closely. Since failing only one section of the test means that the student cannot graduate, a look at the percentage of failures in math, the section of the test in which students of all groups did worst, provides an indication of the maximum number of students in each group who would potentially not graduate from high school.[28] Figure 5 shows the tenth-

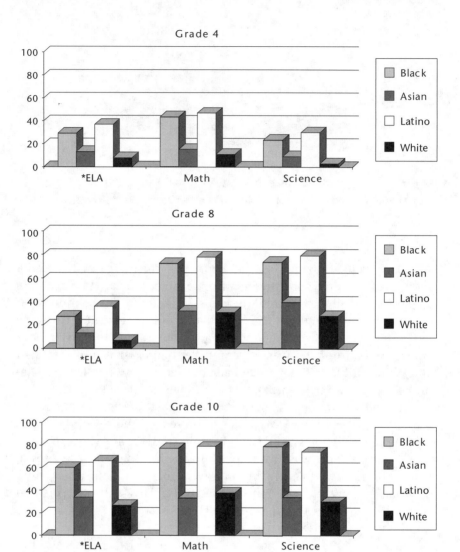

Figures 2–4   MCAS Results by Race, 2000 (% failing)

Source: Massachusetts Department of Education, *Spring 2000 MCAS Tests, Report of State Results,* November 2000.

* ELA = English Language Arts

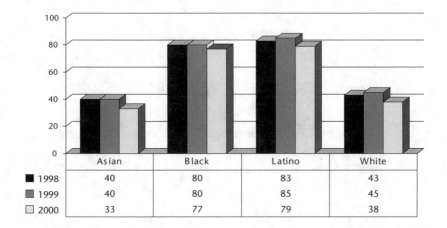

	Asian	Black	Latino	White
■ 1998	40	80	83	43
■ 1999	40	80	85	45
□ 2000	33	77	79	38

Figure 5 Grade-10 MCAS Results in Math by Race, 2000 (% failing)

Source: Massachusetts Department of Education, *Spring 2000 MCAS Tests, Report of State Results,* November 2000.

grade math failure rates by race for the three administrations of the MCAS. In 2000, 79 percent of Latino and 77 percent of Black tenth graders failed the math section of the test — almost double the rates for Asian and White students.

Math outcomes in the year 2000 represent a slight improvement over outcomes of the two previous test administrations. Nevertheless, for all children of color, except Asians, even the 2000 outcomes represent very high rates of failure. The outcomes for Black and Latino children in the Massachusetts high-stakes environment mean that these groups are the most likely to experience the most negative outcomes that derive from the use of high-stakes standardized tests.

When we consider the implications of the results for LEP students, the prognosis is equally bleak. Outcomes for LEP students were first reported by the Department of Education for the spring 2000 test. A comparison of the outcomes for tenth graders listed as "regular" students and LEP students is shown in Figure 6. LEP tenth-grade students did much worse than "regular" students; the rate of failure in all three subjects was more than twice that of "regular" students.[29] Northeast and Islands Regional Educational Laboratory at Brown University analyzed 1998 and 1999 MCAS scores attained by LEP students and found similar patterns. These differences were statistically significant even

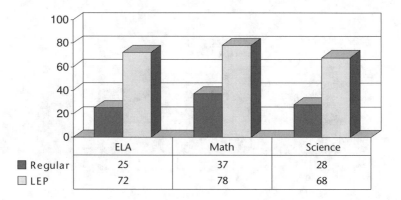

Figure 6   Grade-10 MCAS Outcomes by Student Status (regular and LEP), 2000

Source: Massachusetts Department of Education, *Spring 2000 MCAS Tests, Report of State Results,* November 2000.

when controlling for poverty among students. Although among both groups higher percentages of students who are poor (defined as on free or reduced lunch) fail the test, "in most instances the regular education students who are classified as poor performed better than the LEP students who were not classified as poor."[30]

Magic Bullets and Dropouts

When the Massachusetts Department of Education released the first MCAS results in the late fall of 1998, the failure rates fueled an already heated debate about the testing program. Advocates of the MCAS test emphasize that it is a tool necessary to guarantee accountability for student learning on the part of teachers and schools.[31] It is the "magic bullet" of educational reform, these advocates argue, because "revealing the truth" about student outcomes will force the schools to implement initiatives that will lead to increased student achievement. Holding schools accountable to a high standard will expedite the implementation of improvements in the curriculum and spur the development of advanced placement classes, which will provide increased access to more challenging curricula in math and science. In order to get all students to work at this higher standard, summer school remediation and tutoring programs would be implemented for the weaker students. With high-stakes testing, schools would also have a stake in finding new ways to increase the achievement of all students; schools that show consistent failure over a period of time can easily be identified, placed in receivership, and reorganized.

Opponents of MCAS testing focus on the fact that a "high-stakes" environment creates a climate in schools that does not necessarily lead to improved learning. In the case of school districts where students already excel, a high-stakes environment could affect school culture by forcing teachers to teach to the test and forgo more creative forms of instruction. In many ways, opponents argue, a high-stakes environment undermines good teaching and learning practices that are in place in successful schools.[32]

A powerful argument against the high-stakes test is its impact in school districts already producing lower levels of student achievement. Opponents of MCAS testing argue that a high-stakes environment, rather than improving conditions, may make matters worse, not only by focusing instruction on the test almost exclusively, but also by introducing promotion practices that push children out of school. Holding back weaker students to avoid having them tested is a common practice in a high-stakes environment. It has been documented that retaining weak students in grade without changing the conditions that led to their failure pushes students to drop out of school.[33] Labeling children as failures early in their educational careers may lead them to give up and drop out if they fail the test the first or second time. For all these reasons, the most direct consequence of a high-stakes environment in these weaker school systems seems to be a rapid rise in the dropout rates.

The data in Figure 7 show that there is reason to believe that dropout rates will be a growing concern in Massachusetts. The table shows annual dropout rates for the period between 1992 and 1999, encompassing the whole process of educational reform and the start of the high-stakes environment in Massachusetts schools. Data are presented for each racial or ethnic group so that the differential effect can be discerned. The overall dropout rate began to increase in 1999 after a steady decline over the previous three years. In 1999, the overall dropout rate was somewhat higher (3.6%) than at the start of the process of reform (3.5%) in 1993.

What shows as almost imperceptible change for the overall population hides some larger changes taking place among specific groups.

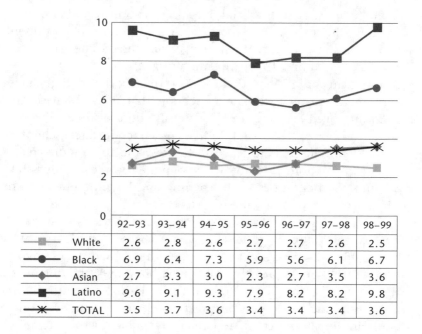

	92–93	93–94	94–95	95–96	96–97	97–98	98–99
White	2.6	2.8	2.6	2.7	2.7	2.6	2.5
Black	6.9	6.4	7.3	5.9	5.6	6.1	6.7
Asian	2.7	3.3	3.0	2.3	2.7	3.5	3.6
Latino	9.6	9.1	9.3	7.9	8.2	8.2	9.8
TOTAL	3.5	3.7	3.6	3.4	3.4	3.4	3.6

Figure 7   Public High School Annual Dropout Rates by Race and Ethnicity, AY1992–1993 to 1998–1999.

Source: Massachusetts Department of Education, *Drop-Out Rates in Massachusetts Public Schools: 1996–1997,* February 1998; *1997–1998,* September 1999; *1998–1999,* August 2000.

In the case of Blacks, after a slow start, dropout rates fell from a high of 7.3 percent in 1994–1995 to a low of 5.6 percent in 1996–1997, but began to rise again by 1997–1998. At that point, dropout rates were almost as high as they were at the start of the reform process in 1993. The pattern for Latinos has been similar, the difference being that the latter rise in dropout rates has been sharper. In 1999, Latino dropout rates were slightly higher than they were at the start of the period of observation. Asian dropout rates in 1999, on the other hand, were almost a full point higher than they were in 1992–1993, after Asians achieved the lowest rates of any group (including Whites) in the middle of the period. Only the dropout rates for White children were lower in 1999 than they were at the start of the process of reform. All children of color, including Asians, have experienced increased dropout rates as the reform process has gone forward. Among Latino children, these rates have reached almost 10 percent per year.

Where Children Go to School

Some argue that the MCAS is an artificially high standard being held against school systems that by and large are doing well in educating children and that Massachusetts school systems are among the best in the United States.[34] They say that the MCAS is too high a standard to hold against an economically and ethnically diverse population of normal children. The fact is that some systems in the state, all wealthier suburban districts, are doing quite well in educating their children to the MCAS standard. What works in the middle-class suburban districts is that the needs of the children are well matched to the resources and methods used to educate them.

This matching of children's needs to educational resources does not appear to take place in the large, multiracial, multicultural urban districts; in these urban districts, children of color and language minority children are performing the worst. Problems with student achievement in these districts are not new. In fact, the process of educational reform began as a way to address the disparities that led to the dysfunction of these systems by bringing equity and fairness to the process of educational funding. The infusion of additional funding, particularly to the poorest districts, was meant to reverse the trend of "benign neglect" of many years.

Conditions in these districts remain fragile. First, the condition of school buildings is often a problem, which affects student performance.[35] Access to books and materials is also unreliable, as evidenced by recent newspaper reports that point out that midway through the year, Boston schoolchildren had not yet received textbooks.[36] Some schools in Massachusetts do not have libraries or may not have appropriate library programs to maximize the use of these resources, according to a recent report.[37] This report also found that MCAS scores are related to student access to a library and a functioning library program.

Another difficulty, as research on local education for the last thirty years has pointed out, is that Latino children are not being taught in ways appropriate to them. Barriers relate to the relevance of curricula and the appropriateness of school practices to the needs of students of color, including Latino students.[38] In the process of educational reform, local participation in the development of curricula that would complement the statewide frameworks was meant to make curricula more relevant to diverse populations. The process of redesigning local curricula, however, is still largely incomplete across the state.

Since the new curriculum frameworks have only recently been put in place, teachers are just preparing themselves to address them. It will take some time for teachers to implement these frameworks with uniformity and with the creativity required to make them relevant to different populations. It will surely take even longer for teachers to build the bridges necessary between the knowledge that students have and the expectations set by the new curriculum frameworks and achievement measures. In general, curricula today still reflect either very low expectations of students or standards that are beyond what students can accomplish with their educational background.

In many schools, children do not yet have access to the content necessary to pass the test. In Boston, for example, a well-documented pattern of tracking of Black and Latino students into the lowest levels of courses[39] leads these students to arrive in tenth grade without either Algebra I or Geometry, which are both essential to passing the tenth-grade math MCAS test. This systematic lack of access to curriculum in math was documented by a 1992 study of Boston high schools, which found that fewer than 20 percent of Black and Latino students in non-exam schools were enrolled in grade-level courses.[40] The study was repeated in 2001, this time focusing on high school students in four Massachusetts districts — Boston, Framingham, Worcester, and Springfield. In Boston, for example, only 16.1 percent of Latino and 38.7 percent of Black students were enrolled in a grade-level math curriculum or above when they took their MCAS test in the tenth grade.[41] The study also indicated that in all districts, in all grades, and in both math and science, the differences in grade enrollments between White students and Black and Latino students were statistically significant.

Finally, although some funding has been made available, remedial programs are not yet in place to the extent necessary to help vulnerable students achieve at the level required to pass the MCAS. The state has begun a well-publicized initiative to remedy the achievement gap by using college students to tutor failing or almost failing K–12 students. This program has been controversial, however, because it places very unrealistic expectations on the tutoring relationship.

No clear plans exist for children who reach the end of twelfth grade without passing the MCAS. The Board of Higher Education has already said that the state university system will not accept students who have not passed the test.[42] There is nothing yet in place to link these students to jobs or to educational alternatives beyond high school. The transition from school to work, long an unresolved problem for minority youth, will most likely be a problem in this case as well.

Concluding Thoughts

Many observers of the educational situation in Massachusetts refer to 2003 as the year of the "train wreck":[43] this is the year in which the high stakes of the MCAS will become a reality. Students who did not pass the MCAS test either as tenth graders in April 2001 or in subsequent chances to retake the test during their junior and senior years will not be graduating in June 2003. If current conditions prevail, almost one-half of Massachusetts tenth graders will fail the first round of the MCAS and, unless they are offered increased support and instruction, they will likely not be eligible to graduate in 2003. An overwhelming majority (75–80%) of racial and language minority students in Massachusetts will not be able to graduate high school in 2003.

Following the 1998 release of test results, political debate and media attention to MCAS results has grown, focusing primarily on the wisdom and appropriateness of testing. Teachers unions, the Massachusetts Association of School Committees, individual school committees and systems, and even the Boston City Council have issued statements against different aspects of the policy as currently implemented. For advocates, the image of the train wreck alludes to the political impact that the high failure rates will have on the process of educational reform. The fear of many stakeholders is that along with the increasingly politically charged testing, politicians will abandon educational reform and, with that, any hope of transforming the educational system.

The highly publicized testing has made evident to all what many parents and educators already knew — that children of some racial and linguistic minorities from low socioeconomic status are receiving an education that is not on a par with that of majority children. Although in general all students have high failure rates, these rates are highest among Black, Latino, and language minority students. As the state's own data reveal, in 2000, 77 percent of Black tenth graders, 79 percent of Latino tenth graders, and 78 percent of LEP students failed the test, whereas only 38 percent of White students failed. These are staggering indicators that schools are not teaching to the standards required by the MCAS, particularly in the case of Black, Latino, and language minority students.

The most obvious consequence of MCAS testing may be the results of policies that for a very long time abandoned and underfunded urban systems and systematically underserved urban students, particularly Latinos and Blacks. High-stakes testing ignores the fact that children in urban schools are clustered in systems that have not yet undergone substantial transformation to guarantee access to the knowledge being tested. This unfairness is due to the fact that, at this point, only the students — not teachers, not principals or superintendents, not schools of education or state regulators — bear the burden of the gap. Although in time schools whose children consistently show high failure rates on the MCAS will be identified and labeled as "failing schools," at this point the MCAS represents a diagnostic tool rather than a sanction for schools and districts. The consequences for schools, school personnel, districts, and district personnel are neither as clearly specified nor as critical as the consequences borne by students. This means that, come 2003, students alone will bear the consequences of the failure of adults to develop the structures necessary for all children to learn.

Without a doubt, the high-stakes environment in Massachusetts blames the victim. The current testing policy in Massachusetts is inequitable and unjust, and the dire consequences of failing the test are particularly injurious to the most vulnerable students. Clearly, there must be some guarantee that children will have more than one measure of their educational achievement. It is also clear that those who propose standardized tests as the measure of system accountability must be responsible for guaranteeing that all children have access to the material on which they are being tested and that the testing situation be fair. Until these conditions are met, there is no accountability argument that outweighs the damage that is done to the lives of the most vulnerable children. Educational policy should, at the very least, do no harm.

The truth is that the problems with Black and Latino education did not start with MCAS testing. The story of Black and Latino education in Massachusetts is the story of the resistance of school systems' resistance to the changing demographics and demands of an increasingly diverse population of children. The history of segregated and unequally funded schools and the battle for desegregation; the practice of tracking in the lower grades and low expectations throughout; curricula that have no connection to the life of urban minority children; the teachers who, unprepared to deal with children different from themselves, are scared of their students; parents who are alienated from the educational process and, often, from their own children — all are revealed in the light of the sobering evidence brought out by MCAS testing.

The task so often mentioned in any discussion of the education of minority children is constructing public systems that respond to the needs of a diverse population of children. We know many of the ingredients that will promote school success for racially, culturally, and linguistically diverse students. Children must be well fed and drug free if they are to focus on learning. Parents, teachers, and schools must have high expectations and provide strong support for children's achievement of these goals. Curricula must offer multiple points of entry that are relevant to the diverse experience of learners. Professional development for teachers must enhance mastery of subject areas, good teaching strategies, and improved abilities to teach across linguistic and cultural difference. School-based, community-inclusive programs must support the achievement of the most vulnerable students and encourage them to remain in school. After-school programs that address homework completion must be available, particularly for children from families whose educational background or English skills do not permit them to assist their children with homework. Schools must build bridges to parents and connections to communities. Parents need to recognize the importance of education and communicate its value to their children. Families and communities must nurture their children and expect excellent performance of them, despite schools that might not do so. Clearly, schools, teachers, parents, communities, and children themselves are all vital actors in the process of constructing school success.

True educational reform is in the best interests of racial and language minority children. But for them, the priority of the reform should be the creation of an academically rigorous environment that is also responsive to their needs. Educational reform in Massachusetts mobilized positive energy that may have led eventually to positive educational experience for all children. This momentum toward building better schools, however, appears to have been lost as the focus has shifted to the test and the debate surrounding the test.

The image of the train wreck alludes not only to the students who will fail, but also to the political impact that high rates of failure will have on the process of educational reform. Many stakeholders fear that, in the stark light of the increasingly political debate about testing, politicians will abandon educational reform and thus lose the opportunity to initiate the fundamental changes necessary to transform the educational system. The condition of the system revealed by MCAS testing is only one harsh reality. An equally great tragedy would be squandering the opportunity that educational reform initially presented to transform our schools into ones that support the academic achievement of *all* our students.

Notes

1. Throughout this chapter I use the terms *Latino, Asian, and Black* in their aggregate form because finer, more disaggregated categories are not available in educational data. There may be differences among subgroups encompassed globally in these categories that, unfortunately, are not reflected here.
2. Massachusetts Department of Education (1992).
3. See Wheelock (1990, p. 11) for data from the late 1980s.
4. I use the terms *Limited English Proficient* and *LEP* because these are the technical terms used by school systems to refer to children who live in the United States and whose first language is a language other than English. I acknowledge here as valid the position of those who criticize the use of these terms because they define children in terms of the characteristics that they lack rather than those they possess.
5. See Hispanic Office of Planning and Evaluation (1978b) for attendance, dropout, and retention rates in the late 1970s; Wheelock (1990) for dropout and truancy rates through the 1980s; and Uriarte and Chavez (2000) for dropout rates through the 1990s.
6. Massachusetts Department of Education (1995b).
7. Massachusetts Department of Education, "Structuring Schools for Student Success: A Focus on Grade Retention," cited in Wheelock (1990, p. 14).
8. These findings are from Boston and are reported in Dentzer and Wheelock (1990, pp. 78–79).
9. Among the most salient examples are the report of the Massachusetts State Advisory Committee of the U.S. Commission on Civil Rights (1976) and reports by the Hispanic Office of Planning and Evaluation (1978a, 1978b, 1980, 1985).
10. Massachusetts Commission on Hispanic Affairs (1986, p. 5).
11. Boston Public Schools (1989a), Exhibit 2.
12. Boston Public Schools (1989b); see also Ribadeniera (1989, p. 45).
13. See the Massachusetts Department of Education website at http://finance1. doe.mass.edu/chapter70/c70hist.html. The state's share of funding for educa-

tion has increased from $1.2 billion in 1993 to $2.6 billion in 1999 and has been distributed using formulas that attempt to address disparities and establish comparable foundation budgets across districts.

14. Massachusetts Department of Education (1997).

15. Massachusetts Department of Education (1995a).

16. Recent proposals for policy change include an appeals process for students who fail. This appeal may take into consideration students' grades and portfolios.

17. The MCAS was administered at district and regional schools, vocational schools, charter schools, special education schools, and agricultural and technical schools.

18. Massachusetts Department of Education (1999a, Tables 1, 3, 5).

19. Massachusetts Department of Education (1999b, p. 7).

20. Massachusetts Department of Education (2000a, p. 2).

21. Massachusetts Department of Education (2000a, p. 2).

22. Since different numbers of children took the different sections of the test, in this chapter *test-takers* refers to those children who took the math test, since this test had the largest number of participants.

23. Massachusetts Department of Education (2000b, p. 16).

24. Massachusetts Department of Education (2000b, p. 18).

25. At the time of the writing of this chapter, data on the racial breakdown of LEP test-takers had not yet been made available. Data for 1999 are taken from the Massachusetts Department of Education CD-ROM release of 1999 MCAS results.

26. Massachusetts Department of Education (2000b, pp. 4–5).

27. Recent newspaper reports have focused on the extreme difficulty of the fourth-grade English language arts test (see "Some Educators Say," 2000).

28. Using the math section of the test for comparison also minimizes the effects of English proficiency as a factor in the high Latino failure rates. Students with limited English proficiency took this section of the test in Spanish.

29. Although these tables report 2000 data, it is important to know that the quality and accuracy of the 1999 data on LEP students reported by the Department of Education have been criticized for their inconsistencies. Many LEP students eligible to take the test did not take it, or the tests were not scored. In the case of students that took the test in Spanish, there is no indication of how many took it in this language and how they scored. See Beals and Pedalino Porter (2000, p. 1).

30. Lachat (2000, p. 6).

31. See, for example, Mass Insight Education (2000, n.d.) and Taylor (2000), among others.

32. See, for example, McNeil (2000); McNeil and Valenzuela (2000); and the following website: http://www.fairtest.org/catalog.htm

33. Dentzer and Wheelock (1990, ch. 2).

34. Marcus (1999, p. 73).

35. See Darder and Upshur (1993, pp. 133–134, 142) for student reaction to the conditions of school buildings in Boston.

36. Vaishnav (2000).
37. Baughman (2000).
38. See Darder and Upshur (1993); Frau-Ramos and Nieto (1993); Montero-Seibruth (1993); and other works about the experience of Latino children in Massachusetts schools.
39. See Dentzer and Wheelock (1990) for a good documentation of this process in Boston's public schools.
40. Upshur, Freitas, Ahern, Benton, and Carver (1991, pp. 7–15).
41. Upshur et al. (in press).
42. Greenberger (2000a, 2000b).
43. Fair Test and CARE (2000, p. 6).

References

Baughman, J. C. (2000, October 26). *School libraries and MCAS scores*. Paper presented at a symposium sponsored by the Graduate School of Library and Information Science, Simmons College, Boston.

Beals, R., & Pedalino Porter, R. (2000). *Bilingual students and the MCAS: Some bright spots in the gloom*. Washington, DC: Institute for Research in English Acquisition and Development.

Boston Public Schools. (1989a). *Brief report on dropout statistics for Hispanic students in the Boston public schools: Focus on high schools and neighborhoods*. Boston: Author, Office of Research and Development.

Boston Public Schools. (1989b). *Hispanic dropout program*. Unpublished document.

Darder, A., & Upshur, C. C. (1993). What do Latino children need to succeed in school? In R. Rivera & S. Nieto (Eds.), *The education of Latino children in Massachusetts: Issues, research and policy implications* (pp. 127–146). Amherst: University of Massachusetts Press.

Dentzer, E., & Wheelock, A. (1990). *Locked in/ locked out: Tracking and placement practices in Boston public schools*. Boston: Massachusetts Advocacy Center.

Fair Test & CARE. (2000). *The coming "train wreck": Asleep at the switch*. Cambridge, MA: National Center for Fair and Open Testing and the Coalition for Authentic Reform in Education.

Frau-Ramos, M., & Nieto, S. (1993). *I was an outsider: An exploratory study of dropping out among Puerto Rican youths in Holyoke, Massachusetts*. In R. Rivera & S. Nieto (Eds.), *The education of Latino children in Massachusetts: Issues, research and policy implications* (pp. 147–169). Amherst: University of Massachusetts Press.

Greenberger, S. (2000a, September 26). Ed board considers alternative to diploma, *Boston Globe,* p. B1.

Greenberger, S. (2000b, September 28). MCAS required for state colleges, local certificates not acceptable. *Boston Globe,* p. B1.

Hispanic Office of Planning and Evaluation. (1978a). *The Puerto Rican community of Boston: Opportunity and participation in education and employment*. Boston: Author.

Hispanic Office of Planning and Evaluation. (1978b). *Puerto Ricans in Boston: Current conditions in education and employment*. Boston: Author.

Hispanic Office of Planning and Evaluation. (1980). *Juventud Latina de Boston luchando por su futuro: Social realities and the information gap for Hispanic youth in Boston.* Boston: Author.

Hispanic Office of Planning and Evaluation. (1985). *The Education of Hispanic youth: An initial blueprint for public school reform and community action in Boston* (HOPE Working Paper). Boston: Author.

Lachat, M. A. (2000). *The performance of limited English proficient students on the 1998 and 1999 Massachusetts Comprehensive Assessment System.* Providence, RI: Brown University, Northeast and the Islands Regional Educational Laboratory.

Marcus, J. (1999, October). The shocking truth about our public schools. *Boston Magazine,* pp. 70–83.

Massachusetts Commission on Hispanic Affairs. (1986). *Report of the Education Task Force.* Boston: Author. (Available: Massachusetts State House archive)

Massachusetts Department of Education. (1992). *School and school districts profiles* [On-line]. Available: http://www.doe.mass.edu/pic.www/profmain.htm

Massachusetts Department of Education. (1995a, November). *Advisory on school governance* [On-line]. Available: http://www.doe.mass.edu/lawsregs/advisory/cm1115gov.html

Massachusetts Department of Education. (1995b). *Dropout rates in Massachusetts public schools: 1994* [On-line]. Available: http://www.doc.mas.edu/ata/dropout/9394/

Massachusetts Department of Education. (1997). *Educational reform in Massachusetts. A progress report: 1993–1997* [On-line]. Available: http://www.doe.mass.edu/edreform/edreformreport/erprogrpt597-1.html

Massachusetts Department of Education. (1999a). *October report.* Unpublished document.

Massachusetts Department of Education. (1999b). *Massachusetts Comprehensive Assessment System. Report of 1998 statewide and district results by race and ethnicity.* Malden, MA: Author.

Massachusetts Department of Education. (2000a). *Massachusetts Comprehensive Assessment System: Requirements for participation of students with limited English proficiency. A guide for educators and parents* (spring update). Malden, MA: Author.

Massachusetts Department of Education. (2000b). *Massachusetts Comprehensive Assessment System: Spring 2000 MCAS tests, report of state results* [On-line]. Available: http://www.doe.mass.edu/mcas/results/html

Mass Insight Education. (2000). *Up and over the bar.* Boston: Author. Available on-line: www.massinsight.com

Mass Insight Education. (n.d.). *For the first time ever.* Boston: Author. Available on-line: www.massinsight.com

Massachusetts State Advisory Committee of the U.S. Commission on Civil Rights. (1976). *Issues of concern to Puerto Ricans in Boston and Springfield.* Unpublished manuscript.

McNeil, L. (2000). *Contradictions of school reform.* New York: Routledge.

McNeil, L., & Valenzuela, A. (2000). *The harmful impact of the TAAS system of testing in Texas.* Cambridge, MA: Civil Rights Project at Harvard University.

Montero-Seibruth, M. (1993). The effects of schooling policies and practices on potential at-risk Latino high school students. In R. Rivera & S. Nieto (Eds.), *The
education of Latino children in Massachusetts: Issues, research and policy implications* (pp. 217–242). Amherst: University of Massachusetts Press.

Ribadeneira, D. (1989, November 16). Wilson, Hispanics agree on school plan.
Boston Globe, p. 45.

Some educators say scores show fourth-grade test too tough. (2000, December 25).
Boston Globe, p. B1. Available on-line: http://www.boston.com/dailynews/
360/region/Some_educators_say_scores_show:.shtml

Taylor, W. L. (2000, November 15). Standards, test, and civil rights. *Education Week*
[On-line]. Available: http://edweek.com/ew/ewstory.cfm?slug=lltaylor.h20

Upshur, C., Freitas, R., Ahern, S., Benton, R., & Carver, I. (1991). *Analysis of math
enrollments in Boston public high schools: Effects of differential access and tracking*
(Report prepared for the Massachusetts Advocacy Center). Unpublished document.

Upshur, C. C., Vega, R. R., Carithers, N., Jones, C., Lucy-Allen, D., Meschede, T., &
Ndungu, C. (in press). *Access to educational opportunities for Latino students in
four Massachussets school districts*. Boston: Mauricio Gastón Institute for Latino
Community Development and Public Policy.

Uriarte, M., & Chavez, L. (2000). *Latino students and the Massachusetts public schools*.
Boston: Mauricio Gastón Institute for Latino Community Development and
Public Policy.

Vaishnav. A. (2000, November 1). Boston schools short on social-studies texts.
Boston Globe, p. B1.

Wheelock, A. (1990). *The status of Latino students in Massachusetts public schools: Di-
rection for policy research in the 1990s*. Boston: Mauricio Gastón Institute for Latino Community Development and Public Policy.

Revealing Illusions of Educational Progress: Texas High-Stakes Tests and Minority Student Performance[1]

WALT HANEY

For several years the state of Texas has been widely cited as a model of standards-based education reform; some have even called recent educational progress in Texas a miracle. Indeed, Texas has been cited as a model worthy of emulation by other states and even by the federal government. In this chapter I review evidence to show that the "miracle" of education reform in Texas is really a myth and an illusion, particularly when we focus our attention on minority student performance.

We should learn from rather than emulate the Texas experience. First, we should learn to be cautious in drawing sweeping conclusions about large and complex educational endeavors based on only one form of evidence, such as test scores. Second, we should closely monitor the conduct of school districts that may be driven to alter student grade-promotion and placement procedures in order to influence the high-stakes test averages by which their schools are evaluated, and then punished or rewarded. Finally, we must recognize that in a high-stakes environment those students whom the accountability schemes were designed to benefit may actually end up suffering most. In Texas today more minority students are being retained in grade, more are being placed in special education classes, and more end up dropping out of school (Haney, 2000).

Recent Educational Reform Efforts in Texas

Texas has seen several waves of education reform over the last several decades. As with reform efforts in many other states, testing has featured prominently in these efforts. In 1984, the Texas legislature passed a comprehensive education reform law mandating sweeping changes in education. Among other things, the law established a statewide curriculum, known as the Essential Elements, that required students to achieve a score of seventy to pass their high school courses, mandated that students could not participate in varsity sports if they did not pass high school courses, required teachers to pass a proficiency test, and mandated changes in the statewide testing program (Funkhouser, 1990). In addition to taking a basic skills test in each odd-numbered grade, the testing program required that students pass an exit-level test to graduate from high school. The exit-level tests were given for the first time in October 1985; 85 percent of students who took the test passed the math portion, 91 percent passed the English language arts portion, and 85 percent passed both. Students who failed either portion had an opportunity to retake the tests in May 1986. The majority of students who had failed in the fall passed the spring retest (Funkhouser, 1990, pp. 199–201).

In subsequent years, a new wave of educational reforms throughout the country placed a stronger emphasis on "outcomes accountability," that is, holding teachers and schools accountable for student achievement measured by statewide tests. In 1990, changes in Texas law required the implementation of a new criterion-referenced testing program, the Texas Assessment of Academic Skills (TAAS).[2] The TAAS was much more difficult than previous tests and was intended to shift the focus of assessment from "minimum skills" to "academic skills" and to test "higher-order thinking skills and problem solving ability" (Texas Education Agency, 1997, p. 1). Since 1994, the TAAS reading, math, and writing tests have been consistently administered to students in the spring of grades four, eight, and ten.

In addition to assessing student learning, TAAS results are used to hold schools and school systems accountable for student learning. By Texas law, the State Board of Education is mandated to rate the performance of schools and school districts annually according to a set of academic excellence indicators, including TAAS results, dropout rates, and student attendance rates (Texas Education Agency, 1997). State law also prescribes that student performance data be disaggregated by ethnicity and socioeconomic status. The performance rating system holds that school performance is not acceptable if the performance of all subgroups is not acceptable. Based primarily on the percentage of students passing each of the TAAS tests, public schools in Texas have been rated since 1994 as "exemplary," "recognized," "acceptable," or "unacceptable."

TAAS passing standards for school performance ratings are based on the passing rates for all students and the disaggregated rates for four student groups: Hispanic, African American, White, and economically disadvantaged. Of the four categories, only the "exemplary" rating has had a consistent passing standard, requiring at least 90 percent of all students and each student group to pass each subject area. The "recognized" rating has increased from at least 65 percent of students passing in 1994 to a current 70 percent, the "acceptable" rating has gone from at least 25 percent passing to 30 percent passing, and the "unacceptable" rating from less than 25 percent to less than 30 percent (Gordon & Reese, 1997, pp. 347–480). Schools are eligible for cash awards for high ratings; if they are rated as low performing two years in a row, they are subject to sanctions from the Texas Education Agency, including possible closure.

In short, over the past decade TAAS has become an extremely high-stakes test for students, educators, and schools in the state of Texas. Regardless of grades in their high school courses, students cannot graduate unless they pass all three portions of the exit-level version of TAAS in reading, math, and writing. Schools' reputations, funding, and even continued existence depend on student performance on TAAS. Given the consequences attached to TAAS, it is not surprising that this test has had a major impact on schools and education in Texas. At first glance, this impact appears to have been largely positive, and it is evidence of the apparent positive impact of TAAS, along with the Texas system of school accountability, that has helped give rise to the story of an education reform miracle in Texas.

Four kinds of evidence seem to have been most widely cited as indicative of major improvements in education in Texas: sharp increases in the overall pass rates on TAAS during the 1990s; apparent decreases in the achievement gap between White and minority students in Texas, again based on TAAS scores; seemingly decreasing rates of students dropping out of school before high school graduation; and apparent confirmation of TAAS gains by results on the National Assessment of Educational Progress (NAEP).

The main evidence contributing to the perception of dramatic educational gains in Texas during the 1990s seems to have been sharp increases in overall passing rates on the TAAS. Table 1 shows the testing results.

For grade-ten testing, there was steady improvement from 1994 to 1998, with the percentage of students passing the TAAS reading test rising from 76 percent to 88 percent, the percentage passing the TAAS math test rising from 57 percent to 78 percent, and the corresponding increase for the TAAS writing test going from 81 percent to 89 percent. The percentage of grade-ten students passing all three tests increased from 52 percent in 1994 to 72 percent in 1998.

Even as test scores were improving overall, the gaps in achievement between White, African American, and Hispanic students appeared to have been narrowing. Comparing groups of tenth-grade students who passed all three TAAS tests in 1994, there was a large disparity in pass rates of Black and Hispanic students compared to White students. Table 2 shows the percentages of Black, Hispanic, and White students who passed all TAAS tests from 1994 to 1998.

In 1994, the Black student pass rate of 29 percent and the Hispanic passing rate of 35 percent were much lower than the White student passing rate of 67 percent. By 1998, the White passing rate jumped to 85 percent, but the Black and Hispanic rates jumped even further, to 54 percent and 59 percent, respectively. It appeared as if over time the race gap was narrowing.

During the same period, dropout rates in Texas seemed to be declining as well. Dropout rates decreased for all high school students in Texas from 1994 to 1998, as well as for each of the three race groups for which data were disaggregated. Table 3 shows Texas annual dropout rates from grades seven to twelve from 1994 to 1998.

Statewide, dropout rates for all students decreased from 2.8 percent to 1.6 percent from 1994 to 1998. Over the same four years, dropout rates for Black students declined from 3.6 to 2.0 percent; for Hispanic students from 4.2 to 2.3 percent; and for White students from 1.7 to 1.0 percent.

Finally, in 1997, release of results from the NAEP indicated that, among the states participating in the state-level portion of the math assessment, Texas showed the greatest gains in percentages of fourth

TABLE 1

Texas Assessment of Academic Skills, Grade 10, Percentage of Students Passing, 1994–1998; All Students Not in Special Education

	1994	1995	1996	1997	1998
TAAS Reading	76	76	81	86	88
TAAS Math	57	59	65	72	78
TAAS Writing	81	86	85	88	89
TAAS All Tests	52	54	60	67	72

Source: Selected State AEIS Data: A Multiyear History
(www.tea.state.tx.us/student.assessment/swresult/gd10sp98.htm)

TABLE 2

Texas Assessment of Academic Skills, Grade 10, Percentage of Students Passing All Tests by Race, 1994–1998; All Students Not in Special Education (Does Not Include Year-Round Education Results)

	1994	1995	1996	1997	1998
Black	29	32	38	48	55
Hispanic	35	37	44	52	59
White	67	70	74	81	85

Source: Selected State AEIS Data: A Multiyear History
(www.tea.state.tx.us/student.assessment/swresult/gd10sp98.htm)

TABLE 3

Texas Annual Dropout Rate, Grades 7–12, 1994–1998, in Percentages

	1994	1995	1996	1997	1998
All Students	2.8	2.6	1.8	1.8	1.6
Black	3.6	3.2	2.3	2.3	2.0
Hispanic	4.2	3.9	2.7	2.5	2.3
White	1.7	1.5	1.2	1.1	1.0

Source: Selected State AEIS Data: A Five-Year History
(www.tea.state.tx.us/perfreport/aeis/hist/state.html)

graders scoring at the proficient or advanced levels. Between 1992 and 1996, the percentage of Texas fourth graders scoring at these levels had increased from 15 percent to 25 percent. The same NAEP results also showed North Carolina to have posted unusually large gains at the grade-eight level, with the percentages of eighth graders in North Carolina scoring at the proficient or advanced levels, improving from 9 percent in 1990 to 20 percent in 1996 (Reese, Millert, Mazzeo, & Dossey, 1997). Putting aside for the moment the fact that the 1996 NAEP results also showed that math achievement in these two states was no better (and in some cases worse) than the national average, these findings led to considerable publicity for the apparent success of education reform in these two states. The apparent gains in math, for example, led the National Education Goals Panel in 1997 to identify Texas and North Carolina as having made unusual progress in achieving the national education goals.

These developments led to a flurry of praise for the apparent educational progress in Texas. For example, Skrla, Scheurich, and Johnson (2000) wrote a report based on research in four fairly large Texas districts. Based on analysis of district-generated documents, on-site observations, and more than two hundred individual and group interviews, they concluded that these districts had had dramatic changes in "teaching and learning practices in the classroom." The authors claimed that because of "changes in equity beliefs" and "the pursuit of educational equity and excellence," these school systems had produced "equitable educational success for literally all the children in their districts" (pp. 6, 7, 39).

In this chapter, I refute claims of success based on the four kinds of evidence briefly reviewed above and show that the Texas miracle is a myth when we take a closer look at the student achievement and student enrollment data. Although there has been some rise in TAAS scores in recent years, we should not be unduly surprised by this trend. Anyone familiar with the recent education history of the United States must view with some skepticism the meaningfulness of the almost inevitable increases in performance that follow introduction of a new testing program. When a new testing program is first introduced, students and teachers have little familiarity with the specifics of the new tests. After a few years, students become familiar with the style and format of the tests; hence, average test scores almost inevitably increase.

Furthermore, students can be coached specifically for the test in question, which has been shown time and again. Indeed, what happens when students are coached for a specific test has come to be called the "sawtooth" phenomenon by educational researchers because of the regular pattern in which scores steadily rise after the introduction of a new testing program, only to fall dramatically when a different test is introduced (Linn, 2000, p. 7). Scores may be raised by focusing narrowly on test objectives without improving achievement across the broader domain that the test objectives are intended to represent (Haney, 2000). Worse still, students may spend class time practicing on nearly identical or even the actual items that appear on a test. Rising scores on statewide tests such as TAAS are not a real indication of improved student learning when similar gains are not evident on other standardized tests, such as NAEP or SAT, measuring similar math and verbal skills.

In the following pages, I focus on evidence that shows that, despite seeming overall improvement in TAAS pass rates, the achievement disparities among racial groups are not decreasing. In fact, high-stakes tests are having a disproportionately adverse effect on Hispanic and African American students. Specifically, I show that, since the implementation of high-stakes tests in Texas, an increasing number of minority students are excluded from taking the TAAS test each year, either because they are placed in special education classes, or retained in grade nine before taking the test, or because they drop out. Thus, the exclusion of low-achieving minority students from TAAS tests is creating an illusion that the racial achievement gap in Texas is decreasing. Finally, I reveal illusions of educational progress in Texas by showing that SAT scores of students in Texas have not improved, and indeed "college readiness" test scores have plummeted.

Increasing Special Education Placement of Minority Students and the Illusion of Progress

Some portion of the apparent gains in TAAS pass rates of tenth-grade students between 1994 and 1998 appears to be due to increased exclusion of minority children from the test by placement in special education classes. Texas reports the TAAS scores of mainstream students and special education students separately. Table 4 shows the numbers and percentages of grade-ten TAAS test-takers in special education.

TABLE 4

Numbers of Grade-10 TAAS Takers in Special Education, 1994–1998

Year	All Groups	Afric. Amer.	Hispanic	White
1994	7,602	833	1,991	4,685
1995	9,049	1,032	2,351	5,581
1996	11,467	1,500	3,017	6,810
1997	13,005	1,518	3,707	7,617
1998	14,558	1,818	4,271	8,284

Percentages of Grade-10 TAAS Takers in Special Education, 1994–1998

Year	All Groups	Afric. Amer.	Hispanic	White
1994	3.9	3.3	3.3	4.5
1995	4.5	4.0	3.7	5.2
1996	5.3	5.4	4.5	6.1
1997	5.8	5.3	5.1	6.6
1998	6.3	6.3	5.7	7.1

The numbers and percentages of Texas students taking the grade-ten TAAS but classified as special education students have increased steadily between 1994 and 1998. The percentage of African American grade-ten TAAS takers in special education almost doubled in four years, from 3.3 percent in 1994 to 6.3 percent in 1998. The percentage of Hispanic tenth-grade TAAS takers in special education increased from 3.3 percent in 1994 to 5.7 percent in 1998. Finally, White TAAS takers in special education increased from 4.5 percent in 1994 to 7.1 percent in 1998. This means that increasing percentages of students who have made it to grade ten are excluded from school accountability ratings by virtue of having been classified in special education. The increase in percentage change was more pronounced for African American and Hispanic students than for White students, although the percentage of White students counted as special education grew less rapidly but remained higher. This means that a portion of the increase in pass rates on the grade-ten TAAS is attributable simply to the increases in the rates at which students were diverted into special education and hence excluded from school accountability ratings and from summary statistics showing pass rates for students not in special education.[3]

Increasing Retention of Minority Students and the Illusion of Progress

Some portion of the apparent overall gains and decreasing racial gap in TAAS pass rates of tenth-grade students in Texas seems to be due to increased exclusion of minority children from taking the test by being retained in grade. The 1998 statewide retention rates in K–12 (Texas Education Agency, 1998) illustrate the widening (not diminishing) gap in White and non-White retention rates. Compared with only 10 percent of White students, 25–30 percent of Black and Hispanic students were "failing" grade nine, instead of being promoted to grade ten.

Table 5 shows that, across all ethnic groups, total retention rates for students in ninth grade were much larger than retention rates for any other grade. Overall, 17.8 percent of the entire public school population, meaning one in five or six public school students in the state of Texas, was retained in ninth grade. A close look at the retention rates by ethnicity reveals that retention in ninth grade was much more common for Hispanic and Black children than for White children. Specifically, compared with 9.6 percent of White students who were retained in ninth grade, 24.2 percent of Black and 25.9 percent of Hispanic students were retained in ninth grade. In other words, the rate at which Black and Hispanic students were retained in grade nine was 2.5 to 3 times the rate at which White students had to repeat grade nine. One cause for the apparent decrease in the racial gap in the TAAS test scores is that Hispanic and Black students are being retained in ninth grade *before* they take the high-stakes tests in grade ten. It is clear that the apparent diminution in the racial gap in TAAS grade-ten pass rates is in some measure an illusion when a large percentage of low-achieving minority students did not even make it to tenth grade to take the exit-level TAAS test.

The grade-nine retention rates in Texas are far in excess of national trends. For example, a recent report of the National Research Council (NRC) shows that Texas has one of the highest grade-nine retention rates for 1992 to 1996 among the states for which such data are available (Heubert & Hauser, 1999, Table 6.1). Supporting previous

TABLE 5

Texas Statewide Rates of Retention in Grade, 1996–1997, by Ethnicity

Grade	White % Retained	Afric. Amer. % Retained	Hispanic % Retained	Total %
K	2.30	1.40	1.60	1.80
1	4.40	7.00	6.60	5.60
2	1.60	3.20	3.40	2.50
3	0.90	2.10	2.10	1.50
4	0.70	1.30	1.40	1.10
5	0.60	0.90	1.00	0.80
6	1.00	2.10	2.30	1.60
7	1.60	3.70	3.80	2.70
8	1.30	2.10	2.90	2.00
9	9.60	24.20	25.90	17.80
10	4.80	11.60	11.40	7.90
11	3.20	8.30	7.90	5.40
12	2.50	6.30	7.20	4.40
Total	2.70	5.70	5.80	4.20

Source: Texas Education Agency (1998), Table 4.2, p. 53.

research that demonstrates grade retention as a common precursor to dropping out of school, the NRC report concludes, "In secondary school, grade retention leads to reduced achievement and much higher rates of school dropout" (p. 285). The next section examines the applicability of the retention-dropout link for Texas students.

Increasing Minority Student Dropouts and the Illusion of Progress

A portion of the seeming rise in TAAS scores and the highly touted diminishing racial gap can also be explained by the increase in students who drop out before tenth grade and do not take the test. Distrusting the dropout rates listed by the Texas Department of Education, I used a different method of calculating dropout rates, one that takes into account the student enrollment and student retention rate in each grade.[4] Figure 1 shows student enrollment by grade, actual rates reported by the state, and predicted rates based on my calculations for the 1996–1997 academic year. As can be seen in Figure 1, there is a close match between the actual student enrollment rates for each grade level until ninth grade, with the exception of first grade.[5] For grades ten and eleven, there are much larger disparities between student dropout rates reported by the state and those that I calculated. Overall, enrollments in grades ten and eleven in 1996–1997 were lower than predicted by more than 65,000, based on the previous year's enrollments. The missing students were predominantly Black and Hispanic. Most probably the missing students are those who dropped out of school before the tenth or eleventh grade.

It is highly possible that students who were retained in ninth grade, disproportionately Black and Hispanic students, dropped out before completing high school. A study recently released by Texas state senator Gonzalos Barrientos supports this argument. Focusing on 41,334 freshman high school students who repeated the ninth grade in all Texas districts in the 1992–1993 academic year, this study found that five years later, in 1997–1998, only 19.5 percent of them had

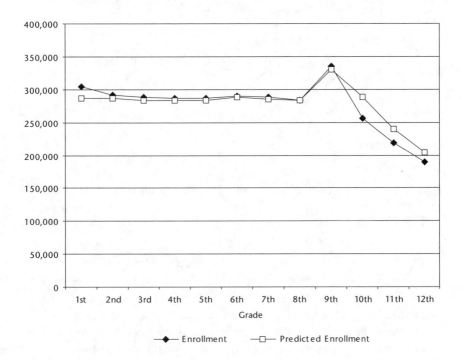

Figure 1 Texas Enrollment by Grade, 1996–1997, Predicted and Actual

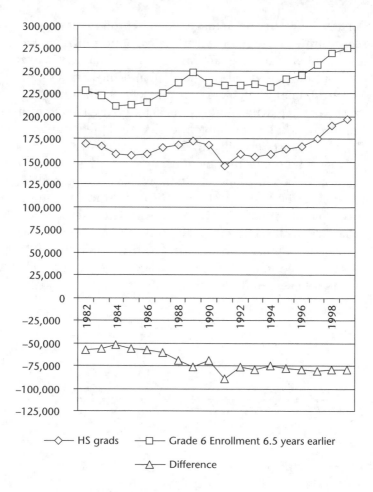

Figure 2   Progress from Grade 6 to High School Graduation, Texas Classes of 1982 to 1999

graduated from high school, and another 15.6 percent had received GED certification. In other words, an overwhelming majority of students who repeated the ninth grade in Texas did not receive a high school diploma. Only one in five students persisted in high school until graduation after repeating the ninth grade.

It is ironic that, by 1999, dropout rates were actually worse in Texas than the dropout rates before the so-called education reform movement started. Increasing dropout rates since the initial year of TAAS testing (1990–1991) show that it is a myth that fewer students are dropping out of Texas public schools. A close look at the grade enrollment patterns from 1982 to 1999 reveals that there is an increase in the number of students dropping out of school since the implementation of the standards-based education reform in Texas. Figure 2 shows the total number of students who progressed from grade six to high school graduation six years later for Texas high school classes of 1982 to 1999. Also shown are the differences; that is, the numbers of students who do not make it from grade six to high school graduation six years later.

The number of children lost between grade six and high school graduation in Texas was in the range of 50,000 to 60,000 for the classes of 1982 to 1986. The number of lost children started to increase rapidly for the class of 1987 and jumped to almost 90,000 for the class of 1991. For the classes of 1992 through 1999, 75,000 to 80,000 children were being lost in each cohort. Cumulatively, for the classes of 1992 through 1999, 2,226,003 White, Black, and Hispanic students were enrolled in grade six (in the academic years of 1984–1985 through 1992–1993). The total number graduating from these classes was 1,510,274. In other words, for the graduating classes of 1992 through 1999, more than 700,000 children in Texas were lost or left behind before graduating from high school. This implies that in the 1990s, about one in three students in Texas dropped out and did not graduate from high school.[6]

Diminishing College Readiness and the Illusion of Progress

An educational system in which 30 percent of students overall and 40 percent of minorities do not even complete high school is one to be deplored rather than applauded. Some may argue, however, that having 30 percent of young people fail to graduate from high school is an unfortunate but necessary price to pay for boosting the achievement of those who do finish high school. We can see that this is not true by looking at Texas students' performance in other nationwide and statewide tests. The results of Texas college-readiness tests (the Texas Academic Skills Program [TASP] tests) from 1993 to 1998 show that the college readiness of Texas students in high school classes has fallen precipitously. For the members of the high school class of 1998 who sought to attend college in Texas and hence had to take the TASP tests, only 31.8 percent of students overall and just 17.6 percent of Black and 23.2 percent of Hispanic students passed all three tests (reading, writing, and math). These were students who would have taken the TAAS in 1996 when they were in grade ten. Furthermore, evidence indicates that, at least as measured by performance on the SAT, the academic learning of secondary school students in Texas has not improved since the early 1990s, compared to SAT takers nationally. Results from 1993 to 1999 on the SAT-M indicate that the learning of Texas students has deteriorated relative to students nationally, and this result holds even after controlling for percentage of high school graduates taking the SAT. Similarly, on another nationwide test, NAEP, the magnitude of the gains apparent on NAEP for Texas fails to confirm the dramatic gains apparent on TAAS. These results indicate that the dramatic student progress as measured by TAAS during the 1990s is more illusory than real (see Klein, Hamilton, McCaffrey, & Stecher, 2000, for a similar conclusion). In other words, the huge cost of having three or four out of ten students in Texas drop out of school cannot be justified in terms of the increased achievement of students who do graduate from high school.

Lessons from the Myth of the Texas Miracle

The TAAS was introduced in Texas in the 1990–1991 school year. Since then, TAAS testing has been the linchpin of educational accountability in Texas, not only for students but also for educators and schools. A variety of evidence in the late 1990s led many observers to conclude that the state of Texas had made nearly miraculous educational progress on a number of fronts. Between 1994 and 1998, the percentage of students passing the math, reading, and writing parts of TAAS tests was reported to have grown from 52 percent to more than 70 percent. In addition, the racial gap in TAAS results seemed to have narrowed. Statistics from the Texas Education Agency showed that during the same interval dropout rates had declined steadily. These developments led to a flurry of praise for the apparent educational progress of Texas.

Despite such ongoing boosterism, a wide range of evidence indicates that the Texas miracle is mainly a myth and an illusion. A substantial portion of the apparent increases in TAAS pass rates in the 1990s are due to such exclusions as increased dropouts, increased retention rates, and increased placement in special education. Dropout rates, retention rates, and special education placements have increased substantially since Texas implemented high-stakes testing.

The Texas story should lead us to pause and consider the broader aims of education in our society. It is a sad reminder of what we have seen again and again, namely, that when enough pressure is brought to bear on schools, test scores can be increased. Such increases frequently come at great cost to the broader learning of students and to the meaningfulness of test results themselves (Cannell, 1987, 1989; Koretz & Barron, 1998; Koretz, Linn, Dunnbar, & Shepard, 1991; Linn, Graue, & Sanders, 1989). The Texas story reminds us clearly that, quite apart from raising test scores, surely one of the main outcomes of precollegiate education is the proportion of students who complete and graduate from high school. By this measure, the Texas system of education, in which only two out of three young people actually graduated from high school in the 1990s, surely should not be deemed a success, much less a miracle.

The TAAS testing program in Texas seems to have been spawned mainly by a desire to hold schools accountable for student learning. It is an unfortunate and common manifestation of what has come to be called "outcomes accountability." Quite apart from test scores, however, one of the most important outcomes of public education is how many young people complete twelve years of schooling and graduate from high school. Accountability, after all, refers to providing an account or explanation not just of consequences but of conduct as well.

The most devastating impact of high-stakes testing seems to have fallen on the students it was supposed to help: the lower-achieving minority students. By setting clear standards and measuring results, state-mandated tests were intended to make schools accountable for the basic education to which all children are entitled. Unfortunately, the real impact of high-stakes tests in Texas has been the opposite: more minority students are held back in grade nine, more minority students are placed in special education classes, and more minority students drop out of school.

The Texas story underlines the importance of inquiring into conduct as well as consequences when judging educational endeavors. When we look behind the myth of the Texas miracle, educators, parents, and policymakers must be concerned and investigate further the apparent changes in school and district student grade-promotion and placement procedures that appear to have so adversely affected Black and Hispanic students. Is it merely a coincidence that average TAAS scores have risen across the state at the same time that students have increasingly been held back in ninth grade and not promoted to tenth grade, in which TAAS tests are administered? Is it merely a coincidence that the percentage of minority students classified as special needs and therefore not counted in schools' accountability ratings has doubled while TAAS scores have appeared to rise? What are the forces that have moved Black and Hispanic students in Texas to drop out of school in large numbers and thereby helped create the illusion of rising TAAS scores? The Texas experience shows us the hazards of high-stakes testing and the need to return standardized testing to its rightful place, as a source of potentially useful information to inform human judgment, and not as a cudgel for implementing education policy.

Notes

1. This chapter has been adapted with permission from the *Education Policy Analysis Archives*, with generous editorial assistance from Zeynep F. Beykont, from two longer works (Haney, 2000, 2001). More documentation and several other kinds of evidence are discussed in these sources.
2. End-of-course tests for selected high school course subjects were also established at this time. Also, it should be mentioned that though the TAAS was supposed to have been a criterion-referenced test, as implemented, it is in effect a norm-referenced test.
3. Beginning in 1999, students classified as in special education were no longer excluded from the pool of students counted in schools' accountability ratings. As a result of this change, between 1998 and 1999 the percentage of students whose scores on TAAS counted in schools' accountability ratings went up from 76 percent to 85 percent (Fuller, 2000, p. 2). However, "at the same time, the percentage of students given special education exemptions [from taking TAAS] increased from 5.8 percent in 1998 to 7.8 percent in 1999" (p. 4).
4. I used the retention rates listed in Table 5 and the statewide enrollment data for 1995–1996 and 1996–1997 to calculate the grade levels at which students are dropping out of school in Texas. The logic of these calculations is as follows: if we assume no net immigration of students into Texas, the number of students enrolled in, say, grade six in 1996–1997 ought to be equal to the sum of the number of students enrolled in grade five in 1995–1996 times the rate of nonretention in grade five, plus the number enrolled in grade six times the grade-six retention rate. Using this approach we may calculate the predicted grade enrollments in 1996–1997 and compare them with the actual 1996–1997 enrollments. Given that during the last decade or more, there has been positive net migration into the state of Texas (Murdock, Hoque, Michael,

White, & Pecotte, 1997), these calculations almost surely underestimate the extent of the dropout problem.

5. The difference for first grade presumably derives from the fact that across all groups kindergarten attendance was not universal in 1995–1996 hence the grade-one enrollments in 1996–1997 are larger than those predicted from 1995–1996 kindergarten enrollments.

6. Some of these dropouts may have received GED equivalency degrees, but GED certification is by no means equivalent to regular high school graduation.

References

Cannell, J. J. (1987). *Nationally normed elementary achievement testing in America's public schools: How all 50 states are above the national average.* Daniels, WV: Friends for Education.

Cannell, J. J. (1989). *The "Lake Wobegon" report: How public educators cheat on standardized achievement tests.* Albuquerque, NM: Friends for Education.

Fuller, E. (2000) *Special education exemption rates and school accountability ratings in selected Texas school districts for the 1997–98 and 1998–99 academic years.* Austin: University of Texas at Austin, Charles A Dana Center.

Funkhouser, C. (1990). *Education in Texas: Policies, practices and perspectives* (5th ed.). Scottsdale, AZ: Gorsuch Scarisbrick.

Gordon, S. P., & Reese, M. (1997). High stakes testing: Worth the price? *Journal of School Leadership, 7,* 345–368.

Haney, W. (2000, August 19). The myth of the Texas miracle in education. *Education Policy Analysis Archives, 8* [On-line]. Available: http://epaa.asu.edu/epaa/v8n41/

Haney, W. (2001, January). *Revisiting the myth of the Texas miracle in education: Lessons about dropout research and dropout prevention.* Paper prepared for the HCRP/Achieve conference, Dropout Research: Accurate Counts and Positive Interventions, Cambridge, MA. Available: http://www.law.harvard.edu/civilrights/publications/dropout.html

Heubert, J., & Hauser, R. (Eds.). (1999). High stakes: Testing for tracking, promotion, and graduation (Report of the National Research Council). Washington, DC: National Academy Press.

Klein, S., Hamilton L., McCaffrey, D., & Stecher, B. (2000, October). What do test scores in Texas tell us? *Education Policy Analysis Archives, 8.* Available: http://epaa.asu.edu/epaa/v8n49/

Koretz, D. M., & Barron, S. I. (1998). *The validity of gains in scores on the Kentucky Instructional Results Information System* (Report No. MR-1014-EDU). Washington, DC: RAND.

Koretz, D. M., Linn, R. L., Dunbar, S. B., & Shepard, L. A. (1991, April). *The effects of high stakes testing on achievement: Preliminary findings about generalization across tests.* Paper presented at the annual meeting of the American Educational Research Association, Chicago.

Linn, R. L. (2000). Assessments and accountability. *Educational Researcher, 29*(2), 4–15.

Linn, R. L., Graue, M. E., & Sanders, N. M. (1989, March). *Comparing state and district test results to national norms: Interpretations of scoring "above the national average."* Paper presented at the annual meeting of the American Educational Research Association, San Francisco.

Murdock, S., Hoque, M. N., Michael, M., White, S., & Pecotte, B. (1997). *The Texas challenge: Population change and the future of Texas.* College Station: Texas A&M University Press.

Reese, C. M., Millert, K. E., Mazzeo, J., & Dossey, J. A. (1997). NAEP 1996 mathematics report card for the nation and the states. Washington, DC: National Center for Education Statistics. Available: http://www.ed.gov/NCES/naep

Skrla, L., Scheurich, J., & Johnson, J. (2000). *Equity-driven achievement-focused school districts.* Unpublished manuscript, University of Texas at Austin, Charles A. Dana Center.

Texas Education Agency. (1997). *Texas student assessment program technical digest for the academic year 1996–97.* Austin: Author.

Texas Education Agency. (1998). *1998 comprehensive biennial report on Texas public schools.* Austin: Author.

University of Houston. (1998, November). Freshman admission requirements [Online]. Available: http://www.uh.edu/enroll/admis/freshman_req.html

A Quest for Quality: Providing Qualified Teachers for California's English Learners

JULIE MAXWELL-JOLLY AND PATRICIA GÁNDARA

As the nation's English-learner (EL) student population has increased, our educational system has not demonstrated a commitment to provide them with a quality education. In California, the nation's most culturally and linguistically diverse state, English learners are the most likely of all students to have underqualified teachers (Rumberger & Gándara, 2000). These California students, who make up 25 percent of the state's student population, most often have teachers who have neither state credentials nor relevant experience specific to the educational needs of English learners (Shields, Young, Marsh, & Esch, 1999). They are also most likely to attend schools that are overcrowded and in poor condition and have a less rigorous curriculum (Betts, Reuben, & Donnenberg, 2000; Finkelstein, Fury, & Huerta, 2000).

California has never supplied enough qualified teachers for its English learners. In 1997, among the EL students in classrooms designated as bilingual (about one-third of all such students), nearly two-thirds had a teacher who had not been properly trained to work with this population or lacked competency in the language of the students or both (California Department of Education [CDE], 1999a). Furthermore, fully 16 percent of English learners were receiving no special services designed for those who are learning English. In fact, the vast majority of English learners were in some kind of program that provided instruction mostly or solely in English, with a teacher who may or may not have had any training in teaching English learners.

In this chapter, we examine the issue of building a corps of qualified teachers to serve EL students in California. First, we demonstrate that Proposition 227 and other competing reform efforts in California have had an unforeseen adverse effect on EL students' education largely because these reforms have increased the demand for qualified teachers. Furthermore, unanticipated effects are likely to continue as the consequences of the new policies unfold. In the second part of the chapter, we discuss the changing composition of California's teaching force, the impact of Proposition 227 on the recruitment of bilingual teachers, the effect teachers have on student performance, and the qualities of exemplary teachers for English learners. Finally, we offer strategies to select, recruit, and train individuals to become effective teachers of EL students.

Proposition 227

Recently, California's English learners have been affected by various school policy changes. Principal among the changes affecting these students was Proposition 227, which resulted from a movement begun in 1997 to ban primary language instruction in California for most English learners. As evidence of bilingual education's failure, proponents of the proposition cited the continuing underachievement of English learners and the fact that only 5 percent of Limited English Proficient (LEP) students were being reclassified to Fluent English Proficient (FEP) status annually. The California Department of Education countered that, in addition to being inaccurate (it was actually 7%), the 5 percent figure was calculated from an ever-growing base of students. Thus, 7 percent of EL students in 1997 represented far more students than 7 percent in 1995. More important, however, the California Department of Education noted that two-thirds of English learners were not in bilingual classrooms; therefore, their academic underachievement could not be attributed to these programs.

Proposition 227 became law as soon as it passed, requiring that "all children in California public schools shall be taught English by being taught in English." The mandated pedagogical strategy was to place English learners in "sheltered English immersion" classes for a period not normally to exceed one year.[1] Sheltered English immersion was defined in the law as a program with multi-age, multilanguage classrooms, including non-native English-speaking students at the same level of English proficiency, in which the focus of instruction is the development of English language skills. The assumption was that most English learners would acquire enough English in one year to be reclassified and join the mainstream of students in the school. The only exception to the English-only mandate was for students whose parents sought a specific waiver of the English-only program. According to Proposition 227, waivers could be allowed on one of three conditions: 1) the child already knew English well enough to be considered fluent; 2) the child was over ten years of age and school staff believed that another approach, such as bilingual instruction, might be better suited to the student; or 3) school staff determined that the child had special needs that could be better met in a program other than structured English immersion. Much about the implementation of Proposition 227 remained vague, however, including what procedures would be used to determine if students were ready to be mainstreamed after one year, what to do if they were not, and how teachers were to ensure these students' learning without the aid of primary language support or instruction.

The State Board of Education issued regulations in October 1998 to clarify some aspects of the new law. The regulations specified that students could be reenrolled in the structured English immersion program if they failed to gain sufficient fluency in English to successfully move to a mainstream classroom within one year. They also provided that "parents must be notified of the opportunity to apply for a parental exception waiver." Moreover, the board ruled that all "parental exception waivers shall be granted unless the school principal and educational staff determine that an alternative program (i.e., bilingual education) would not be the best choice for the educational development of the student." This clarification shifted the burden of proof from parents seeking the waiver to those who would deny the waiver, thus opening the door for more primary language instruction than had been envisioned initially when the initiative passed.

Competing Education Reform Efforts

Although the popular press has been quick to attribute many things to the passage of Proposition 227, a major theme in its implementation is the extent to which it has been affected by other changes in state education policy. Proposition 227 was enacted in an era of prolific education reform activity. During this period a class size–reduction statute was enacted for grades K–3 and some high school courses. Although the program was optional and required school districts to provide some matching funds, it was extremely popular with teachers and the public and was adopted in an overwhelming majority of California schools. Thus the state's overcrowded classrooms went from a cap of more than thirty students to only twenty. Although the program has been lauded by educators and parents, it has created a statewide teacher shortage. This shortage has had a disproportionate impact on rural and urban minority students, who attend schools that have traditionally been harder to staff, even in times of high teacher supply (Shields et al., 1999).

A series of additional policy changes resulted from a cluster of initiatives intended to encourage the accountability of schools, teachers, and students. The state legislature, with strong impetus from the governor, established a plan to implement statewide curriculum standards and to test students based on these standards. The plan, encompassed in several pieces of legislation, provides monetary rewards for schools and individual teachers whose students meet or exceed improvement goals and imposes sanctions and mandated improvement actions for those that do not. It requires that students who do not meet specific annual content and promotion standards (as measured by the Stanford Achievement Test, or SAT 9) not be promoted to the subsequent grade.[2] The plan also introduces a new high-stakes high school exit examination that determines who will graduate and who will not. For students who are in danger of flunking a grade, the plan provides the option of remedial summer school, thus giving them the opportunity to meet grade-level promotion standards before the ensuing school year. Finally, the plan includes a process of teacher review and either mandatory or optional peer assistance.

An unfortunate feature of the plan is that the sole accountability measure currently in use is the SAT 9 standardized test, which is not correlated with the state's curricular standards for each grade. Although the reform calls for the development of assessment instruments based on these standards, for the time being teachers are in the unenviable position of having their teaching skills judged by how well their students score on a test that does not reflect the curriculum that students are supposed to be learning. In addition, few districts provide additional resources to schools or teachers to help them carry out these reforms.

Teachers, having to respond to all these mandates with minimal support, have been under considerable pressure. With the expansion of the class size–reduction initiative came many new, untrained, and inexperienced teachers, and they were most likely to be assigned to classrooms serving English learners (Shields et al., 1999). Trying to juggle new standards, a high-stakes test, and the teaching of English learners without any additional resources or specialized training has proven to be a daunting and demoralizing task for many teachers. In addition, the thousands of EL students who, due to Proposition 227, are now in mainstream classrooms with teachers who have no specific training and no primary language support to assist their students reveals the extent to which the education system has been challenged by these policy changes.

The Impact of Proposition 227 on Classroom Instruction

In 1997–1998, a team of University of California researchers conducted observations in twenty-two schools in sixteen districts as Proposition 227 was being implemented.[3] In discussions with dozens of teachers at these sites, we came to understand the impact of the new law on teachers and their classrooms (see Gándara et al., 2000). The greatest impact of Proposition 227 was found at the level of classroom instruction. Teachers of English learners, whether they had previously adhered to an English-only or full bilingual curriculum, had to alter their practices to accommodate the new law without materials, training, or time to plan for the precipitously implemented policy changes. In addition, at the level of classroom instruction, much more was operating than Proposition 227: teachers were also grappling with new standards, especially with the new statewide testing. The convergence of these mandates left many in a quandary about how to approach instruction. One teacher in a large suburban district talked about feeling that she had "no protection" and worried that she might lose her job if she did not "produce" students who met the new standards. She also noted that students who did not speak English would likely "always score below students who were English speakers," and so she felt she was in a catch-22 situation: Should she continue to teach English learners, the students to whom she felt most devoted and committed, or should she move to an environment with more English speakers, who would be likely to score higher on the tests and thus not incur student or teacher sanctions? Other teachers suffered similar anxieties, as expressed below:

> I've spent more time assessing than teaching this year, and on top of that everybody's been complaining about that. That's why the talk of a strike and all the uproar with the teachers. And on top of that we have the 227 on our backs, so it's been an extremely stressful year, to say the least.

At the schools where we observed, we found that English-only testing was having an extraordinary impact on the instruction that English learners were receiving. Teachers often told us that they did not feel good about how they were focusing on English word recognition or phonics bereft of meaning or context. However, they were concerned that if they spent time on broader literacy activities in the primary language, their students would not gain the skills assessed by the standardized English test and, as a result, the school and the students could suffer sanctions. Thus, even in classrooms designated as bilingual in schools where principals contended that little had changed, teachers revealed that they had altered their teaching practices substantially. The following account from a structured English immersion classroom is an example of the increased focus on form over meaning:

> Ms. P. stood at the front of the class and instructed students to circle the long-vowel sound in each of the sentences on their worksheets and write this word in the long-vowel column. She completed the first three sentences with the students. When it was time for students to do the activity on their own, Ruben and Miguel rubbed their hands together excitedly.
>
> Miguel, reading "Will Pat go to the store" in a flat tone with no questioning intonation, pauses for a moment and raises his head from the text. "That doesn't make any sense." Then, almost smugly, "Don't matter." He picks up his pencil and writes the words *go* and *store* in the long-O column.

Thus, Miguel could write words with long O's in a column, but he did not understand the meaning of the sentence. In a focus group with teachers from one large urban district that was attempting to create more English-only classes because of Proposition 227, teachers expressed their views about the type of teaching described above. One teacher critiqued the prevailing pedagogy:

I feel like the children are forced into silence. They're really not getting the opportunity to express themselves as they normally would were they in a bilingual classroom. I think that it's very unfair. I don't think they're receiving equal opportunity, equal education in the sense that they're really not learning to read. They're learning to decode. Their decoding skills are coming along nicely, but the problem is that second language acquisition, it takes time. And you know the district expects us to move these children from ELD level 1 [the lowest level of English language development, indicating that the students have virtually no English language proficiency] to ELD level 4 [out of five levels] in a matter of one year. With ELD level 4, then you can begin to present instruction of all the subjects in English.

Another teacher in the focus group had eliminated a learning strategy she once considered very effective:

One of my frustrations has been journals. This year they were all writing in Spanish in their journals and so I didn't know what to do. I really have just stopped journals because they really can't write what their thoughts are in English. And every once in a while I think about it — they're not doing journals because I didn't want them to write in Spanish because I thought they weren't supposed to write in Spanish, and they don't have enough knowledge to do it in English.

The bilingual classrooms that we observed exhibited activities reflecting a much more reductive notion of literacy in the aftermath of the policy change. In these classrooms, oral English language fluency was increasingly the specific target of instruction and, as a result, a wider range of language and literacy skills was not integrated throughout the curriculum as both a means and an end of learning. Teachers emphasized decoding (phonics) and vocabulary development rather than broader literacy skills, such as reading for meaning or writing, and they attributed this focus to their concerns about the English language testing to which students would be exposed. This emphasis on rote skills can be seen in the test scores of EL students. After the initial increase in scores for second graders, where the emphasis is on rote learning of decoding skills and word and letter recognition, the students' scores began to decline precipitously as more comprehension tasks were introduced (CDE, 2000b).

Test Scores in the Post-227 Era

More than two years after the passage of Proposition 227, the pundits and the policymakers are anxiously making pronouncements about its effects on California's English learners. Ron Unz, the author of the initiative, and his colleagues have declared it a success in spite of the fact that the redesignation rates from LEP to FEP increased by less than 1 percent (from 7% to only 7.6%) in the year following implementation, and by only 0.2 percent the subsequent year, 1999–2000 (CDE, 2000a). Proposition 227 was based on the contention that LEP students normally should need no more than one year of English language development to join the mainstream, and that in a year they would be ready for redesignation as Fluent English Proficient (FEP) in a structured English immersion classroom. The less than one percentage point increase on which the proposition's supporters base their claim for success appears to fall far short of this goal. Proposition 227 proponents also noted that SAT 9 scores were up for LEP students across the state. However, while test scores did indeed increase for LEP students, they increased for students in both bilingual and English-only classrooms. Moreover, they increased more for English-only speakers. In any case, an increase in test scores was predictable, because simple familiarity with the standardized test, and therefore the ability to better prepare for it, normally confers small initial year-to-year gains (Haney, this volume; Herman, Brown, & Baker, 2000).

Figure 1 compares the reading scores on the SAT 9 standardized test of four groups of students. English-only students speak English as their first and primary language. FEP students are those who have bilingual skills but who are classified as English dominant when they enter school. Redesignated FEPs (often called R-FEPs) are those who gained sufficient second language skills over the course of time to demonstrate a level of fluency that identifies them as no longer limited in English. LEP students are not yet proficient in English but may have a range of English language skills. A critical issue overlooked in press reports about test score increases is the enormous gap in performance between English speakers and English learners. Twenty-five percent of EL second graders score above average, that is, above the 50th percentile, but more than twice as many English-only (native English-speaking) second graders score above average. Notably, R-FEPs, that is, those who are bilingual, score higher than all other students in the second grade. As Figure 1 indicates, all students' scores decline after the second grade. This

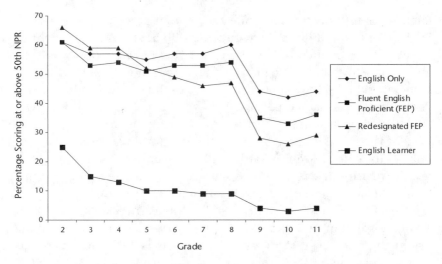

Figure 1   Percentage of Students Scoring above the 50th Percentile, 2000

sharp drop in scores is a striking characteristic of these test data. The reason for it is most likely that second-grade scores reflect test skills that are very basic and highly teachable — whether the student understands the test or not — but as the difficulty of the test increases in each grade, the scores for all children decline. Figure 1 shows that scores for English learners are especially low and that the gap in scores between ELs and students whose primary language is English continues to increase, reaching a fivefold difference by the eleventh grade (CDE, 2000b).

Unfortunately, based on existing data, it is not possible to determine under what conditions EL students have shown the greatest gains; no controlled studies have yet been conducted in which groups of children in different programs are followed over time. Existing data on program placement are also very difficult to interpret because, as has been noted in numerous studies of bilingual education, it is impossible to know what students are actually being exposed to under the title of "bilingual" or "structured English immersion" without doing careful observation in the classroom (Ramirez, Yuen, Ramey, & Pasta, 1991; Dolson & Lindholm, 1995; Lindholm & Molina, 1998). Looking to statistics for help in understanding this issue, we find that the test-score data confuse rather than illuminate. In 1998, at the end of the first year of Proposition 227 implementation, 15 percent of second-grade EL students performed at or above the 50th percentile in

English reading on the statewide test. On an academic skills test in English, one would not expect students who are not yet proficient in English to score much higher than this. These lower scores would be attributable to students' English language limitations, not their lack of academic skills. Yet, by 2000, one-fourth of the second-grade LEP students in California scored at or above the 50th percentile (CDE, 2000b). This gain warrants further investigation because an LEP or EL student is defined, in part, as one who does not understand sufficient English to score above the 35th to 40th percentile on a standardized test in English, such as the SAT 9. Thus, we must ask several questions. How could this percentage of LEP students be performing at such a high level on this test? In addition, if English learners are making such dramatic gains in one year, why aren't we seeing an accompanying rise in the number of students reclassified as FEP? In fact, there has been an increase in the number of English learners rather than in the numbers of these students being reclassified as FEP. In 1998, approximately 231,000 of the second graders tested were identified as English learners. One year later, about 265,000 third graders were classified as EL students. Although the rising test scores indicate that many students significantly increased their English skills and that as a result we should see a decrease in the numbers of EL students, quite the opposite is true. The cohort of LEP students who were tested in 1998 had grown by almost 13 percent, a figure far greater than can be accounted for by new immigrants. This raises serious questions about who the schools are testing and why, indicates confusion and misinterpretation, and calls into question the usefulness of these test scores as indicators of the academic progress of English learners.

The Changing Preparation of the California Teacher Force

All the aggregate estimates of teacher supply and demand — no matter how optimistic or pessimistic — mask the disproportionate effect of teacher shortages on EL students. One-fourth of California's schoolchildren were classified as LEP in the 1997–1998 school year, almost 20 percent received Aid to Families with Dependent Children, and nearly half were poor enough to qualify for free meals (CDE, 1999b). Arguably, these are the very children who need the highest level of teacher quality to meet their educational needs. Yet these children are

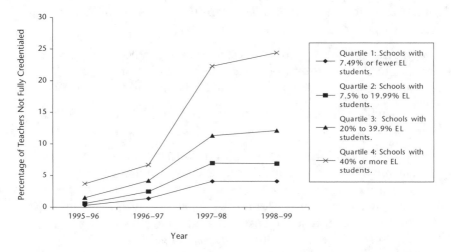

Figure 2 Percentage of English Learners with Uncredentialed Teacher by Percentage of EL Students in School

concentrated principally in the state's urban areas where the greatest numbers of underqualified teachers are working (Shields et al., 1999).

As Figure 2 illustrates, English learners remain three times as likely as other students to have an underqualified or uncredentialed teacher, and the severity of the problem increases with the density of English learners in a school. Thus, for example, in 1998–1999, schools with few EL students (fewer than 7.5%) also had very few uncredentialed teachers (fewer than 5%). Conversely, that same year, schools with 40 percent or more EL students had a teaching staff of which one-fourth did not have a credential. In other words, the more ELs in a school, the greater a child's chances of being assigned to an unqualified teacher (Rumberger, 2000).

Many of the teachers we interviewed, who are qualified on paper to teach English learners because they hold a Crosscultural Language and Academic Development (CLAD) credential or Assembly Bill (AB) 1969 authorization, said that this certification was clearly inadequate to prepare them for the challenges they faced. It is difficult for the CLAD teacher, with as few as forty-five hours of workshops on cultural diversity, language acquisition, and instructional techniques for EL students, let alone a teacher with no specialized credential at all, to meet the unique needs of a room full of students who cannot communicate effectively with their teacher. In the words of one ESL resource teacher,

> CLAD is a start. It's not the best approach, but it's a start. There has to be immersion in culture. We spend a lot of time worried about language. We also need to understand other cultures better.

A teacher who had been an EL student herself had the following perspective:

> There's a lot of teachers that go to these CLAD trainings, and it's all very nice theory, but when it gets down to doing it, I see my colleagues, they just don't have the time, the effort to sit down and give individualized lessons to English language learners, so they [the students] are doing exactly the same thing that I was doing thirty-six years ago, sitting and listening.

Setting the bar lower (i.e., requiring no more than a CLAD credential) for those who would instruct EL students seems to be counter to the current emphasis on strengthening the skills of teachers in California's classrooms. It also contradicts the advice of the California Department of Education, which has reiterated the importance of maintaining the bilingual credential even to teach EL students in structured English immersion programs because of the greater expertise and language skills that this credential requires.

The Impact of Proposition 227 on the Recruitment of Bilingual Teachers

California has always had a shortage of credentialed bilingual teachers, although it was making substantial gains during the 1990s in rectifying this problem. However, the passage of Proposition 227 has severely curtailed the number of teachers seeking bilingual credentials. In 1997–1998, before the passage of Proposition 227, there were 10,894 teachers in the pipeline for the bilingual credentials working in California schools. In 1999, after the passage of Proposition 227, that number had been reduced by half (CDE, 1998). Some of those teachers may still be pursuing their bilingual credential, but without the prospect of a job opportunity it is not clear what their incentive is to continue the additional preparation. This is especially unfortunate, given that, independent of the language used in the instructional program, teachers with Bilingual Crosscultural Language and Academic Development (BCLAD) authorization are usually better prepared to meet the needs of EL students. They have broader training in techniques for teaching these students, understand more deeply the process of second language acquisition, and are able to communicate with the students' parents and communities. At the same time that the bar is being lowered for teachers who work with English learners, the failure to provide LEP students with teachers who are skilled and appropriately matched to their needs is reflected in the startlingly large gaps in performance between these students and all others.

The Effect of Teacher Quality on Student Performance

If teacher quality had little or no impact on student achievement, as was once believed (Coleman, 1966; Jencks et al., 1972), the serious shortage of qualified, credentialed teachers for EL students might be of less concern. However, findings from a new generation of studies that revisit the question of how teacher quality affects student achievement are adding to evidence supporting the notion that teachers matter a great deal (Ferguson, 1991; Hanushek, 1986, 1992; Murnane, 1991). Additional support is provided by studies from New York (Armour-Thomas, 1989, cited in Darling-Hammond, 1997); Dallas, Texas (Archer, 1998, cited in Haycock, 1998); and Boston (Haycock, 1998). Darling-Hammond (1999) investigated how teacher qualifications are related to student achievement across states. She found that "full certification and a major in the field is a much more powerful predictor of student achievement than teachers' education levels (e.g., master's degrees)" (Darling-Hammond, 1999, p. 53). The University of Tennessee Value-Added Research and Assessment Center used a database of individual records of more than three million students across subjects and grade levels to reveal that both good and bad effects of teachers on student achievement persist over time (Sanders & Horn, 1995; Sanders & Rivers, 1996).

Whether they have been convinced by contemporary research or by their own experience, many believe that teachers are the most critical element in improving education. "Educational change depends on what teachers do and think — it's as simple and as complex as that" (Sarason, cited in Fullan, 1991, p. 117). Some qualities of exemplary teachers are discussed in the next section.

The Qualities of Exemplary Teachers for English Learners

Gándara (1997) synthesized research describing some of the qualities necessary for effective teachers of English learners. These include (a) proficiency in two languages and the ability to deliver instruction in both; (b) the ability to determine and integrate a mix of students' academic level and degree of English language proficiency; and (c) knowledge of the rules of appropriate behavior for at least two ethnic groups. Other attributes that are mentioned in the literature include the ability to work collaboratively with specialists and nonspecialists who serve these children, an understanding of how to arrange classroom settings to support a variety of instructional strategies, the ability to help students build on their existing knowledge, an eagerness to involve parents, and the skill to create ample opportunities for students to speak, listen, read, and write. The importance of ongoing and appropriate assessment of student learning and the use of active teaching behaviors (Garcia, 1988, 1996; Milk, Mercado, & Sapiens, 1992) are two additional features of effective teaching for English learners.

Teachers who recognize that education is not a politically or ideologically neutral endeavor and who acknowledge their responsibility to transform sociopolitical and economic realities that limit student achievement may increase the chances for success of these students (Bartolomé, this volume). The importance of teacher ideology can be conceptualized in a variety of ways. The notion of "political clarity" (Bartolomé, 2000) includes the capacity of teachers to think critically about their stereotypical beliefs. According to Bartolomé, "uncritical prospective teachers often end up blindly following lockstep methodologies and promulgating unexamined beliefs and attitudes that can compound the difficulties faced by linguistic minority children in school" (2000, p. 167). Garcia (1991) found that successful EL teachers questioned the fairness of the existing social order while rejecting the notion that schools can do little to teach students from low socioeconomic status backgrounds. Foster (1990) stressed the importance of teachers who recognize the societal limitations on themselves and their students and are not overwhelmed by them. Ladson-Billings (1994) discussed the importance of circumventing "assimilationist" teaching, that is, teaching that replicates in schools the larger social order, in which minority students occupy the lowest rungs of the social ladder, and that ultimately contributes to the maintenance of this social order. "Teaching against the grain" is Cochran-Smith's (1991) conception of how teachers need to become aware of schooling practices that sustain an unfair status quo and must seek to avoid these in their teaching. Therefore, although teacher preparation programs need to teach specific skills and methods, they must go beyond this and help prospective teachers develop positive attitudes and beliefs about their students' ability and desire to learn. In addition, programs can help teachers evaluate the social, political, and economic status quo that does not adequately cultivate the academic achievement of these students (Nieto, 2000).

Strategies for Building the Teacher Corps for English Learners

Three principal strategies emerge as both practicable and potentially effective for building a corps of teachers who are competent to work with California's diverse learners: selection and recruitment strategies, preparation of the corps of prospective teachers, and professional development for those who are already in the field.

Selection and Recruitment: The Case for Minority Teachers

Although California's students are diverse, its teachers are much less so. While 61 percent of the state's students are ethnic minorities, only 22 percent of teachers are from minority groups (Center for the Future of Teaching and Learning, 1999; Shields et al., 1999). The greatest discrepancy is between Latino students and teachers. Latino students represent 41 percent of the student population, whereas Latino teachers comprise only 12 percent of the state's teachers. Given the lack of diversity in the teacher corps, recruitment and selection strategies might be used to much greater advantage than they are.

An approach that maximizes existing resources and competence is to recruit individuals who already have the desire to teach EL students and the language, along with other experience that enables them to teach these students competently. Screening of prospective teacher candidates on the basis of cultural sensitivity and commitment to the education of all students is a useful selection strategy (Zeichner, 1996). A teacher we interviewed reiterated the importance of having a specific desire and interest in teaching EL students:

Now, everyone has to have a CLAD, but I think that it goes be-yond that because it takes a kind of a person who really is inter-ested [in teaching EL students]. Anybody can get a paper and be a teacher almost, but they aren't all teachers. I think this calling is a very specific calling just like a math specialist is a specialist. And, I think that people should be only admitted into this type of pro-gram if they are trained, if they do have an interest, and if they are able to carry out the demands. I think then they're a special-ist. It isn't just walking in with a teaching credential and doing it.

Teachers from backgrounds similar to their students are likely to have insights, experiences, and skills that are difficult to duplicate in the short amount of time that teacher preparation programs have to train new teachers. Certainly, the acquisition of a second language rarely occurs in that time frame.

A growing body of literature reveals the positive influences of teachers of color on personal development and academic achievement of minority students overall (Haberman, 1996). For example, a num-ber of studies have shown the importance of positive role models from similar backgrounds in the lives of ethnic minority students (Bu-chanan, 1999; Foster, 1990, 1997). Others hypothesize that the ab-sence of role models in positions of authority in schools hinders stu-dents' development of an academic self-image (Ladson-Billings, 1994). Moreover, research with Latino students finds that the presence of La-tino teachers in the classroom goes beyond simply creating role mod-els and is positively correlated with increased academic performance. Teachers of the same ethnic heritage, for example, are less likely than other teachers to place Latino students in remedial programs and are more likely to identify them as gifted (Tomás Rivera Center, 1993).

Teacher preferences and expectations can also be powerful contri-butors to students' success or failure. There is evidence that few pro-spective teachers choose to work with diverse students (Wayson, cited in Avery & Walker, 1993) and that new teachers prefer working with students like themselves, that is, middle-class children from the suburbs (Gómez, 1996; Wildeen, Mayer-Smith, & Moon, 1998). Other studies indicate that these teachers tend to be more effective with the middle-class students they prefer to teach than with other students (Zeichner, 1996). Research also documents mainstream teachers' failure to appre-ciate the unique educational challenges that minority students face (Delpit, 1995; Foster, 1997; Ladson-Billings, 1994; Quintinar-Sarellana,

1997) or the linguistic and other knowledge that these students bring to the classroom from their homes and communities (Moll, 1988, 1992; Moll & Vellez-Ibanez, 1992). Some of the most disturbing findings in the literature on learning come from studies of teacher expectations. Mainstream teachers and counselors of low-income and minority students are more likely to perceive these students as having low ability, and therefore they hold lower aspirations for them (McDonough, 1997; Romo & Falbo, 1996; Tettegah, 1997; Webb & Crosbie, 1994). Teachers habitually send nonverbal messages about the amount of confidence they have in students' abilities: they call on favorite students more often, wait longer for an answer from a student they believe knows the answer than from one they view as less capable, and are more likely to provide students in whom they have little confidence with the correct answer, or move on quickly to another student (Brophy & Good, 1974). Students have been shown to be very sensitive to these subtle teacher behaviors and to "read" their teachers' attitudes quite accurately (Weinstein, 1989). Sprinthall, Sprinthall, and Oja (1998) describe how teachers' attitudes and beliefs can moderate students' assessment of their own abilities. If teachers do not believe some students are capable of excelling, there is a great likelihood that these students will confirm their teachers' expectations.

Students, teachers, and families all benefit when teachers can communicate with parents. Such teachers can call on parental expertise for help in the classroom and can consult parents when their children need help. At the same time, parents whose children have a teacher with whom they can communicate know that there is someone who can answer their questions and are thus more likely to stay in touch with their children's school lives. Recent research finds a high correlation between parental involvement in their children's education and minority students' academic outcomes (Arvizu, 1996; Desimone, 1999; Keith et al., 1998; Zellman & Waterman, 1998). In low-income and largely minority schools, teachers commonly complain of lack of parental involvement and therefore perceive a lack of caring on the part of the parents (Metropolitan Life, 1998). With little connection among parents, teachers, and schools, however, along with an increasing number of parents and teachers who literally do not speak the same language, it is difficult for parents to create a role for themselves in their children's schooling. Thus, evidence clearly supports increasing the cadre of teachers with cultural and language backgrounds similar to their students. This is not a panacea, however; there can be division within ethnic groups, for example, due to socioeconomic differences, and a teacher from one minority ethnic or language group is not necessarily the best teacher for students from another. Therefore, all teachers, no matter what their ethnic or linguistic backgrounds are, need high-quality instructional and field experiences designed to better prepare them to work with diverse students. Moreover, given the growing numbers of English learners, this means that all teachers should be prepared to work effectively with students whose first language is not English (Nelson-Barber, 1991).

Teacher Preparation

Although knowledge about effective teaching practices for linguistic minority students is increasing, evidence on effective staff development and preservice instruction based on these principles is lacking (Hakuta & August, 1997). Furthermore, Merino's (1999) review of research on reforms in teacher education programs aimed at preparing teachers to work in culturally and linguistically diverse settings reveals few empirical studies. She finds a scarcity of rich descriptions of what teacher preparation programs actually do to address cultural and linguistic diversity and cites a widespread failure to describe or evaluate the impact of course work and experience on student teachers and their practice.

Teacher education often falls short of preparing teachers for diversity, according to teachers themselves (see Friedman, this volume). Periodic surveys of credential program graduates one year after program completion are a tradition of research in teacher education. These surveys are periodically submitted to the California Commission on Teacher Credentialing as part of the external evaluation process. The 1990 survey conducted by the California State University system revealed that credential program graduates were generally satisfied with the competencies surveyed. One exception was their low level of satisfaction with the expertise in teaching culturally and linguistically diverse students, and in particular the aspects of the program dealing with instructional strategies for teaching English learners (Merino, 1999). However, there is some guidance in the literature about effective preparation of teachers for diverse learners.

Several researchers emphasize the importance of infusing issues of cultural and linguistic diversity into the teacher preparation curricu-

lum and activities (Nieto, 2000; Olmedo, 1997; Varvus, 1994; Zeichner, 1996). Programs that take this infusion approach either focus on
preparing teachers to work with diverse students without reference to
any particular culture or language group, or they concentrate on preparation for teaching a specific ethnic group. Grant (1994) found that
preservice programs that infuse multicultural education and provide
immersion field experience, including residence in a culturally diverse
community, offer a strong possibility of successfully preparing effective teachers for diverse learners. His research also revealed the importance of university supervisors and, in particular, cooperating teachers
who have a thorough knowledge of, and belief in, the importance of
multicultural education. Wildeen et al. (1998) also found the role of
the cooperating teacher to be as critical as it is overlooked. Finally, student teachers in these most effective programs participate in projects
that require them to critically analyze race, class, and gender issues
(see Gebhard, Austin, Nieto, & Willett, this volume). Few programs,
however, take Grant's recommended approach.

Certain learning activities or strategies have proven successful in
preparing teachers to work with diverse students, regardless of the
kind of teacher preparation program in which the strategies are employed (Zeichner & Melnick, 1996). These include providing prospective teachers with models of successful teaching for culturally and linguistically diverse learners, exploring their own ethnic and cultural
identity, examining their attitudes toward ethnic groups other than
their own, studying cases and readings by people of color about their
personal schooling experiences, and having field experiences outside
the classroom that give them opportunities to interact with parents
and other adults from backgrounds unlike their own. (However, the
link between this kind of experience and the work teachers will eventually carry out in the classroom has not been made in the research.)
Successful programs also teach aspiring teachers about the histories of
various ethnic groups and their historical and contemporary contribu-
tions to all aspects of life in the United States, as well as giving the
teachers information about unique characteristics and learning styles
of different ethnic groups (Banks, 1993).

Exemplary teacher education programs provide teachers with a
knowledge base that will contribute to their effectiveness as teachers
of linguistically diverse students. This knowledge includes familiarity
with appropriate instructional strategies, such as the challenges of

learning a second language (Reagan, 1997; Wong Fillmore & Snow, 2000) and how EL students' strengths and experiences serve as a foundation for building new learning (Moll, 1992). Moll notes that for teachers of English learners it is critical to utilize all "available resources, including the children's or the parents' language and knowledge, in creating new, advanced instructional circumstances for the students' academic development" (p. 23). Knowledge about appropriate assessment strategies is particularly important for teachers of English learners. Without such knowledge, these students risk grade retention and misdiagnosis of learning difficulties (Figueroa & Hernández, 1999; Figueroa & Valdes, 1996).

Finally, research by Guillaume and her colleagues (Guillaume, Zuñiga-Hill, & Yee, 1994) on teachers at all levels of a preparation program, including those in the bilingual strand, found that the prospective teachers produced essay responses devoid of reference to diversity issues despite course-work activities meant to address diversity concerns. This research provides a reminder of the need to continually examine the effects of efforts to change prospective teachers' reasoning about diversity. In view of the importance of the task, we cannot assume the success of current approaches (Cochran-Smith, 1995).

Professional Development

In-service professional development is a critical avenue for helping teachers understand and meet the challenges of teaching linguistically and culturally diverse students by equipping them with skills they may have not gained in their teacher preparation programs. Unfortunately, many teachers report that they learn very little from the professional development programs in which they participate. A primary reason for this is that these activities tend to be a disjointed series of workshops with little relationship to each other and little follow-up (Shields, Marsh, & Powell, 1998).

Programs that have met with considerable success in this area can provide suggestions for potentially effective strategies. One such program is Puente, an intervention program supported with both state and foundation funding to help underrepresented high school students, particularly Latinos, make a successful transition into college. Puente offers a number of services directly to students and also provides extensive and integrated professional development for high school English teachers. Workshops cover Latino literature, including methods for incorporating it into the core college preparatory curriculum; Latino culture, including how to incorporate cultural artifacts and folklore into the core curriculum and how to use local community resources in developing curriculum; collaborative learning and teaching strategies, with opportunities to engage in collaborative activity; and instruction in writing and assessment that incorporates a Latino perspective and voice. An evaluation of the Puente professional development program has yielded exceptionally high satisfaction rates on the part of participating teachers (Gándara, Mejorado, Molina, & Gutierrez, 1997, Gándara, Mejorado, Gutierrez, & Molina, 1998).

Second language institutes are another important professional development strategy for teachers of English learners. California sponsored many of these institutes during the 1970s and 1980s, before they became casualties of the budget cuts. The second language institute model was geared to providing intensive professional development for teachers and other ancillary school personnel working with English learners. The state-subsidized institutes included three components: language immersion (often in a Spanish-speaking or Asian-speaking country), instruction in target cultures, and instruction in appropriate assessment of English learners. The programs were residential and lasted an average of six weeks during the summer. An evaluation of the institutes showed that participants were generally quite satisfied with the instruction they received, especially in language and assessment, and their supervisors were especially pleased with the added expertise that this training brought to their campuses (Gándara & Samulon, 1983). Teachers we interviewed believed that the experience of learning another language was critical for teachers of English learners:

> To take a second language makes teachers more sensitive and understanding. It lets them give some allowance to these students for the incredible task that they are doing.

> Nothing is as convincing as personal experience. You know, struggling in another language in another culture [makes you] realize how totally stupid and inadequate you can feel.

Conclusions

The effort to increase the pool of teachers prepared to work with English learners must begin immediately. The greater focus on accountability and high-stakes testing, the increasing number of bilingual students in mainstream classrooms, class size reduction, and an increasingly diverse student population all indicate an urgent need for qualified teachers in California who can address the needs of EL students. We propose several strategies to build a corps of qualified teachers that will serve California's EL students well. These strategies include recruitment and selection of minority teachers, preservice teacher preparation, and in-service professional development.

In order to diversify the teacher corps, the easiest strategy is to recruit aspiring teachers who have the background and the inclinations that give them the most potential for success with culturally and linguistically diverse students. Teachers from backgrounds similar to those of their students are likely to have insights, experiences, and skills that are difficult to replicate in the short space of time that teacher preparation programs have to train new teachers. Certainly, the acquisition of a second language will rarely occur in that time frame. Moreover, because teachers are drawn to teaching near where they live (Murnane, Singer, Willett, Kemple, & Olsen, 1991; Shields et al., 1998), the recruitment of more teachers from these underrepresented communities could have a long-term salutary effect on the problem of unequal distribution of the teaching force. Further, there is reason to believe that teachers who share the backgrounds of these students are more likely to persist both in the teacher corps and in schools with large minority populations (Murnane et al., 1991).

School districts and teacher education programs can adopt proven approaches to attract and prepare minority teachers. For example, in California, most first-time college-goers from underrepresented groups attend community colleges, but the majority leave college before they complete a bachelor's degree, due to financial pressures, inadequate career counseling, and lack of focus in their studies. Therefore, one strategy to encourage minority students to become teachers might include a teacher preparation program that begins at the community college. Students would participate in focused course work and counseling toward a specialized associate of arts degree, be awarded grants and forgivable loans to support both the teacher and his or her education, and end up at a four-year college to complete the undergraduate degree and a teaching credential. Another potential strategy is a system of signing-up bonuses paid to qualified teacher candidates who have the skills, background, and experience that are needed to teach diverse students. Helping low-income students pay for their studies through the expansion of grants and forgivable loans to allow teacher candidates to focus solely on obtaining credentials is another way to increase the pool of teachers with more diverse backgrounds. Finally, attracting back former teachers who have bilingual and other demonstrated skills in working with diverse students would help increase the pool of teachers prepared for the state's diverse school population. Districts may be able to attract teachers who do not want to return to the classroom full-time by offering these teachers nonclassroom work, such as mentoring novice teachers, as well as the option of part-time work.

In addition to recruiting and preparing minority teachers, it is also important to reorganize the teacher preparation and professional development experiences of European American teachers, who constitute over 90 percent of the U.S. teaching corps. Experience and research have shown that European American teachers can be fine teachers of culturally and linguistically diverse students (Bartolomé, this volume; Brisk, Dawson, Hartgering, MacDonald, & Zehr, this volume; Hornberger, this volume). Preparing teachers who have a different background, experiences, and language from those of their students is an involved process. Teacher preparation programs should be guided by the research and experience of scholars, colleagues, and teachers that provide information on successful preservice teacher preparation approaches and caveats regarding less successful approaches. Case studies of successful teacher education programs can also provide guidance on what is necessary to prepare White teachers who can effectively teach diverse students (Gebhard et al., this volume; Friedman, this volume). Finally, another way of preparing European American teachers to teach minority students effectively is to provide comprehensive in-service professional development programs. Evaluation studies of well-conceived in-service professional development programs might identify the best ways to provide continued support to White teachers in meeting the needs of changing student populations.

Notes

1. While Proposition 227 proposed a "sheltered English immersion" approach, it did not provide a clear definition for the program and regulatory language came to adopt the term *structured English immersion* after the literature that describes a pedagogical approach that integrates English teaching with content teaching.

2. The Stanford 9 is a norm-referenced test that has replaced the many different tests used by districts to assess student academic progress for the purposes of standardizing these data and to allow for comparison among schools, districts, and population groups.
3. Researchers from the University of California Davis, Berkeley, and Los Angeles campuses joined in a consortium to share data from individual studies for the purpose of publishing a joint policy document to highlight issues in the implementation of Proposition 227.

References

Arvizu, S. F. (1996). Family, community, and school collaboration. In J. Sikula (Ed.), *Handbook of research on teacher education* (pp. 814–819). New York: Simon & Schuster Macmillan.

Avery, P. G., & Walker, C. (1993). Prospective teachers' perceptions of ethnic and gender differences in academic achievement. *Journal of Teacher Education, 44,* 27–37.

Banks, J. A. (1993). Multicultural education as an academic discipline: Goals for the 21st century. *Multicultural Education, 1,* 8 –11.

Bartolomé, L. I. (2000). Democratizing bilingualism: The role of critical teacher education. In Z. F. Beykont (Ed.), *Lifting every voice: The pedagogy and politics of bilingual education* (pp. 167–186). Cambridge, MA: Harvard Education Publishing Group.

Betts, J., Rueben, K., & Dannenberg, A. (2000). *Equal resources, equal outcomes? The distribution of school resources and student achievement in California.* San Francisco: Public Policy Institute of California.

Brophy, G., & Good, T. (1974). *Teacher-student relationships: Causes and consequences.* New York: Holt, Rinehart & Winston.

Buchanan, L. A. (1999). *Recruiting minorities into the teaching profession. Students address the issue: An analysis of four focus groups in Long Beach and Sacramento.* Burlingame: California Teachers Association.

California Department of Education. (1998). *Language census report* [On-line]. Available: www.cde.ca.gov

California Department of Education. (1999a). *Language census report: Bilingual staff providing services to English learners* [On-line]. Available: www.cde.ca.gov

California Department of Education, Education Data Partnership. (1999b). *California student trends* [On-line]. Available: www.ed-data.k12.ca.us

California Department of Education. (2000a). *Language census* [On-line]. Available: www.goldmine.cde.ca.gov/demograpphics

California Department of Education. (2000b). *Star test data* [On-line]. Available: www.star.cde.ca.gov

Center for the Future of Teaching and Learning. (1999). Unpublished data.

Cochran-Smith, M. (1991). Learning to teach against the grain. *Harvard Educational Review, 61,* 279–310.

Cochran-Smith, M. (1995). Color blindness and basket making are not the answers: Confronting the dilemmas of race, culture, and language diversity in teacher education. *American Educational Research Journal, 32,* 493–522.

Coleman, J. (1966). *Equality of educational opportunity.* Washington, DC: U.S. Government Printing Office.

Darling-Hammond, L. (1997). School reform at the crossroads: Confronting the central issues of teaching. *Educational Policy, 11,* 151–165.

Darling-Hammond, L. (1999). *Professional development for teachers: Setting the stage for learning from teaching.* Unpublished manuscript.

Delpit, L. D. (1995). *Other people's children: Cultural conflict in the classroom.* New York: New Press.

Desimone, L. (1999). Linking parent involvement with student achievement: Do race and income matter? *Journal of Educational Research, 93,* 11–30.

Dolson, D., & Lindholm, K. (1995). World class education for children in California: A comparison of two-way bilingual immersion and European school models. In T. Skutnabb-Kangas (Ed.), *European studies of multilingualism, 4.* Lisse, The Netherlands: Swets & Zeitlinger.

Ferguson, R. F. (1991). Paying for public education: New evidence on how and why money matters. *Harvard Journal on Legislation 28,* 465–498.

Figueroa, R., & Hernández, S. (1999). *Testing Hispanic students in the United States: Technical and policy issues.* Unpublished manuscript for the President's Advisory Commission on Educational Excellence for Hispanic Americans.

Figueroa, R., & Valdes, G. (1996). *Bilingualism and testing: A special case of bias.* Victoria, Australia: Ablex.

Finkelstein, N., Fury, W., & Huerta, L. (2000). School finance. In E. Burr, G. Hayward, B. Fuller, & M. Kirst (Eds.), *Crucial issues in California education: Are the reform pieces fitting together?* (pp. 45–78). Palo Alto, CA: Stanford University, Policy Analysis for California Education.

Foster, M. (1990). The politics of race: Through the eyes of African-American teachers. *Journal of Education, 172,* 123–141.

Foster, M. (1997). *Black teachers on teaching.* New York: New York Press.

Fullan, M. G. (1991). *The new meaning of educational change.* New York: Teachers College Press.

Gándara, P. (1997). *Review of the research on instruction of limited English proficient students: A report to the California legislature.* Davis: University of California, Davis, Language Minority Research Institute.

Gándara, P., Maxwell-Jolly, J., Garcia, E., Asato, J., Gutierrez, K., Stritikus, T., & Curry, J. (2000). *The effects of proposition 227 on the instruction of English learners: Year one implementation.* Santa Barbara: University of California Linguistic Minority Research Institute.

Gándara, P., Mejorado, M., Gutierrez, D., & Molina, M. (1998). *Final evaluation of high school Puente. 1994–1998.* Davis: University of California, Davis.

Gándara P., Mejorado, M., Molina M., & Gutierrez, D. (1997). *Year III evaluation of high school Puente.* Davis: University of California, Davis.

Gándara, P., & Samulon, M. (1983). *Evaluation of second language institutes.* Sacramento: California Department of Education, Office of Special Education.

Garcia, E. E. (1988). Attributes of effective schools for language minority students. *Education and Urban Society, 20,* 387–398.

Garcia, E. E. (1991). Effective instruction for language minority students: The teacher. *Journal of Education, 173,* 130–141.

Garcia, E. E. (1996). Preparing instructional professionals for linguistically and culturally diverse students. In J. Sikula (Ed.), *Handbook of research on teacher education* (pp. 802–813). New York: Simon & Schuster Macmillan.

Gómez, M. L. (1996). Prospective teachers' perspectives on teaching "other people's children." In K. Zeichner, S. Melnick, & M. L. Gomez (Eds.), *Currents of reform in preservice teacher education* (pp. 109–132). New York: Teachers College Press.

Grant, C. A. (1994). Best practices in teacher preparation for urban schools: Lessons from the multicultural teacher education literature. *Action in Teacher Education, 16*(3), 1–18.

Guillaume, A., Zuñiga-Hill, C., & Yee, I. (1994). Prospective teachers' use of diversity issues in a case study analysis. *Journal of Research and Development in Education, 28*(2), 69–79.

Haberman, M. (1996). Selecting and preparing culturally competent teachers for urban schools. In J. Sikula (Ed.), *Handbook of research on teacher education* (pp. 747–760). New York: Simon & Schuster Macmillan.

Hakuta, K., & August, D. (1997). *Improving schooling for language-minority children: A research agenda.* Washington, DC: National Academy Press.

Hanushek, E. A. (1986). The economics of schooling: Production and efficiency in public schools. *Journal of Economic Literature, 24,* 1141–1177.

Hanushek, E. A. (1992). The trade-off between child quantity and quality. *Journal of Political Economy, 100,* 84–117.

Haycock, K. (1998). Good teaching matters: How well-qualified teachers can close the gap. *Thinking K-16, 3,* 1–8.

Herman, J., Brown, R., & Baker, E. (2000). Student assessment and student achievement in the California public school system. In E. Burr, G. Hayward, B. Fuller, & M. Kirst (Eds.), *Crucial issues in California education: Are the reform pieces fitting together?* (pp. 113–152). Berkeley: University of California, Policy Analysis for California Education.

Jencks, C., Smith, M., Acland, H., Bane, M. J., Cohen, D., Gintis, H., Heynes, B., & Mickleson, R. (1972). *Inequality.* New York: Harper & Row.

Keith, T. Z., Keith, P. B., Quirk, K. J., Sperduto, J., Santillo, S., & Killings, S. (1998). Longitudinal effects of parent involvement on high school grades: Similarities and differences across gender and ethnic groups. *Journal of School Psychology, 36,* 335–363.

Ladson-Billings, G. (1994). *The dreamkeepers.* San Francisco: Jossey-Bass.

Lindholm, K., & Molina, R. (1998). *Learning in a dual language education classroom in the U.S.: Implementation and evaluation outcomes.* Proceedings of the Third European Conference on Immersion Programs, Barcelona, Spain.

McDonough, P. (1997). *Choosing colleges: How social class and schools structure opportunity.* Albany: State University of New York Press.

Merino, B. (1999). Preparing secondary teachers to teach a second language: The case of the United States with a focus on California. In C. J. Faltis & P. M.

Wolfe (Eds.), *So much to say: Adolescents, bilingualism, and ESL in the secondary school* (pp. 225–253). New York: Teachers College Press.

Metropolitan Life Insurance Company. (1998). *The American teacher 1998: Building family-school partnerships. Views of teachers and students.* New York: Lou Harris and Associates.

Milk, R., Mercado, C., & Sapiens, A. (1992, Summer). Re-thinking the education of teachers of language minority children: Developing reflective teachers for changing schools. *NCBE Focus: Occasional Papers in Bilingual Education, 6* [Online]. Available: www.ncbe.gwu.edu

Moll, L. C. (1988). Some key issues in teaching Latino students. *Language Arts, 65,* 465–472.

Moll, L. C. (1992). Bilingual classroom studies and community analysis: Some recent trends. *Educational Researcher, 21*(2), 20–24.

Moll, L., & Vellez-Ibanez, C. (1992). Funds of knowledge for teaching: Using a qualitative approach to connect homes and classrooms. *Theory Into Practice, 31,* 132–141.

Murnane, R. (1991). Interpreting the evidence on "Does money matter?" *Harvard Journal on Legislation, 28,* 456–463.

Murnane, R., Singer, J., Willett, J., Kemple, J., & Olsen, R. (1991). *Who will teach? Policies that matter.* Cambridge, MA: Harvard University Press.

Nelson-Barber, S. (1991). Considerations for the inclusion of multicultural competencies in teacher assessment. *Teacher Education Quarterly, 18*(2), 49–59.

Nieto, S. (2000). Bringing bilingual education out of the basement and other imperatives for teacher education. In Z. F. Beykont (Ed.), *Lifting every voice: Pedagogy and politics of bilingualism* (pp. 187–208). Cambridge, MA: Harvard Education Publishing Group.

Olmedo, I. M. (1997). Challenging old assumptions: Preparing teachers for inner city schools. *Teaching and Teacher Education, 13,* 245–258.

Quintinar-Sarellana, R. (1997). Culturally relevant teacher preparation and teachers' perceptions of the language and culture of linguistic minority students. In J. King, E. R. Hollins, & W. C. Hayman (Eds.), *Preparing teachers for cultural diversity* (pp. 40–52). New York: Teachers College Press.

Ramirez, D. J., Yuen, D. R., Ramey, D. R., & Pasta, D. J. (1991). *Final report: National longitudinal study of structured-English immersion strategy, early-exit strategy, and late-exit transitional bilingual education programs for language minority children* (vols. 1, 2). San Mateo, CA: Aguirre International.

Reagan, T. (1997). The case for applied linguistics in teacher education. *Journal of Teacher Education, 48,* 185–196.

Romo, H., & Falbo, T. (1996). *Latino high school graduation: Defying the odds.* Austin: University of Texas Press.

Rumberger, R. (2000). Post-227 enrollment in bilingual classes continues to decline. *Linguistic Minority Research Institute Newsletter, 10,* 1–2.

Rumberger, R., & Gándara, P. (2000). The schooling of English learners. In E. Burr, G. C. Hayward, B. Fuller, & M. W. Kirst (Eds.), *Crucial issues in California education: Are the reform pieces fitting together?* (pp. 23–44). Berkeley: University of California, Policy Analysis for California Education.

Sanders, W. L., & Horn, S. P. (1995). The Tennessee Value-Added Assessment System (TVAAS): Mixed model methodology in educational assessment. In A. J. Shinkfield & D. Stufflebeam (Eds.), *Teacher evaluation: Guide to effective practice* (pp. 337–350). Boston: Kluwer Academic.

Sanders, W. L., & Rivers, J. C. (1996). *Cumulative and residual effects of teachers on future student academic achievement.* Knoxville: University of Tennessee Value-Added Research and Assessment Center.

Shields, P. M., Marsh, J. M., & Powell, J. P. (1998). *An inventory of the status of teacher development in California.* Menlo Park, CA: SRI International.

Shields, P. M., Young, V. M., Marsh, J. A., & Esch, C. (1999). *The supply and demand of teachers for California's classrooms.* Unpublished draft, Center for the Future of Teaching and Learning, Menlo Park, CA.

Sprinthall, R. C., Sprinthall, N. A., & Oja, S. (1998). *Educational psychology: A developmental approach* (7th ed.). Boston: McGraw-Hill.

Tettegah, S. (1997). The racial consciousness attitudes of White prospective teachers and their perceptions of the teachability of students from different racial/ethnic backgrounds: Findings from a California study. *Journal of Negro Education, 65,* 151–163.

Tomás Rivera Center. (1993). *Resolving a crisis in education: Latino teachers for tomorrow's classrooms.* Claremont, CA: Author.

Varvus, M. (1994). A critical analysis of multicultural education infusion during student teaching. *Action in Teacher Education,* 16(3), 46–57.

Webb, S. A., & Crosbie, P. V. (1994). Teaching in California public schools: More than academics. In *1994 Yearbook of California education research* (pp. 191–205). San Francisco: Caddo Gap Press.

Weinstein, R. (1989). Perceptions of classroom processes and student motivation: Children's views of self-fulfilling prophecies. In R. Ames & C. Ames (Eds.), *Research on motivation in education. Goals and cognition* (vol. 3, pp. 187–221). New York: Academic Press.

Wildeen, M., Mayer-Smith, J., & Moon, B. (1998). A critical analysis of the research on learning to teach: Making the case for an ecological perspective on inquiry. *Review of Educational Research, 68,* 130–178.

Wong Fillmore, L., & Snow, C. E. (2000). *What teachers need to know about language* [On-line]. Available: www.ncbe.gwu.edu

Zeichner, K. (1996). Educating teachers for cultural diversity. In K. Zeichner, S. Melnick, & M. L. Gómez (Eds.), *Currents of reform in preservice teacher education* (pp. 133–175). New York: Teachers College Press.

Zeichner, K., & Melnick, S. (1996). The role of community field experiences in preparing teachers for cultural diversity. In K. Zeichner, S. Melnick, & M. L. Gomez (Eds.), *Currents of reform in preservice teacher education* (pp. 133–175). New York: Teachers College Press.

Zellman, G. L., & Waterman, J. M. (1998). Understanding the impact of parent school involvement on children's educational outcomes. *Journal of Educational Research, 91,* 370–380.

PART TWO

Successful Teaching Across Language Difference

"Remember I Said": Cambodian Students' Second Language Literacy Development in a Mainstream Classroom[1]

NANCY H. HORNBERGER

A growing number of Cambodian students attend U.S. public schools. Their parents sought refuge in the United States after the Vietnamese invasion of Cambodia and the overthrow of Pol Pot, during whose four-year reign of terror an estimated one to two million Cambodians died as a result of torture, execution, disease, and starvation (López, 2000). More than 131,000 Cambodian refugees arrived in the United States between 1979 and 1986; by 1997, the total was 147,000. Most of them were ethnic Khmer, although some were ethnic Vietnamese and Chinese Cambodians. Today, the greatest concentration of Cambodians in the United States is in the West (59%), followed by 19.7 percent in the Northeast, 13.4 percent in the South, and 7.9 percent in the Midwest (López, 2000, pp. 241–242).

By the end of the 1980s, when I began my long-term ethnographic study of language and literacy attitudes and practices in the Cambodian community of Philadelphia, approximately eight thousand Cambodians lived in Philadelphia, constituting about 5 percent of the total Cambodian population in the United States (Dubois 1990, p. 4; Tollefson, 1989, p. 4). Philadelphia's Cambodian population is still strong, with significant numbers in the schools, including the "1.5 generation," that is, those born in Cambodia or in the refugee camps of Thailand, who arrived in the United States as small children and are being educated here.

Philadelphia's Cambodian community supports several contexts in which Cambodian literacy is used and cultivated. These contexts include religious and cultural organizations, such as the Philadelphia Buddhist Temple and the Cambodian Association, and educational and social service outreach programs, such as Cambodian classes for children and translation services in hospitals and museums. Some individuals practice Cambodian literacy and have a clear sense of specific functions for Khmer literacy: as an aid in learning English, a skill for employment, a vehicle to preserve Cambodian language and culture in a new land, or an essential for going back to Cambodia (Hornberger, 1996). There are also Cambodian children who are developing Khmer literacy skills in home and community contexts (Hornberger, 1992).

Nevertheless, it is true that community institutions do not focus primarily on the Khmer language. Indeed, Khmer literacy in the United States starts with a number of strikes against it, including the tradition of little or no schooling of Cambodia's rural farming population, the recent history of schooling disrupted by war and turmoil, the current scarcity of printed material in Khmer amid a relative abundance of audiovisual stimuli, not to mention the strong assimilatory power of English (Hornberger, 1996). Further, U.S. public schools offer little or no support for the maintenance and development of Khmer literacy. Most Cambodian children do not have the option of enrolling in Khmer-English bilingual programs. Instead, most are instructed in mainstream classrooms along with native English-speaking children and at best are offered English as a Second Language (ESL) services. Consequently, Cambodian children who are developing Khmer literacy skills acquire these skills at home and most likely do so before or after acquiring English literacy rather than simultaneously with it.

In this chapter, I report on my observations of Cambodian children's second language literacy development at the Henry C. Lea School in Philadelphia. When my long-term ethnographic study began in 1989, Lea School counted some 37 percent of its students as Southeast Asian, of which the vast majority were Cambodian. The program at Lea School began during the 1980s in response to the influx of Southeast Asian children into the school. This program paid no explicit attention to the Cambodian children's first language and literacy, but mainstreamed them into their second language, English, by means of a pull-out English for Speakers of Other Languages (ESOL) program.

Children took most of their classes along with native English speakers, except when they were pulled out of mainstream classes for some period each day and taught English as a second language.

I conducted observations in a fourth-grade mainstream classroom at Lea School. The teacher, L. McKinney, a third-generation Italian immigrant, was an experienced teacher who was recognized for her excellence in teaching. The year I started my ethnographic observations in her class, she had eleven students from Southeast Asia, including nine Cambodian, one Vietnamese, and one Vietnamese Laotian. She also had sixteen African American students and one Ethiopian.[2]

As a believer in bilingual education and in the value of students being able to develop and apply their first language literacy skills in their acquisition of second language literacy, I was perplexed to see that the Cambodian children were thriving despite the fact that they were not receiving any instruction in their first language, Khmer. Students showed great progress in reading level, and their oral and written performance in literacy tasks improved noticeably throughout the school year. I was eager to learn the teaching strategies for students' second language literacy development in this monolingual instructional setting, which appeared to compensate for the lack of Khmer instruction in the school. Although I focused my observations on the teacher, the children's response was evidence of the efficacy of her approaches. Although I report on the teaching of reading, writing, spelling, and language arts, many of the characteristics of this teaching were also observable in McKinney's teaching of math, science, and social studies.

Shulman (1987) has argued that pedagogical excellence must be defined by a model that goes beyond a set of globally effective teaching skills considered without reference to the adequacy or accuracy of the content being taught, classroom context, student characteristics, and the accomplishment of purposes not assessed on standardized tests. I attempt to contribute to our understanding of pedagogical excellence by describing this teacher's content- and context-specific ways of promoting Cambodian children's English literacy development. The content is the children's second language and literacy; the context is discussed in terms of four themes drawn from the literature on bilingualism, literacy, second and foreign language teaching, and the teaching of reading and writing. This literature identifies critical aspects of context for teaching second language literacy: motivation, purpose, text, and interaction.

Motivation

McKinney made membership in the classroom community desirable through affective and experiential bonds while maintaining the successful execution of literacy tasks as the criterion for membership. She explicitly included herself in the community, for example, by sharing personal anecdotes with her students and holding herself accountable to them for her own absences. McKinney did not share a common cultural and linguistic background with her students but made up for that by creating classroom-based shared experiences. One shared experience was the annual three-day camping trip on which she and another teacher took their classes in May. Throughout the year she referred frequently to the future camp trip, linking class activities to what they would do, see, and experience at camp — for example, camp buildings and natural features were the reference points for a map lesson in social studies. The students participated in a candy sale to raise money for the trip. Students who presented consistent behavior problems were warned, and if necessary excluded from the trip. McKinney worked conscientiously, often with the help of the home-school coordinator, to convince parents that their children would benefit from the trip and be well supervised, and she was genuinely sorry that each year a few parents did not allow their children (usually girls) to go. Furthermore, she made every effort to ensure that no child was excluded because the family could not pay the $30 contribution toward a $50 per-child cost.

Another way she created classroom-based shared experience was by use of various games in which she participated with the students. One of the most popular was a panel game modeled on a television quiz show. The panel game exemplified important aspects of membership in the community: membership was made desirable through affective and experiential bonds and depended on the successful execution of literacy tasks. The questions used in the game were comprehensive review questions composed by the teacher covering social studies, math, and language arts lessons from the preceding weeks.

Aside from creating a desirable, literacy-based classroom community, the other way McKinney built her students' motivation was through taking an interest in and holding accountable each person as an individual. Her attention to each student's ability, activities, and current status achieved the double purpose of demonstrating the teacher's concern for that student and making clear her expectation that each and every student participate fully. This good teaching practice requires the teacher to be attentive to specific community, program, and classroom characteristics. In McKinney's class, attention to individuals required keeping track of which ESOL students had been pulled out for which ESOL class at which time. For example, she arranged for ESOL children in her class to be excused from ESOL to attend the special Settlement Music School assembly program with the rest of their classmates. She might ask them to copy an outline from the board, make up a social studies test, or go get their library books — all missed because of ESOL. Her instructional tasks were further complicated by the fact that different groups of both ESOL and non-ESOL students were regrouped for Chapter 1 and supplementary instruction for the statewide test — Testing Essential Literacy and Learning Skills (TELLS) — separately from the rest of the class at different times during the week.[3]

At its best, McKinney's ability to focus on individuals allowed each student to experience a coherent learning activity in the context of a group lesson. Consider the experience of one Cambodian student as the teacher worked with her group using the book *Increasing Comprehension* (Kravitz & Dramer, 1978). When the students took turns reading aloud, this Cambodian girl read the second paragraph. After all three paragraphs were read, McKinney asked which sentence in each paragraph was similar to the "main idea sentence" given in the exercises. The girl volunteered, "I got it," and correctly identified "It is the lung that makes this one-foot-long fish different from other fish" as the sentence expressing the paragraph's main idea. Although several student turns intervened between the girl's reading and her answer to the main idea question, she successfully answered the question relating to the paragraph she read aloud. Her experience epitomized the way motivation worked in this classroom: as an individual she was held accountable *and* given the opportunity to execute the literacy task successfully, and as a member of the classroom community she valued, she wanted to do so.

Purpose

The teacher established both broadly social and more narrowly task-focused purposes for her students' second language literacy development. McKinney noted that, although she did not want the Cambodian children to lose their culture, she saw it happening, just as it had happened in her own family's history. Although she appreciated linguistic and cultural diversity, she tended to see it as a contribution to a "mix." McKinney was aware of Southeast Asian students' different language and culture, yet she intentionally mixed Southeast Asians with other students at their work tables. A U.S.-born student gave evidence of his teacher's awareness when, on being frustrated because a Cambodian child kept saying "wolleyball" instead of "volleyball," he finally remembered that his teacher told him that Cambodians do not have "v" in their language. Her tolerant assimilation approach was congruent with the school's pull-out ESOL/mainstream program and the community's relative lack of institutional support for literacy in Khmer.

At the level of task-focused purpose in McKinney's classroom, tasks were clearly defined, teacher correction was focused on the task and included acknowledging her own mistakes, and the teacher continually adapted the definition of the task to the immediate situation. All of these are good teaching practices, but what is interesting is how the teacher's task definitions, corrections, and adaptations show her responsiveness to the particular configuration of the second language literacy context. In McKinney's classroom, where Cambodian children were becoming literate in their second language without recourse to their first, it was significant that her correction of students' oral reading and of their writing emphasized meaning rather than phonological or grammatical form. For example, one student read a paragraph from *Increasing Comprehension* fluently, but substituted "Joe's" for "Joseph's" and "train track" for "railroad track." McKinney did not correct these errors and the child went on to answer the multiple-choice comprehension question correctly.

Such instances are consistent with McKinney's expressed approach to student writing. In correcting written work, she said, she looked for complete sentences and for answering the question, but did not pay much attention to spelling; for creative writing, especially, she preferred not to grade at all because the primary purpose was the expression of ideas. Her emphasis on meaning over form was also reflected in her adaptation of literacy tasks to the situation. In a lesson based on a reading about Native Americans, she adapted to the ambiguity present in an exercise involving fill-in-the-blank sentences followed by a word-search puzzle: when she noticed that the sentence could be meaningfully filled by more than one word, she told the class she would accept an answer if it made sense, even if it was not the one she was looking for, but that they should be aware that they might not find that word on the word search.

Text

McKinney felt constrained to use basal reading series by district policy and curricular guidelines and accountability requirements. Such texts can be used in narrow and limiting ways. McKinney, however, not only used them in more open and challenging ways, but also sought to expose her students to genres beyond those in the basal readers and workbooks. The variety of genres in McKinney's classroom derived primarily from exposing students to both oral and written texts and both receptive and productive interaction. She said, "Reading is very important to me, and I want the kids to feel that reading is enjoyable, not just a burden." Besides the many books and magazines in the classroom, she kept a well-stocked and well-organized classroom library, complete with card catalog, designated librarians, and borrowing rules. The library collection encompassed fantasy, adventure, biography, and social studies and science reference works.

Every day, in the twenty-five minutes between recess and lunchtime, McKinney read aloud to the class. During this time, she read books of her own choice that she had liked as a child and that she found to be good, such as *The Lion, the Witch, and the Wardrobe* by C. S. Lewis (1950). To a certain degree, she followed the sequence of genres indicated in the district curriculum guide, but her main goal was that the children would "like being read to." Her variations on the storytime included reading a story brought in by a student (e.g., *The Lost Prince: A Droid Adventure*). Toward the end of the year, each student chose, practiced, and read a story to their classmates.

McKinney gave students an opportunity to gauge their oral reading of a story in their reading group at least once during the year by taping and playing back their reading. "I explain in the beginning that this is . . . a learning tool, . . . that we're not making fun of each other. We all sound pretty bad when it comes down to it. . . . But you want to really be able to say, 'What is it that I have done wrong?' And somebody else might be able to pick something up that you didn't. . . . It's what we call constructive criticism."

Basal readers were put aside for a couple of weeks each year, and the children read book-length stories. McKinney tried to bring out . . . what an author puts into writing a book . . . and that language is very important. Like in *The Ghost of Windy Hill* [by Clyde Robert Bulla], we point out all the dark language that's in the story, and events that are leading up to, foreshadowing . . . Why is this person in the story? Why did this happen? And why didn't the author tell you this? . . . So it's a great way to [engage children] — a short story is hard to get children . . . into . . . as much.

In writing, students explored a variety of genres, including autobiography, personal letters, poems, and fantasy stories. In exposing her students to a wide range of genres and opportunities to listen, discuss, read aloud and silently, and write in those genres, McKinney was aware that different students in her class were at different points in their second language literacy development. For example, she observed that the written work of one student was much better than her oral reading or her speaking, which were barely intelligible. The writing sometimes took her by surprise because it did not seem that the student could have understood so well.

Interaction

In McKinney's class, interaction with and around texts was characterized by opportunities for a range of participant structures (Philips, 1983); the activation of prior knowledge (Anderson, Spiro, & Anderson, 1978); and the development of strategies for signaling understanding of text, analyzing features of text, and reasoning about text (Lytle, 1982). All of these are good teaching practices, but the interactions around text in McKinney's classroom pointed to options that went beyond what was simply good teaching to good teaching for second language literacy development.

Participant Structures

Small-group peer interaction in McKinney's classroom was planned and tightly controlled. The children were seated at nine worktable areas (created by pushing four desks together) and did a minimum of moving around. The teacher came to them when, for example, she wanted to work with a reading group made up of two or three adjacent worktables. She encouraged the children to interact with the others at their worktable, and distinguished between "busy noise," which is directed noise, evidence that students are working, and "noisy noise," which is not. She also specified when such interaction should or should not occur. Thirty minutes into the children's writing of fantasies, she would tell them, "Let someone at your table read your story and see if they understand it." On another occasion, she told three students, "Sometimes you girls help each other, and that's OK sometimes, but sometimes you have to get it yourself."

Prior Knowledge

McKinney was not able to exploit a common reservoir of community-based knowledge, but she compensated for that by emphasizing the students' classroom-based prior knowledge. She did draw on their experience outside the classroom and school, but more characteristic were her frequent appeals, usually through display questions, to students' knowledge from previous lessons or shared class experiences. She might encourage students to connect stories; for example, a story about Pablo Picasso included a picture of his painting *Harlequin*, and she reminded the group of an earlier story they had read about a harlequin. She also drew on shared class experience in discussing vocabulary: for the word *exhibit*, she referred to class trips to the Academy of Natural Science, the zoo, and the art museum; for *meadow* and *camper*, she tied discussion to their future camp trip; for *germ*, she discussed the flu going around the class and school.

Perhaps most representative of her activation and reinforcement of students' classroom-based prior knowledge were her "remember" statements: "Remember I said English is hard because when you learn a rule, you have to learn five more that have broken it"; "Remember I want you to get a little more independent. Read the directions yourselves"; "Remember we talked about the main sentence in the paragraph in our workbooks? What sentence usually tells us what the main idea of the paragraph is?" Indeed, McKinney insisted that remembering was the sign of learning: "You learn something, you remember it. If you learn something and forget it, you haven't really learned it."

Students' Strategies with Texts

McKinney encouraged her students to signal understanding by defining word meanings, identifying the main idea in paragraphs, and following a story line as it unfolds. She called on students to analyze features of the texts they read, ranging from minimal units such as letters, sounds, morphemes, or words, to sentence-level features such as punctuation and complete thoughts, to discourse-level features such as title information, the structure of paragraphs, main characters, author's purpose, and genre. Furthermore, she wanted students to reason about the texts they read by exploring alternative interpretations and expressions in the text and by inferring, guessing, and predicting from the text. McKinney sought to develop these strategies by pointing out features or giving definitions and rules, or by asking the students to do so and, at all times, insisting on precision. When children signaled understanding by giving definitions or answering comprehension questions, McKinney required that the children be precise. For example, she did not accept "to sweep" as a definition of *broom* because "it tells me what you can do with it but it does not tell me what it is," nor would she accept "a screw" as a definition of *tool* because "it is a type of tool, but not a definition."

The same precision was required in analyzing features of text. *Spoon* was not acceptable as a word with the same sound pattern as *room*, and "apostrophe *s*" was not acceptable as the mark of contractions and possessives since "there's not always an *s*." A definition of a homonym as "same word, different meaning," clarified as "same spelling, different meaning," was not acceptable since "the important thing is 'sound the same,' even though they're spelled differently in most cases." Complete sentences were always required in students' written work and often in oral answers, for example, "Who was the man that was responsible? Try to answer me with a good sentence."

Finally, she required precision as students reasoned about a text. She guided them toward precision in their reasoning about alternative word meanings: both a book and a person can be "firm"; the suffix *er* can be used to compare things (e.g., *bigger*) as well as to mean "one who does"; *center* means not only "middle" but also "building," as in "health center"; and you cannot always tell the meaning of compound words by taking them apart — for example, although "a blueberry is a berry that is blue, a strawberry is not a berry that is straw."

As students chose, in succession, each sentence in the following paragraph as the main idea, she guided them toward the correct response (sentence 2). She did not deny the "main ideaness" of their responses, however, since in this case all the sentences seem to carry only part of the main idea:

Most zoos keep the animals in special pens, or fenced-in areas. But there is another kind of zoo. This kind of zoo lets animals go free and puts the people in cages! These zoos put all the animals in a big park. The visitors can see the animals from their car or from a bus or train.

As she guided students to infer, guess, or predict from the text, the goal of precision remained, whether they were inferring at the level of grammar, vocabulary, or discourse:

Look at these words (it's, its). One's a contraction, one's a possessive. Remember I told you there are some possessives that don't use an apostrophe; so which one of these is the contraction? You should know the answer from what I just said.

I'm not going to tell you what *flummoxed* means, you'll have to figure it out from the story. [After reading the story "The Woman Who Flummoxed the Fairies" to the class, she guided students through some of the things that the woman did to elicit the meaning "tricked" for *flummoxed*.]

In the following dialogue, McKinney guided Tyjae and the other students to infer exactly why Bob, the character in the story they were reading, justified continuing to work for a man whom he had begun to suspect of doing something illegal:

McKinney: Why does Bob say, "Oh, he's rich, he won't break the law"? Can't rich people break the law?

Tyjae: Rich people can do anything they want to 'cause they have money.

McKinney: Sometimes it can seem that way. . . . Does Bob want the job? Why? [She went on to elicit the idea that he wants to keep the job because he is making good money and therefore does not want to admit that there might be something wrong.] So in a way, Bob is trying to make himself feel good.

Good Teaching for Second Language Literacy Development

McKinney found ways to create successful learning contexts for promoting the English literacy development of her Cambodian students without recourse to their first language, Khmer. Many of the things she did could be characterized simply as "good teaching" anywhere, not just for language minority children. However, although good teaching in this classroom looked a lot like good teaching anywhere, it actually reflected sensitivity to a wide range of factors unique to this classroom. In this chapter, I highlighted the strategies this teacher used that went beyond good teaching to good teaching for second language literacy development (i.e., for biliteracy; see also Hornberger, 1989; Hornberger & Skilton-Sylvester, 2000). I discussed McKinney's teaching strategies in terms of four themes identified as critical for teaching to promote second language literacy development: motivation, purpose, text, and interaction.

McKinney built motivation in her students by creating a classroom community in which membership was made desirable through affective and experiential bonds, and simultaneously was made dependent on the successful execution of literacy tasks. In the absence of common cultural experiences, she established these bonds by creating classroom-based shared experiences and by taking an interest in each student in the classroom community. She held herself and all students accountable for learning, an accountability that required accommodation to a complex, multilayered pull-out program structure; for example, making sure that students caught up with work that they missed during the time they were pulled out of class for remedial reading or ESOL instruction.

She established meaningful purposes for her students by keeping them focused on literacy tasks that were clearly defined and suited to the immediate situation. These literacy tasks embodied a broad social purpose that was congruent with the tolerant assimilationist program and community context; for example, she paid greater attention to the meanings expressed by the children than to the form in which they expressed them.

McKinney exposed her students to a variety of texts and provided opportunities for oral and written, receptive and productive interaction with a wide range of genres. A well-stocked and well-organized classroom library and daily reading of interesting stories chosen by the teacher or by a student aimed to inculcate a love of reading in her students. She taught her students to give and receive constructive criticism from peers on their oral reading as they prepared to read a story of their own choice to the whole class toward the end of the year.

Class interaction with and around text took advantage of a variety of participant structures and developed students' strategies for signaling understanding of text, analyzing features of text, and reasoning about text. While guiding her students in understanding text, McKinney compensated for her inability to exploit a common reservoir of community-based knowledge by drawing on students' classroom-based knowledge from previous lessons. She relied on carefully structured small-group interaction in which students received feedback on their writing and helped one another. Most important, she insisted on precision as her students analyzed, inferred, guessed, and predicted from text.

Mainstream teachers like McKinney are confronted with a complex teaching challenge as schools across the country seek to serve an increasingly linguistically and culturally diverse student population. These teachers do not necessarily share a common culture and language with their students. Such a teaching challenge requires not one uniform solution but a repertoire of possibilities and alternatives. This chapter described some of these alternatives by focusing on one fourth-grade mainstream teacher who appeared to be successfully creating learning contexts for her students' academic success.

This teacher rose to the challenge in ways that have since been further corroborated in the ever-growing literature on language minority education.[4] For example, her teaching exemplifies the importance of teaching decontextualized and academic uses of English across the curriculum (Corson, 1998, 2001; Cummins, 2000). Students in McKinney's class get significant exposure to and practice in decontextualized and academic uses of English because of, among other things, her focus on precision as students interacted with texts; her creation of a language-rich classroom filled with books; and her insistence on thorough analysis of text (from minimal units, to sentence-level features, to discourse-level features). Indeed, her teaching is permeated with a conscious focus on academic language use across the curriculum, evidenced not only in reading and language arts lessons, but also in her teaching of science, math, and social studies.

McKinney's teaching is also consistent with the literature advocating the teaching of mainstream expectations and socially valued discourse styles in an explicit manner (Delpit, 1986, 1988). Explicit teaching of mainstream expectations and discourse styles is evident, for example, in McKinney's insistence on complete sentences in student writing and talk, in her assignment for each child to read a whole story to the class toward the end of the semester, and in her encouragement of students' independent comprehension of tasks.

Finally, McKinney's teaching exemplifies the kind of political clarity that translates into her holding high expectations for each child while providing appropriate classroom supports for them to succeed (Bartolomé, 2000; Brisk, 1998; Brisk, Dawson, Hartgering, MacDonald, & Zehr, this volume; Friedman, this volume). Her individual accountability system illustrates the high expectations she holds, while her emphasis on reading, inferring, predicting, guessing from text, exploring alternative interpretations — all important strategies that students need to develop in order to succeed throughout their school years in all content classes — demonstrates the kinds of classroom supports she provides to enable them to succeed. Her guidance of each student to infer from text without simply giving them the right answer is another example of high expectations combined with adequate support.

It is not surprising that McKinney's successful teaching strategies addressing the motivation, purpose, text, and interaction so critical to her Cambodian students' English literacy development also instantiate best practices — attention to academic English, explicit teaching of academic discourse, and the communication of high expectations — that have been documented in other research in language minority education. After all, this teacher excelled in finding content- and context-specific ways of promoting her students' learning, and that is, in the end, what good teaching is about.

Notes

1. Adapted from Hornberger (1990), with permission of *Teachers College Record*.
2. I want to thank L. McKinney for permitting and welcoming me into her classroom and sharing with me both the successes and the difficulties of her teaching. I also thank the Philadelphia School District and the principal of the Lea School at that time, John Grelis, who consented to the study. I am grateful for a National Academy of Education Spencer Fellowship, which enabled me to devote my full time to this research during 1989; and for the Dean's Fellowships, the Literacy Research Center, and the Research Fund at the University of Pennsylvania Graduate School of Education, which provided support for graduate students to work with me on the project.
3. "Chapter 1" refers to Chapter 1 of the Education Consolidation and Improvement Act of 1981, revised from Title 1 of the Elementary and Secondary Education Act of 1965, and specifically to the Chapter 1 Local Educational Agency

Grant program, which provided financial assistance for supplemental remedial instruction for educationally deprived students in school districts with
high concentrations of low-income students. TELLS was the statewide testing
program initiated in the Commonwealth of Pennsylvania in the 1980s. Both
programs provided for supplementary instruction for children whose test
scores fell below a certain level.

4. I am indebted to volume editor Zeynep F. Beykont for pointing out these connections.

References

Anderson, R. C., Spiro, R. J., & Anderson, H. J. (1978). Schemata as scaffolding for
the representation of information in connected discourse. *American Educational Research Journal, 15,* 433–480.

Bartolomé, L. I. (2000). Democratizing bilingualism: The role of critical teacher education. In Z. F. Beykont (Ed.), *Lifting every voice: Pedagogy and politics of bilingualism* (pp. 167–186). Cambridge, MA: Harvard Education Publishing Group.

Brisk, M. E. (1998). *Bilingual education: From compensatory to quality schooling.*
Mahwah, NJ: Lawrence Erlbaum.

Corson, D. (1998). *Changing education for diversity.* Buckingham, Eng.: Open University Press.

Corson, D. (2001). *Language diversity and education.* Mahwah, NJ: Lawrence Erlbaum.

Cummins, J. (2000). *Language, power and pedagogy: Bilingual children in the crossfire.*
Clevedon, Eng.: Multilingual Matters.

Delpit, L. (1986). Skills and other dilemmas of a progressive Black educator. *Harvard
Educational Review, 56,* 379–385.

Delpit, L. D. (1988). The silenced dialogue: Power and pedagogy in educating other
people's children. *Harvard Educational Review, 58,* 280–298.

Dubois, T. A. (1990). *Growing up in education: An ethnography of Southeast Asian ado-
lescent life in Philadelphia schools.* Unpublished doctoral dissertation, University of Pennsylvania, Philadelphia.

Hornberger, N. H. (1989). Continua of biliteracy. *Review of Educational Research, 59,*
271–296.

Hornberger, N. H. (1990). Creating successful learning contexts for bilingual literacy. *Teachers College Record, 92,* 212–229.

Hornberger, N. H. (1992). Presenting a holistic and an emic view: The Literacy in
Two Languages Project. *Anthropology and Education Quarterly, 23,* 160–165.

Hornberger, N. H. (1996). Mother tongue literacy in the Cambodian community of
Philadelphia. *International Journal of the Sociology of Language, 119,* 69–86.

Hornberger, N. H., & Skilton-Sylvester, E. (2000). Revisiting the continua of
biliteracy: International and critical perspectives. *Language and Education: An
International Journal, 14,* 96–122.

Kravitz, A., & Dramer, D. (1978). *Increasing comprehension.* Cleveland, OH: Modern
Curriculum Press.

Lewis, C. S. (1950). *The lion, the witch, and the wardrobe.* New York: Macmillan.

López, M. G. (2000). The language situation of the Hmong, Khmer, and Laotian communities in the United States. In S. L. McKay & S. C. Wong (Eds.), *New immigrants in the United States: Readings for second language educators* (pp. 232–262). New York: Cambridge University Press.

Lytle, S. L. (1982). *Exploring comprehension style: A study of twelfth-grade readers' transactions with text.* Unpublished doctoral dissertation, University of Pennsylvania, Philadelphia.

Philips, S. U. (1983). *The invisible culture: Communication in classroom and community on the Warm Springs Reservation.* New York: Longman.

Shulman, L. S. (1987). Knowledge and teaching: Foundations of the new reform. *Harvard Educational Review, 57,* 1–22.

Tollefson, J. W. (1989). *Alien winds: The reeducation of America's Indochinese refugees.* New York: Praeger.

Teaching Bilingual Students in Mainstream Classrooms

MARÍA ESTELA BRISK, MARY DAWSON, MILLICENT HARTGERING, ELIZABETH MACDONALD, AND LUCINDA ZEHR

Learning to read and write in a second language is a challenge, particularly when there is no native language support. Students need three types of knowledge to be able to read and write in their second language: linguistic knowledge, literacy knowledge, and world knowledge (Bernhard, 1991). In the United States they must learn the English language; that is, acquire a degree of mastery of the sound system, the vocabulary, the rules of grammar, and the discourse conventions (Menyuk, 1999). They need to develop literacy skills, such as orthography, directionality, symbol-sound correspondence, automatic recognition of words, conventions of text structure, and uses of literacy. Making sense of reading texts written by English speakers requires world knowledge based on a different cultural experience than the rich storage of world knowledge the student already has. Teachers working with bilingual learners must simultaneously assume the roles of language teacher, literacy coach, and cultural broker. Not only must they teach students oral and written language, they must also help them understand the new culture and how it influences interpretation and creation of text. Students need to command the academic language of texts, understand and create text for many disciplines, and learn new concepts that come from acquiring new knowledge as well as understanding a new culture.

Students' level of language proficiency should not deter teachers from having high expectations, but it should alert them to the need to provide appropriate assistance so that students can meet those expectations. The use of effective literacy strategies developed for monolingual English learners is not enough to teach bilingual students. This chapter presents the reflections and observations of four mainstream teachers working with bilingual learners in the regular context of their classroom, and concludes with a summary of the lessons we can draw from these experiences.

Teachers' Experiences

Four mainstream teachers, Millicent, Lucinda, Mary, and Liz, experimented with successful literacy practices for bilingual learners. Millicent taught third grade at an urban Catholic school. As a reading specialist in a school with a predominantly Spanish bilingual student population, Lucinda alternated between working with bilingual students in small groups and with the rest of the class. Mary and Liz worked at an elementary school in which the student body represented seventeen languages besides English. Mary, a reading specialist, helped students with reading difficulties either individually or in small groups within the classroom. Liz taught in a self-contained fourth-grade classroom with bilingual learners from various language groups.

These teachers explored students' backgrounds and linguistic abilities and observed their performance. They carried out the projects described in this chapter in the context of their usual classroom routines. They tried four teaching approaches: dialogue journal, reader-generated questions, shared reading, and word cards (for a detailed description of these approaches, see Brisk & Harrington, 2000). The teachers adapted these strategies to the needs of their students and to the context of the whole class. In dialogue journals the teacher and students carry out a conversation in writing (Kreeft Peyton, 1990; Stanton, 1988): students write in their journals and the teacher responds. The students' writing is not corrected, but teachers model correct language forms in their responses. Dialogue journals are a nonthreatening way to introduce students to writing in their second language. Reader-generated questions (RGQs) follow the steps of the reading process (Henry, 1984): students are introduced to the theme of the reading through a variety of stimuli, they propose questions that they think may be answered in the reading, and they guess the answers before reading. After reading they check their answers and synthesize the content of the reading. The preparation for reading helps students develop the vocabulary and background knowledge to engage the text. Often when reading in a second language, students are so concerned with pronunciation and decoding that they fail to understand what they read. RGQs help bilingual learners focus on the content of reading while developing good reading strategies.

A third strategy, shared reading, helps second language learners by modeling the reading of text with expression and by providing a lot of repetition. Teachers read aloud stories, songs, or poems with repetitive language and invite students to chime in. Once students have gained confidence, they can individually direct the reading. Follow-up activities give students practice in fluency, vocabulary, phonics, and other skills (Holdaway, 1984; Peregoy & Boyle, 1996). Finally, word cards help students learn to read using their own words. Teachers write daily on index cards the words that each student gives them. Students then practice their old words and give new ones (Ashton-Warner, 1963). Once they have collected a certain number of words, they practice reading through follow-up activities. This activity appeals to students working in their second language because all they need to know to contribute is one word. Chosen by students, these words frequently are connected to students' interests, daily lives, and cultural backgrounds.

The four teachers implemented these instructional approaches with the whole class or a small group of students, depending on their usual classroom organization. To understand the effectiveness of the approach with bilingual students, the teachers analyzed the performance of one bilingual student per class; the accounts that follow reflect these case studies. Any individual attention given to the focus student was comparable to that given to other students. The assessment strategies described were part of the teachers' normal assessment procedures.

Millicent's Experience: Teaching a Newcomer

I have been teaching at an urban Catholic school while completing a master's degree in reading. There are 250 students in kindergarten through eighth grade, most of whom come from the surrounding neighborhood. My school attracts students from several Caribbean islands, including Haiti, Dominica, Jamaica, Trinidad, and Barbados, as well as a few from Latin America. Due to limited resources there are no

ESL or bilingual teachers to help bilingual learners. Volunteers assist the teachers in tutoring students who need extra help and the Haitian secretary assists in communicating with Haitian families.

The topic of teaching bilingual learners is embedded in several of the courses in my master's program. My interest in teaching in settings with multilingual populations emerges from growing up in a bilingual environment. My cousins were raised bilingual in Spanish and English; interacting with them and their father, a native of Peru, helped develop my fluency in Spanish. I also studied Spanish in high school and college. My Spanish is extremely useful when working with Spanish-speaking students and their families.

Soon after school started, the principal brought a new arrival from Honduras to my third-grade class. Although it meant putting Isabel down a grade, the principal felt it would be an easier adjustment for her to have third-grade content material and a teacher who could speak Spanish. At the end of the year Isabel had made so much progress that she was promoted to fifth grade. Isabel came with strong literacy skills in Spanish, a love of math, and a wonderful attitude toward learning and the challenges of a new environment, but her knowledge of English was extremely limited. Her father wanted her to attend our small parochial school even though he knew there were no special services for second language learners. She joined our third-grade class in November, and as the classroom teacher I was faced with the responsibility of helping her acquire fluency in English.

In Isabel's home, the predominant spoken language was Spanish, but all the family members encouraged Isabel to improve her English skills. Isabel's father wanted her to acquire English literacy skills and conversational abilities quickly: "My goal for her is to maintain a conversation in English with friends or whoever." When her father picked her up after school, he always wanted to know how she was doing in class and with her English skills. It was also important to him that Isabel continued speaking Spanish: "I want her to know both languages, to have a choice. That is powerful. Perhaps one day she will want to return to Honduras. Not now, not when she is older, but maybe when she is ready to retire, she will want to go back. And of course, she will always keep in touch with her family there."

Teaching Isabel English seemed like a daunting task. I was very worried about how I would meet Isabel's learning needs as the classroom teacher, especially since we did not have any staff to offer additional assistance. Initially I used Spanish to help Isabel understand the content of the class and help her with participation. I explained in my less than perfect Spanish the main points of a lesson. To help me assess her reading comprehension I asked my Spanish-speaking cousins and uncles to write questions about the readings and to check her answers written in Spanish.

I was fortunate to have the help of a volunteer who worked individually with Isabel for the first month. Isabel made rapid progress in English. Reading and writing assessment of Isabel after three months also revealed that her reading and writing in Spanish were above grade level. With English texts that were familiar to her, her oral reading showed 94 percent accuracy (instructional level);[1] most of her problems were with word endings. Testing for comprehension was more successful when I gave her multiple-choice answers than when she had to write her answers. She was beginning to understand some English, but it was difficult for her to write in English: the ideas were there, but she did not have the vocabulary needed to express those ideas. Her English spelling was generally accurate.

At this point I decided to use dialogue journals for two reasons. First, I wanted to improve Isabel's ability to write in English. Second, because Isabel's life had changed so drastically — in moving from Honduras to Boston she had left her mother, brothers, other family, and friends behind and come to a new country speaking very little English — I thought it was important to give her an avenue to express her feelings about the dramatic changes in her life.

Dialogue journals allow a private and written conversation between teacher and student. Students write freely in a notebook and the teacher responds briefly in writing without correcting. In dialogue journals, no direct teaching is involved. Changes in spelling, use of conventions, and organization are not as quick to happen. The student does not go back and revise the work, and the teacher does not individually address writing difficulties seen in the journals. Rather, the student's writing gains from whole-class lessons in English, the reading and writing curriculum, and the modeling the teacher does when responding to journal entries.

I had implemented dialogue journals at the beginning of the school year, but for a variety of reasons this first attempt did not last long. Looking back, I think I made a mistake in not making a scheduled time for journal writing in the classroom and by not being consistent about collecting students' journals. I also had not done a complete job of explaining this type of writing to my students. The second time, I was determined to make the experience successful. After reading other articles about dialogue journals, I decided that each student would write in his or her personal journal twice a week, on Monday and Thursday, as the morning work assignment. I used this strategy with my entire class of twenty-one third graders because I was confident that it would benefit all of them.

I introduced the journals by discussing why people write in journals, what they might write about, and how it could improve their writing skills and help them with anything they were thinking about. Dialogue journals also helped me as their teacher, because I would know a little bit more about them and they would know more about me. We discussed how a journal was kept, the importance of writing the date, and what they would write about. I explained that our journals were called "dialogue journals" because the students would write an entry and I would respond. I told the students to pick what they wanted to write about, within a few parameters: journal entries had to be about them, their family, or friends; they had to be real experiences; and they had to concern something that was important to them. Most students wanted to know how much they would be required to write. I explained that my focus was on quality writing that was thoughtful rather than on quantity, and that each entry should be as long as it took for the student to write what she or he wanted to write about. I did not want entries that were two sentences and I wanted students to put some thought into each entry. Their journal writing would become a routine, so they could think about what to write before Monday or Thursday morning. I finished the lesson by writing on the board a journal entry about my family and a dinner we had eaten together. I made sure to include my thoughts and emotions in this model so that students would know it was appropriate to write about what they were feeling.

When the students came in the next day, they started their journals. On the board, I had written the morning message reminding them of this assignment. Generally, everyone was excited about it and got straight to work. Many students had questions about spelling, punctuation, and other grammatical concerns. I reminded and assured them that they were writing a private conversation and I wasn't going to correct or grade these journals. I also wasn't going to tell the students what to write about. After everyone had completed their entry, I collected the journals. Later I read them and responded in a few short sentences. When I handed the journals back the next day, all the students were excited about reading my replies. Some immediately wrote back to me, especially if I had asked a question.

After a few entries, some students said that they didn't know what to write about, and a few spent most of the time either trying to think of a subject or to avoid the work, and so their journal entries were either very short or nonexistent. To address this problem, we brainstormed a list of things that the students could write about, including family, pets, trips, classroom happenings, dreams, hopes, fears, and the future. The students copied this list and kept it in their journals in case they ever had a problem deciding what to write about. For students who continued to have trouble, I occasionally gave them a choice between a prompt that I wrote on the board and what they wanted to write about.

Generally, their topics included personal feelings toward classmates, frustration and difficulty in learning, and thoughts on field trips or lessons. Many students wrote about their families and important events in their lives. New pets, visitors, and trips they took or would like to take were other frequent subjects. Students sometimes asked me a question about my life, family, and friends, or they asked for advice. Isabel's journal entries also covered this broad range. In the beginning, her journal entries reflected her spirituality and belief in God through a type of written prayer. In other entries, she wrote about her family in Honduras, memories of her friends there, and why she came to America. Even though I gave her the choice of writing in English or Spanish, she always wrote in English.

In my responses to Isabel, as with all the students, I wrote short replies, usually no longer than two sentences. When responding, I always modeled correct grammar, spelling, and punctuation. I usually tried to pick up on a common error the student was making and model the correction in my response. For example, Isabel continued to write *whith* for *with*, so for several journal entries I used that word. Modeling and explicitly pointing at the appropriate spelling helped Isabel.

From the beginning, Isabel's journal entries were focused and organized. Early entries showed that she had developed her ability to write simple sentences, but she still had difficulties with English vocabulary, grammar, and spelling, as in this example:

In the weekend I go whith Mariana's father to go visit him. And I go to see Mariana's step Brother at the cemetery. He died. I was having a good time whis Mariana's father. Mariana's father is a good people whith others. That was hapening in this wheekend. The En.

My response to this entry was as follows.

I'm glad you had a good weekend with Mariana and her father. I didn't know she had a stepbrother who died.

Later journal entries revealed her language development: her ideas were clearer, the sentences better developed, and spelling errors were typical of a Spanish speaker learning English. Isabel responded to a comment I had written about her mother, who was still in Honduras:

Yes, Ms. Hartgering I will call her or I will write to her. But I miss her A lot. I remember when my mom was with me I allways cry when my mother was living [leaving]. I allways remember my mom when I'm allone. I don't know when I'm going to see her, I don't know when I'm going to hear her voice, I know that Jesus is with her. The End.

Over the many weeks that Isabel wrote in her journal, her vocabulary showed definite signs of improvement. On several occasions, she turned to her Spanish-English dictionary and then used the word in her writing. These words appeared again later in her writing, and she understood them when reading.

Throughout the journal entries, Isabel continued to show growth and development in her writing, for example, using verb tenses appropriately, correctly spelling words she had misspelled before, and increasing her vocabulary. Because of Isabel's strong literacy in her first language, Spanish, she was able to make quick gains in English reading, writing, and speaking.

Isabel's journal entries gave me a lot of information about her as a learner, which I used to inform my classroom teaching. The entries helped me understand her spelling needs, word use, and vocabulary, and so I was able to plan lessons to meet her individual needs more easily. For example, if I noticed she was having difficulty with a specific word, I would include it on her spelling list. When I conferred with her during the writing process, I focused on helping her write sentences that included descriptions and time, especially of events in the past.

Through my experiences with dialogue journals, the first of which failed and the second of which succeeded wonderfully, I have come to believe that they are an essential element in any classroom, particularly one including students with a variety of cultural and linguistic backgrounds. Dialogue journals create a correspondence between student and teacher that gives the teacher some insight into the student's life while providing an opportunity for the teacher to model correct English writing skills. There is rarely time during the day to sit down with students and talk about their lives, their triumphs, and problems. Built into the day's schedule, dialogue journals open a window into each student's life, thinking, and learning while allowing the teacher to regularly assess students' writing development over time.

Lucinda's Experience: Using Reader-Generated Questions to Engage a Passive Learner

I am a reading specialist in a culturally diverse urban school of nine hundred children. Previous experience as an ESL teacher of adults and the courses that I took made me aware of the instructional needs of bilingual learners. I am a native English speaker and do not speak a second language. I report here on my work with one bilingual student, whom I call Elias. Elias was born in Puerto Rico and moved to the United States when he was three. His mother, stepfather, and brother spoke both Spanish and English at home; his mother read in Spanish, and his stepfather read in both languages. Elias had some productive language delays in both Spanish and English and was receiving services from a bilingual speech therapist. His teachers described him as struggling with literacy skills and motivation; however, it was not clear to the teachers whether his problems came from English language proficiency, language-processing problems, or lack of motivation.

Elias was one of several students in his third-grade classroom who were identified as being at risk for retention. His scores on formal literacy assessments were well below grade level. Elias had strong decoding skills in English and he seemed to have a large sight-word vocabulary that helped him with reading and spelling. He could read grade-level texts with more than 90 percent accuracy, even when his comprehension of what he read was low.

Elias did not seem to be making meaning of print; when he read, he demonstrated little comprehension. For example, after he accurately read the book *Tiger Runs Away,* we discussed why the girl in the story goes back to her old house. According to the text, she went back with her mother to retrieve a hose they had left behind and unexpectedly found their runaway cat. Even after text-based discussion, Elias said, "She go back to find Tiger [the cat]."

Elias's writing lacked cohesion, development, and mechanical accuracy. In a composition about Benjamin Franklin in which he was supposed to answer what invention Franklin might find interesting in today's classrooms, Elias wrote, "I have invention about school about book. Benjamin Franklin like book he read he brother get so angry when he read an write."

In addition, Elias's work habits themselves seemed to be an obstacle to learning. He was not an independent learner, he had trouble attending to classroom instruction, and he was easily distracted. It took a long time and much teacher prompting for him to finish assignments.

Most of my work with Elias took place in a group of four students from his class four days a week for about forty minutes. I also worked with Elias in a whole-class setting when teaching English language arts to his class. The primary strategy used in the small-group setting to build reading comprehension skills was RGQs. RGQs follow a student-centered approach that includes six basic steps:

1. Stimuli. Introduce the topic of reading through pictures, semantic maps, title, and so on.
2. Generating questions. Ask students to generate questions as a large group, small group, or individually.
3. Predicting responses. Have students guess responses to the questions.
4. Presenting the text. Read or tell the story, as a group or individually.
5. Checking out responses. Have students check the accuracy of their responses.
6. Final activity. Have the students synthesize the reading content through writing, drawing, or another activity (see Brisk & Harrington, 2000, for more detail).

The basis of this approach lies in understanding what effective readers do: they spontaneously pose questions to themselves when they begin to read, and then seek answers to their questions through reading. According to Henry (1984), the traditional method of requiring students to demonstrate comprehension by answering questions posed by others is not a natural part of the reading process and actually interferes with normal reading strategies.

These procedures were adapted to fit the particular instructional situation with Elias's group. The most significant modification involved eliminating step three, that is, students were not asked to predict answers to their questions. After formulating their questions, they read the text and looked for answers to the questions. This allowed the whole cycle, from stimulus to final activity, to take place within one class meeting, which was an important consideration, given the short attention spans and the overall weak learning strategies of these students.

I used this methodology not only because it was pedagogically sound and related to Elias's area of greatest academic need (i.e., reading comprehension), but also because it suited his learning style. As mentioned earlier, he struggled to attend to instruction and to stay involved in lessons. He had a hard time working independently and generally did not take ownership of his learning. The active nature of this approach, as well as the shift of responsibility from the teacher to the student, seemed an appropriate challenge for Elias.

The presentation of this methodology moved gradually from more teacher guidance (i.e., modeling and cooperative group discussion) to more student independence. Most of the books used were at students' instructional level for reading comprehension (i.e., below grade level). Along with RGQs, reading instruction also included activities to build background and world knowledge. The follow-up activity was usually writing paragraph responses to key questions related to the literature they read. Answering key questions was congruent with the statewide standards and testing format. When appropriate, I incorporated drawing activities into the lessons.

Elias read and used RGQs for five books over the course of eight weeks. These books were chosen to reflect the students' interests. We spent from one day to two weeks on each book, depending on the curriculum needs. I gradually adapted the approach from a more group-oriented format, which offered students a lot of modeling and support from their classmates, to a more individualized format, which required students to work more independently. The more group-oriented format involved students developing questions together, which I wrote on chart paper with the contributors' names. After reading the book, we worked as a group to answer the questions. The follow-up activity was usually answering key higher-order questions about the book that required evidence from the book for support; we developed these questions as a group.

The first change in the RGQ format was implemented during lessons eight and nine, whole-class lessons, when students wrote their own questions without discussing them as a group. After reading the book, students answered their own questions. The next step toward a higher level of independence was implemented during lesson ten. Students chose between two books, developed their own questions on a worksheet, and read independently to find answers to their questions. The worksheet was set up the same way the group charts had been, with two columns: "Questions I have" and "Answers I found."

From the beginning of the implementation of this approach, Elias was eager to participate, was on-task most of the time, and engaged in the academic tasks at hand. His predictions about the book during the stimulus phase moved from questions or comments related specifically to the book cover to questions and comments that went beyond the cover. "Is Triceratops going to kill Tyrannosaurus Rex?" he asked when shown the cover of *Brave Triceratops,* which showed a tyrannosaurus rex approaching a triceratops. Elias was good at formulating questions and finding answers in the text and was quite capable of retelling the story in detail afterward. He had great difficulty, however, finding the main idea when asked for a key question. He responded, "A girl Emily and her dog Clifford," when asked for the main idea of the book *Clifford's First Valentine's Day*. In subsequent books, he would sometimes accurately find the main idea, other times he would answer based on some detail of the story.

Although Elias exhibited difficulties and often did not get the big picture, it was exciting to see him make text-to-text connections and text-to-life connections at unexpected times. During lesson seven he gave an example from the previous story when asked to define a topic sentence, which showed that he recalled information and could apply it to a new context. A text-to-life connection occurred during lesson six, when the group was discussing how to handle conflict. Elias offered a solution that was used by a character in *Brave Triceratops*, a book we had read earlier, as a possible solution to the conflict in his own life:

Lucinda: What should you do when someone bothers you?
Elias: Scare them like Triceratops in the book.

Elias stayed most involved and on task when the tasks were finite, clear, and active. He responded well to the short lessons and quick pace of the instruction. Most of the instruction was quite teacher-directed and involved a lot of student-teacher interaction, thus Elias did not have a chance to get off task. RGQs were well suited to Elias's learning needs in that they contained several finite steps that were active and could be completed quickly. I adapted the methodology further to involve students getting up to write on the chart paper and to note verbally during reading when they found an answer to a question. In addition, RGQs demanded Elias's own input, which made him responsible for making meaning from text. He was invested: they were his questions and he wanted to find answers to them.

When I first worked with Elias, I noticed that he had problems working independently. During the implementation of the RGQ approach, Elias worked diligently even when the activities began to require more and more independent work. When we implemented RGQs with the whole class, Elias wrote a question and then the answer without prompts from the teacher or other students. In lesson ten he worked independently, using yet another format for his questions, a worksheet. As Elias became more familiar with the questioning process, his syntax improved and he was increasingly able to formulate questions using appropriate English structure.

RGQs helped Elias improve reading comprehension to a certain degree. There are two ways to measure growth in reading comprehension. First, it can be measured relative to overall reading ability, that is, has the student grown in his or her overall ability to understand text? The other way is relative to a certain text, that is, has the student grown in understanding of this particular text? It is difficult to determine how much Elias grew in his overall ability to comprehend text in eight weeks. His ability to state the main idea of something he read only once did not seem to improve consistently, nor did his ability to answer a key question and support it with relevant details from the story.

Despite constraints in implementation and numerous personal and family factors affecting Elias's schooling, he did grow academically during my work with him. There was more evidence of the second type of measurable growth. For each of the books we read, there were many opportunities to explore the text at different times and levels, from prereading to follow-up activities. In follow-up activities and discussion, Elias showed growth in understanding each text. For example, on the third day we worked with *Tiger Runs Away,* Elias wrote a sentence in which he stated accurately a main point that he had misunderstood during his initial reading. Moreover, his correct answers to the questions he posed for each book were evidence that he grew in his understanding of each book. RGQs can be credited with promoting this comprehension; by involving students as thinkers, this strategy prepared and motivated them to make meaning from the text.

A particularly valuable aid for Elias was that the process of using RGQs as a reading comprehension strategy was introduced to him gradually, with a lot of teacher modeling and support. As he became more comfortable with the process of generating and answering questions, I adapted the approach in several stages that challenged him to work and apply the strategy more independently. He also responded well to consistent, teacher-structured instruction in which he had some control over the content and the content matched his interests and reading level. In addition, he was able to exercise one of his strengths, drawing, in the context of these reading activities, which increased his interest and validated his abilities. Most important, however, was the fact that I encouraged him to take a more active role in his own learning.

Mary's Experience: Teaching English Literacy while Supporting Bilingualism

I am a reading specialist trained in reading recovery.[2] I have been teaching for two years, working exclusively with students of diverse language backgrounds. I am not proficient in Spanish, but a few courses I took for my master's degree addressed the educational needs of bilingual learners and helped me in my teaching and in my interactions with parents.

My school is located in a lower-middle-class neighborhood that has welcomed many waves of immigrants. Our 350 students reflect the linguistic and cultural variety of the neighborhood, and of the seventeen languages represented in the school, Spanish and Portuguese are the most commonly spoken. Some students are themselves immigrants, others come from immigrant families but were born in the United States and have some proficiency in both English and their heritage language. The school offers a pull-out ESL program for students with limited proficiency in English.

While working with a group of first graders with reading difficulties, I chose to focus on Michael, a student with a number of learning difficulties. Michael was a U.S.-born, six-year-old first-grade student who was fluent in spoken English. He could understand some Spanish but spoke it only a little. His parents spoke English and Spanish at home but encouraged him to speak only English. His ability to read or write in either language was very limited, and included a few high-frequency words, such as *to, the, and,* and *yes,* and a few patterned, predictable books that would be appropriate for a first grader to be reading in October.

Michael was first placed in a two-way Spanish-English bilingual classroom for kindergarten and first grade. After two months, Michael's mother decided to move him to a mainstream classroom because he was performing significantly behind his first-grade peers and she believed that he was getting confused between the two languages. When we met, Michael talked openly about his desire to become a better Spanish speaker even though he preferred to speak in English. He seemed to be very aware of the difference between the two languages and that he was more proficient in English. In general, he had a very positive attitude toward learning and was eager to learn how to read.

Michael's classroom was traditional and structured and filled with students from various language backgrounds. The schedule of the day was always the same: journal writing, repetitive writing of ten weekly spelling words, reading group, phonics worksheets, snack, math worksheets, lunch, special (e.g., art, music), science or social studies, and dismissal. Students sat in rows and the teacher taught from basal readers and worksheets. I worked with Michael in a group with two other children within the classroom, five days a week for fifteen minutes each day. I also saw him five days a week for thirty minutes each day in one-on-one reading-recovery sessions.

I implemented two approaches with the goal of improving Michael's reading ability: word cards and shared reading. Combined, these approaches helped Michael to read new words and improve his reading fluency. Every day during reading group I asked each student for a word, which I wrote on an index card so that they watched me writing it correctly (left to right) and listened to me sounding it out. They read their words to me, to other members of their group, and to their families at home. Once we had collected ten to fifteen word cards, we played word games such as "Concentration" or "Go Fish." Through this procedure it was my hope that Michael would learn new words and their meanings and become interested in learning and taking on more words.

The first word Michael chose was *heart*. As he sat beside me, I held the paper in front of him and spelled out the word slowly as I wrote, "h-e-a-r-t". I then had him trace the letters with his finger and say the word slowly, sounding out each part. Next I told him to run his finger under the whole word and say "heart." He repeated this three times. On the second day we used word cards, Michael recognized the word *heart* right away. He then read the word twice while he underlined it with his finger. On the third day, the words *heart* and *house* confused Michael because they both begin with *h*, so I showed him a way to discriminate between the two: *heart* ends with the letter *t*, and *house* ends with the letters *se*. I demonstrated this strategy by putting emphasis on the final word sounds and looking for the best match. When I presented the two cards to him and asked him to read the words, he read them correctly. Over the next few days he added *pig* and *octopus* to his collection of word cards. When I presented him with all four cards, he was able to read each of them correctly. He told me that he was "checking the first letter and the last letter" (if the first letter was the same as a first letter of another word). I then had him read his cards to another student in the group and show the other child how he knows which word is *house* and which word is *heart*. He proceeded to explain that he first looks at the beginning of the word, and if the first letters are the same, as in *heart* and *house*, he then looks at the ending. Michael began to take words apart whenever he encountered difficulty, even while reading on his own. While reading the story *Fishing*, we came to a page that read, "On Wednesday I went fishing with my *big* brother" (italics added). He noticed the word *big* and said, "Hey! That word looks like *pig*. If I change the first letter to b, it will be *big*." From then on he consistently solved words by association. He used *there* to get to *then* and *they*, and *clock* to get to *rock*.

I then began to use the shared reading approach with Michael's group. In this approach the teacher and students read together while looking at the same text. Teachers use big books or an overhead when working with a large group. After the teacher models the reading, students venture to read by themselves and model for other students. Books with repetitive language are recommended. During our first meeting, we used the book *Birthday Cakes*. In the story, each person, from a two-year-old to a grandmother, has birthday candles that need to be blown out. The pattern "they blew them out with one big blow" is repeated on every page. The first time Michael read this with the group, he said, "The blew out the candles with one big blow." We read through the first page again, practicing the pattern, and he read, "They blew them out with a big blow." Finally, on the third practice, Michael read, "They blew them out with one big blow." We then read through the story as a shared reading.

On the following day, we revisited *Birthday Cakes*. This time I noticed Michael read, "And they blew them out with one big blow," inserting the word *and*. After reading, I asked him to point to the word *and*. "Oh!" he said, "it doesn't say *and*," and he self-corrected to, "They blew them out with one big blow." During the weeks I used the shared reading strategy, Michael's phrasing and fluency increased in several ways. Early on, Michael read a passage from the book *Ben's Teddy Bear* in two- to three-word phrases: "Mom! Mom!" "where is," "teddy bear?" Four weeks later, as he read a passage from *A Friend for Little White Rabbit,* I observed that his reading fluency had increased to four-to five-word phrases: "Hello little brown rabbit," "said the little white rabbit," "please will you play with me?" "Yes said the little brown rabbit," "come on." His reading sounded very natural, like talking, and he was reading with expression, for example, "Yes! said the little brown rabbit." Shared reading was very effective for improving Michael's oral reading skills as well as his phrasing and fluency.

In addition to classroom observations, I assessed Michael's progress using Marie Clay's observation survey (1992, 1993) (see Table 1). I administered it before I started using these approaches and again after two months of implementation. Michael improved in every aspect measured by the survey, significantly increasing his reading ability.

To support Michael's literacy development I worked with both his classroom teacher and his parents. For his teacher, I demonstrated the teaching strategies I used with Michael so that these approaches could be transferred to other work in the classroom. I talked with his mother concerning language choice and consistency of language use with her children. I explained that it was important that she and her husband

TABLE 1
Michael's Reading Performance[a]

Reading Subtests	February	April
Letter Identification	40/54 letters	54/54 letters
Word Test	3/20 words	15/20 words
Concepts about Print	19/24 concepts	22/24 concepts
Writing Vocabulary	9 words in 10 minutes	26 words in 10 minutes
Dictation Task	19/37 sounds	36/37 sounds
Text Reading	Reading Recovery Level 3	Reading Recovery Level 9
Record of Oral Language	Level 1	Level 3

[a] Based on Mary Clay's Observation Survey, 1992, 1993.

use their strongest language, Spanish, when they spoke with their children, while continuing to support the school's efforts to develop Michael's English language and literacy. Michael's mother accepted my advice as informed knowledge. She talked with her children about speaking more Spanish in the home. Later, Michael announced to me that during breakfast his family sang a Spanish song and he told me they had been speaking Spanish during breakfast and dinner.

Michael also progressed socially. When he entered our school he had few friends and rarely spoke with anyone other than his twin brother. By March he talked animatedly with both adults and children, as his English oral language continued to improve. He enjoyed participating in group work. He liked sharing his word cards, reading with the group during shared reading time, and helping his peers who were still struggling. After two months of implementing the word cards and shared reading approaches, Michael improved his English reading skills, became a strategic reader, and seemed more social and sure of himself.

Liz's Experience: Helping One Bilingual Learner while Teaching Twenty-Five Students

I am a fourth-grade teacher with a self-contained mainstream classroom in the same school as Mary. Although I took Spanish in high school, I never felt I had mastered a second language, so I felt insecure working with bilingual students. A few ESL workshops and graduate courses helped me understand bilingualism and second language learning and gave me the confidence to work with bilingual learners. I concluded that learning English did not have to compete with students' native languages and cultures. I also realized that strategies that are helpful for these students are also effective with all my students.

Several of the students in my class come from Spanish, Haitian Creole, and other linguistic backgrounds. I decided to focus on Javier because, although he was able to comprehend text, he had difficulty with pronunciation and spelling. I worked with him during our reading group time. The description that follows concerns Javier, but all the activities were carried out with the whole group. I gave equal attention to all my students.

Javier was a ten-year-old boy born in the United States. His mother was from Puerto Rico and his father from the Dominican Republic. Javier lived with his mother and his younger brother, who was in the first grade. His Puerto Rican grandmother often took care of the children. He had learned both English and Spanish at home before entering school. He had always been in a monolingual classroom where he spoke only English. Javier demonstrated enthusiasm when Spanish words appeared in a reading during class; he always volunteered to read the word and explain the meaning to the rest of the class. His academic performance had been a concern of mine since I had administered an adaptation of the Developmental Reading Assessment (DRA) to Javier in the second week of school. This test measures decoding and reading comprehension ability through a variety of tasks, using a series of leveled storybooks. Javier understood the readings, but his oral reading showed many miscues. A second-grade book, *Worms for Breakfast,* was used for the reading assessment. Javier answered both literal and inferential questions about the story correctly and he was able to retell the characters, the important details, and the events of the story in sequence. His oral reading was not as successful: he mostly read word by word in short phrases, although a few times he read fluently with expression. He did not use picture cues but did monitor his reading by sounding out some words and rereading. He self-corrected two times. Javier relied heavily on the initial letters to decode words, read *place* for *pieces,* and did not attend much to the middle or end sounds of words.

Javier's reading continued to be a concern after I conducted the midyear reading assessment. Before administering the midyear assessment to see if any progress had been made, I had been meeting with

Javier three to four times a week for guided reading. Guided reading is an approach to teaching reading that aims at developing strategies to help students interact with increasingly difficult text (Fountas & Pinell, 1996). During these sessions I would meet with Javier and three other students to read and practice reading strategies. We would focus on isolated phonics lessons during our 20-minute guided reading sessions. Javier also met with the special education teacher in a resource room setting with six other students four times a week for a 45-minute guided reading session.

When tested again at midyear, Javier had advanced in reading level and his comprehension continued to be acceptable. He was able to retell the story in sequence including character names and specific details. He answered both the literal and inferential questions correctly; he took his time answering and appeared to think carefully about his responses. His oral reading, however, was not appropriate: he read the text in short phrases with no intonation at an inconsistent rate. Javier continued to rely heavily on the initial letters to decode words. He had increased the use of final cues but demonstrated a weakness in attending to the middle graphemes. He read *Perer* for *Putter, Tibby* for *Teaberry,* and *what* for *when.*

Javier's writing showed comparable qualities and problems. After a visit to a haunted house he wrote, "This weeked [weekend] I went to hunt [haunted] house in Bocktion [Brockton] it was really scarey [scary] at the begeeing [beginning]." A number of middle and final sounds were missing and he left out punctuation, but for the most part his writing made sense.

Given Javier's abilities, I decided to do two things: 1) move him to a group that was reading higher-level books and 2) use the word-card approach to help him with decoding and spelling. I felt that moving Javier to a higher level would challenge him in the area of reading comprehension. I thought that the move also would boost Javier's self-esteem, since he was aware of the fact that he was in a low-level reading group and this seemed to discourage him from coming to guided reading group. After Javier moved into the higher reading group, I saw a change in his attitude: he was more willing to come to the reading table and he stayed on task while reading. Javier was able to keep up with the comprehension of the books but continued having difficulty decoding some words. The other students in the group were having more difficulty with comprehension than decoding. I thought this was the ideal mix, giving all students an opportunity to shine at something.

I use word cards to teach the sound-symbol connections of words. I thought that the word cards would be beneficial for a child like Javier, who exhibited a low level of phonemic awareness and poor spelling skills. Since I had been meeting with Javier three to four times a week during guided reading sessions to read instructional-level texts and to work on phonemic awareness skills, I decided to incorporate word cards into our work. The first day I asked the four students to come up with five words each and then wrote those words on index cards while sounding them out. Two of the five words Javier chose were from the vocabulary written on the classroom board. The ones he wrote on his own were missing sounds: *comption* for competition, *mulction* for multiplication, and *subtration* for subtraction. Looking at his classmate's dry-erase board, he recognized the proper spelling of *multiplication,* saying, "Oh, that's how you spell multiplication. I just spelled it the way it sounded." Javier was aware of the strategy of sounding out words, but the problem was that he was not sounding out the middle phonemes. He would say the word slowly, as if he were breaking the word up into syllables, but he was really only paying attention to the initial phoneme and the end phoneme. Javier seemed to enjoy the activity of making word cards because he was on task during the lesson and reread all the words he had chosen when the lesson ended. Javier and the other students were asked to study the words each night and quizzed each other at the start of each guided reading session.

The next day, when a classmate quizzed Javier on the word cards from the previous day, he had difficulty reading the words from the cards. He told his classmate to skip over *vacation* and *attention* because he didn't know how to read them. He also made six miscues when reading: *decision* for *division, expansion* for *explanation, mention* for *mansion, notation* for *nation, otaion* for *lotion,* and *ment-tion* for *mention.* He did read *multiplication* and *station* correctly. Javier appeared discouraged and frustrated while reading the word cards. When he came to the word *nation* he attempted to sound it out several times, but then gave up, saying, "Notation no I don't know just go on." The next day Javier read a few more words correctly but continued to have problems with a number of them. He looked embarrassed when he was unable to read a word. After his classmates told him the word, he would try to cover up by saying, "Oh yeah, I knew that word."

At this point I needed to reflect on the approach I was taking with word cards. It was never my intention to make a child feel discouraged and frustrated; my goals were to instill confidence and help each child feel successful. I realized that my approach of giving the students the words was achieving neither of these goals. The word card approach is based on the notion that students, not the teacher, choose the words they want to learn. Since at these meetings we were also reading instructional-level books, I decided that they could make word cards from words they wanted to learn in the readings. I told everyone in the group that, when they came across a word they could not pronounce, one they had never seen before, or even one they just liked, to point it out to me and we could use it for a word card. The students all read aloud to themselves at the same time while I listened to one student at a time. As I worked with each student, I wrote on cards the words they chose.

I used this approach for four weeks during guided reading sessions, which met three times a week for twenty minutes. While I met with a guided reading group, the other students worked in learning centers around the room. Students learned not to interrupt a reading group but instead to ask a classmate for help or to solve a problem on their own. Most of the students came to realize that reading group was a short period of time that gave them the opportunity to really improve their reading skills, since I could guide their reading in a small group. As a result the students came to respect and adhere to the necessity of not interrupting reading group and to use their time wisely while in reading group.

With the revised approach, Javier enjoyed word cards. He chose words that he was unable to read. As soon as he came across a word that he had difficulty reading, he tried to sound it out using the initial consonant sound. For example, he attempted to sound out the word *serious* by verbalizing "se se se." When he was unsuccessful sounding out a word based on the initial consonant sound, he showed me the word. At that point I took an index card, broke the word up into syllables, and slowly wrote each syllable on the card as Javier watched. Javier was usually able to pronounce the word after it had been broken up into syllables.

The students practiced reading their word cards at the start and at the end of each guided reading session to build fluency. They were then asked to begin their reading with what they had read the previous day. Practicing the difficult words on the word cards before read-

TABLE 2
Javier's Reading Performance[a]

Reading Subtests	1/27/00	4/10/00
Reading Level of Text[b]	I	K
Accuracy	89%	89%
Semantically Acceptable Miscues	33%	32%
Syntactically Acceptable Miscues	83%	50%
Miscues with Similar Initial Graphemes	58%	68%
Miscues with Similar Middle Graphemes	8%	27%
Miscues with Similar End Graphemes	41%	27%
Self-Corrections	0%	9%

[a] Based on the school's adaptation of the Developmental Reading Assessment, 1997.

[b] Books used to assess students are classified from Level A (kindergarten) through W (sixth grade). A Level I corresponds to high second grade, a Level K to low third grade (levels according to Fountas & Pinell, 1996, 1998).

ing helped Javier read more fluently. When he came across a word he had had difficulty with previously, he could read it with confidence and ease.

After using this approach for four weeks, I assessed Javier's reading again (see Table 2). His comprehension was good. Javier read a third-grade-level book, having moved up three levels in the list that graded the books. He read in longer phrases at a consistent rate, and he continued to monitor his reading by rereading, sounding out words, and breaking words up into syllables. Javier continued to rely heavily on initial letters to decode words (68% of his miscues had initial graphic similarity). He was attending more to the middle graphemes, with 27 percent of his miscues having middle graphic similarity. Twenty-seven percent of his miscues had final graphic similarity. Half of Javier's miscues were syntactically acceptable, and 32 percent were semantically acceptable.

During the assessment, Javier proved that he knew the strategy of breaking up words into syllables. When he came to the word *savage*, he initially read it as *rescue*. Realizing that it either didn't look right or didn't make sense, he changed the word to *saving*. After saying "saving," he knew that the word was still not correct. "No, no!" he exclaimed. At that point, I asked him how he could figure out the word. He then put his hand over *sav* and tried to sound out *age*. After saying "age," Javier uncovered *sav* and said "save." When he put the word together he pronounced it "save-age." Even though he was unable to pronounce the word properly, Javier demonstrated that he knew the strategy of breaking up words into syllables.

Javier's writing showed much progress. His thank-you letter to the educational zoo his class had visited read as follows:

> Thank you for having us come to your zoo four times in a row. I like when we went bird hunting. It was fun to go see out some birds. My favorite bird we saw was the Blue Jay. It was cool. I had fun to see so many birds. So I hope you can come back to go bird hunting again.

This letter shows complete sentences with proper punctuation. His spelling was correct. Except for a couple of grammatical problems, the letter is well written and expressive.

Using my own adaptation of word cards helped Javier learn a new strategy to cope with decoding difficulties, gain confidence in reading, and become a more careful speller. Breaking up difficult words into syllables, both orally and in writing, helped Javier take ownership of reading the word rather than losing control by having me simply tell him the word. Practicing reading difficult words in isolation before reading them in context increased Javier's fluency. Freedom to choose the words, breaking them up into syllables, and repeated practice helped Javier's fluency and confidence in oral reading. In turn, his comprehension increased, allowing him to read higher-level books.

Lessons Learned

Mainstream teachers can efficiently educate bilingual learners, as these experiences illustrate. Millicent undoubtedly had an advantage over the other teachers because she knew the language of her student. This skill not only facilitated her teaching and communication with the learner, but was also essential in developing a rapport with the father.

These four teachers learned many lessons that other mainstream teachers working with bilingual learners can apply: help the whole class by educating bilingual learners; make approaches for bilingual learners part of the class routine; get to know the students; teach bilingual students as bilinguals; use students' languages and cultures to facilitate acquisition of English; have high expectations of all students;

adapt approaches carefully; enlist support from others; and encourage positive attitudes toward bilingualism.

Help the Whole Class by Addressing Bilingual Learners' Academic Needs

Teachers should make approaches that are beneficial for bilingual learners their preferred approach to teaching, either with the whole class or selected groups. Millicent's entire class benefited from the writing practice provided by dialogue journals. Lucinda developed good reading habits with the whole group of students by using RGQs.

Approaches recommended for bilingual learners usually include modeling, explicit instruction of procedures, drawing on students' experiences, connecting new concepts with those that are part of the students' existing knowledge, doing cooperative work in both heterogeneous and homogeneous groups, and allowing students to regulate the level of difficulty of content. Such characteristics are helpful instructional approaches for all students. Facilitating instruction for bilingual learners renders highly adaptable teaching that addresses classes with a variety of skills and backgrounds.

Make Approaches for Bilingual Learners Part of the Class Routine

Approaches chosen to address the needs of bilingual learners will be sustained if they are incorporated in the regular class routine. When the needs of bilingual students are seen as extra, the changes will never take place or may not last because they are perceived to be an added burden.

These approaches can be implemented with the whole class or a group of students. It is best to use approaches with the whole class when all students can benefit, for example, using graphic organizers to introduce concepts or a book. Limiting the instruction to a group is better if the needs are specific to a group of students, if the class usually works in groups, or if the teacher feels more comfortable trying something new first with a small group. Teachers need to analyze their routines and their students' needs in general in order to decide how best to implement these new ideas. Liz determined that the best way to use word cards with Javier was to include them with the already organized group work during the literacy block. By carefully choosing the students in the group, she sought to benefit all. Millicent wanted to use dialogue journals to help Isabel, but she implemented the strategy with the whole class. Twice a week Millicent started class with journal time, and making it a routine for all students made the experience successful for her and her students.

Get to Know the Students

Bilingual students are very different from one another, and their patterns of language ability and use vary greatly. Three of the students reported on in this chapter showed difficulties with the reading and writing process, and the fourth, Isabel, was a skillful, literate learner. Isabel, however, was the least proficient in English.

Knowing their educational and cultural backgrounds and their language ability helps the teacher choose approaches and strategies. Liz's careful evaluation of Javier's reading ability allowed her to take advantage of his strengths while aiming at improving his weaknesses. Using strategies that allow the students to express themselves, such as the dialogue journal, and communicating with families help teachers discover more about their learners. Mary's contact with parents made her aware of the many educational and linguistic environments her student had experienced. It also made her aware of the parents' dilemma about language choice for communication and education.

Teach Bilingual Students as Bilinguals

Bilingual students must be approached as individuals with another language and cultural experience who have varying degrees of English proficiency; they should not be taught as students with poor English. Bilingual students such as Isabel, who have strong ability and literacy in their home language, use this ability to develop English and to function in school. Javier had difficulty with spelling because of how he had acquired his oral English. He developed his own notion of how words such as *multiplication* are pronounced and spelled. Liz's careful pronunciation and breaking up of words helped him reformulate how these words were pronounced and spelled.

Recognizing students as bilinguals means allowing them to use their native languages in school. Use of the students' home languages in no way interferes with their acquisition of English. Within a year, most students switch to speaking primarily English long before they are proficient in it (Wong Fillmore, 1991). They always like to have access to their native language for social and academic purposes (Pease-Alvarez & Winsler, 1994). Millicent's acceptance and use of Isabel's language constituted an important support in her English development. At no time did the use of Spanish discourage Isabel from trying her English, and her progress in English was steady. By the time Millicent used dialogue journals, Isabel wanted to write only in English.

For emotional, linguistic, and cognitive reasons, students who live in a bilingual world benefit from fostering both languages. Recognition of their bilingualism helps them take advantage of the knowledge they have (Jimenez, García, & Pearson, 1995).

Use Students' Languages and Cultures to Facilitate Acquisition of English

A student's stronger language is the best medium for thinking and understanding. Millicent encouraged Isabel to use Spanish to express herself. She also used it to communicate with Isabel and her father, although her own Spanish was less than perfect. Even when teachers know only English and teach in that language, they can take advantage of students' languages and cultures to enhance learning. Reading books in the home language can build the concepts explained in English, and planning writing in the stronger language allows students to organize ideas. Consulting and collaborating in the native language among peers helps with the tasks at hand (Marsh, 1995; Reyes, Laliberty, & Orbanosky, 1993).

Instructional approaches that allow for students' creativity open a window to their background and cultural knowledge. Using the students' words to teach decoding skills and dialogue journals to stimulate writing allowed Mary and Millicent to learn about their students' interests and experiences. Presenting familiar topics or texts facilitates comprehension because students can relate them to their own knowledge (Carrell, 1987). As Perez further explains:

> Bilingual readers when confronted with reading English texts containing familiar cultural material may comprehend the text content within the larger sociocultural context of their own related experiences rather than as isolated facts. They are more likely to connect implicit as well as explicit information to their prior experience and knowledge. (1998, p. 37)

Furthermore, activating students' background knowledge relative to the topic of instruction facilitates learning and engagement. When Lucinda asked her students to develop their own questions before reading, she opened a window onto their ideas and concepts. Her students became active learners regardless of their ability.

Have High Expectations of All Students

Of paramount importance for teachers is the development of high expectations for themselves as teachers and for their students as learners. "When I expect them to succeed, the children respond, develop, and are alive; and I am refreshed" (Igoa, 1995, p. 9). High expectations must be accompanied by appropriate instructional support. Liz moved Javier to a higher reading group while she implemented a teaching approach that helped him with his greatest difficulty, decoding long words. Lucinda taught Elias to take responsibility for his learning by slowly giving him more freedom of choice. Those were the forms of support these two students needed to live up to their teachers' high expectations.

There is no doubt that learning in a new language and in a new cultural setting is difficult. Teachers may avoid being demanding because they feel sorry for students, but bilingual students offer a different view of demanding teachers. As one student put it, "They expected a lot, they cared" (Brisk, 1994, p. 23). Knowledge of second language acquisition processes helps teachers determine the appropriate instructional strategies to help their bilingual students meet high academic expectations.

Adapt Approaches Carefully

Approaches can be adapted to individual teaching styles and student needs, although care must be taken not to completely change the most important features of the approach. When Millicent first tried dialogue journals, she did not respond consistently to them. The purpose and benefits of the dialogue journal come from the interaction with the teacher: students are motivated by the notion that the teacher is interested in what they have to say. Rather than not collecting journals for lack of time to read them, it is better to assign them less frequently. Liz's attempts to tell students the types of words to give for word cards was less successful than telling them to choose words from their textbook. Although the latter method was an adaptation of the approach, it allowed students to choose the words. The key to success with the word card approach is giving students the choice of words to be used for learning, thus enabling students to maintain their ownership of the material and their enthusiasm for learning.

Enlist Support from Others

Teachers who find themselves with students of different language abilities and cultural backgrounds benefit from support from others. Community organizations, colleges, museums, and other institutions often have resources that can support the work of teachers. Millicent secured the help of relatives who knew Spanish, as well as a tutor who worked individually with Isabel.

Students' families can become partners in their children's education by strengthening knowledge through the home language and facilitating the acquisition of English by using both languages. Mary convinced Michael's parents to support his native language development at home because neither Mary nor the school was equipped to do it.

Encourage Positive Attitudes toward Bilingualism

Parents and teachers need not be afraid of bilingualism. Nearly half of the children in the world are raised in more than one language from infancy (Wölk, 1987). Many more acquire another language when they enter school or move to a different country. Supported by good education, bilingualism results in linguistic and cognitive advantages. (For a synthesis of this research, see Brisk, 1998; de Houwer, 1995; Lee, 1996.)

Teachers and parents must realize that bilingual development is not confusing and that bilingual students benefit from a consistent language environment. The fact that students codeswitch, that is, move from one language to the other or interject words from one language when speaking the other, does not mean that they are confused; these are behaviors typical of bilinguals. There are many conscious and unconscious reasons for mixing the languages, but it is not necessarily a reflection of confusion (Romaine, 1995).

Languages develop because of children's innate abilities and the input they receive from their environment. Rich and consistent exposure to first and second languages is essential in the linguistic development of a bilingual learner. Parents and schools must establish and maintain their policies for language use. Michael's parents wanted him to be bilingual but kept changing their minds about which language to reinforce at home and in school. They changed the language of instruction as well as of home use for fear that bilingualism was going to delay his academic development. These changes were problematic, not only for his linguistic development but also for his emotional development. Michael considered himself bilingual but was aware of how quickly his Spanish was weakening. As de Houwer writes:

> Bilingual families have been known to give up being bilingual, much to their social, cultural, and emotional detriment, as a result of worries caused by uninformed warnings by people in authority concerning the supposed negative effects of bilingual upbringing. (1995, p. 222)

Michael's parents started to reinforce Spanish at home as a result of Mary's efforts to overcome their fears and explain the benefits of strengthening both languages. Michael's triumphant announcement of his family's use of Spanish reflected his longing for affirmation of the heritage language.

Conclusion

The steady increase of bilingual learners in U.S. classrooms is a reality of the new century. Teachers must take advantage of the presence of linguistic and cultural diversity in their classroom to challenge their instructional practices and enrich curricular content. Good teaching is not enough. The language and culture of the students must be present in teaching, curriculum, and materials. Studying bilingualism and helpful instructional approaches as well as observing students contributes to developing expertise among mainstream teachers.

Connecting with families and community resources makes the task less onerous. Parents and community members are ready and willing to help teachers who open their classroom doors and acknowledge that they too need support for teaching students of diverse cultural backgrounds.

Instruction that facilitates learning for bilingual students benefits all because it addresses individual differences, enriches everybody's knowledge with experiences of many cultural backgrounds, and creates an accepting classroom atmosphere. Success in educating bilingual learners makes teachers' experiences enjoyable and rewarding. The world of work in a global economy requires workers to have high-level academic and technical skills *and* to have knowledge of languages and the ability to work with people of different cultural backgrounds (Lindholm-Leary, 2000).

Notes

1. Results of reading tests determine if students are reading at independent, instructional, or frustration level. This relates to students' ability to read and comprehend the passage on their own, with instruction or not at all.
2. Reading recovery is an early intervention reading program developed by Clay (1993). Teachers work individually with students to help them achieve grade-level 2 reading.

References

Ashton-Warner, S. (1963). *Teacher.* New York: Simon & Schuster.

Bernhard, E. B. (1991). A psycholinguistic perspective on second language literacy. *Reading in Two Languages: AILA Review, 8,* 31–44.

Brisk, M. E. (1994). *Portraits of success: Resources supporting bilingual learners.* Boston: Massachusetts Association for Bilingual Education.

Brisk, M. E. (1998). *Bilingual education: From compensatory to quality schooling.* Mahwah, NJ: Lawrence Erlbaum.

Brisk, M., & Harrington, M. (2000). *Literacy and bilingualism: A handbook for all teachers.* Mahwah, NJ: Lawrence Erlbaum.

Carrell, P. L. (1987). Content and formal schemata in ESL reading. *TESOL Quarterly, 21,* 461–481.

Clay, M. M. (1992). *Observation survey.* Portsmouth, NH: Heinemann.

Clay, M. (1993). *Reading recovery: A guidebook for teachers in training.* Portsmouth, NH: Heinemann.

de Houwer, A. (1995). Bilingual language acquisition. In P. Fletcher & B. MacWhinney (Eds.), *The handbook of child language* (pp. 219–250). Oxford, Eng.: Blackwell.

Fountas, I., & Pinell, G. S. (1996). *Guided reading: Good first teaching for all children.* Portsmouth, NH: Heinemann.

Fountas, I., & Pinell, G. S. (1998). *Matching books to readers: A leveled book list for guided reading, K–3.* Portsmouth, NH: Heinemann.

Henry, R. (1984). Reader-generated questions: A tool for improving reading comprehension. *TESOL Newsletter,* June, 4–5.

Holdaway, D. (1984). Developmental teaching of literacy. In D. Holdaway (Ed.), *Stability and change in literacy learning* (pp. 33–47). Exeter, NH: Heinemann.

Igoa, C. (1995). *The inner world of the immigrant child*. Mahwah, NJ: Lawrence Erlbaum.

Jimenez, R. T., García, G. E., & Pearson, P. D. (1995). Three children, two languages, and strategic reading: Case studies in bilingual/monolingual reading. *American Educational Research Journal, 32*, 67–97.

Kreeft Peyton, J. (1990). Dialogue journal writing: Effective student-teacher communication. In A. M. Padilla, H. H. Fairchild, & C. M. Valadez (Eds.), *Bilingual education: Issues and strategies* (pp. 184–194). Newbury Park, CA: Sage.

Lee, P. (1996). Cognitive development in bilingual children: A case for bilingual instruction in early childhood education. *Bilingual Research Journal, 20*, 499–522.

Lindholm-Leary, K. (2000). *Biliteracy for a global society: An idea book on dual language education*. Washington, DC: National Clearinghouse for Bilingual Education.

Marsh, L. (1995). A Spanish dual literacy program: Teaching to the whole student. *Bilingual Research Journal, 19*, 409–428.

Menyuk, P. (1999). *Reading and linguistic development*. Cambridge, MA: Brookline Books.

Pease-Alvarez, L., & Winsler, A. (1994). Cuando el maestro no habla Español: Children's bilingual language practices in the classroom. *TESOL Quarterly, 28*, 507–535.

Peregoy, S. F., & Boyle, O. F. (1996). *Reading, writing and learning in ESL: A resource book for K–12 teachers*. New York: Longman.

Pérez, B. (1998). Language, literacy, and biliteracy. In B. Pérez (Ed.), *Sociocultural contexts of language and literacy* (pp. 21–48). Mahwah, NJ: Lawrence Erlbaum.

Reyes, M. de la Luz, Laliberty, E. A., & Orbanosky, J. M. (1993). Emerging biliteracy and cross-cultural sensitivity in a language arts classroom. *Language Arts, 70*, 659–668.

Romaine, S. (1995). *Bilingualism*. New York: Basil Blackwell.

Stanton, J. (1988). *Dialogue journal communication: Classroom, linguistic, social, and cognitive views*. Norwood, NJ: Ablex.

Wölk, W. (1987). Types of natural bilingual behavior: A review and revision. *Bilingual Review/La Revista Bilingüe, 14*, 3–16.

Wong Fillmore, L. (1991). When learning a second language means losing the first. *Early Childhood Research Quarterly, 6*, 323–346.

Agents of Literacy Change: Working with Somali Students in an Urban Middle School

AUDREY A. FRIEDMAN

The changing demographics of U.S. urban schools are creating classrooms that are more culturally and linguistically diverse than ever (Faltis, 2001). Second language learners are found in urban mainstream classrooms throughout the nation; although they are best served by bilingual specialists, the demand for these specialists is significantly higher than availability in most urban school districts (Maxwell-Jolly & Gándara, this volume). Due to the scarcity of trained personnel, these students are instructed either by mainstream teachers who are inadequately prepared to work with second language learners, or by ESL teachers who are prepared (Garcia, 1996). In either case, second language learners are taught by teachers who usually do not speak their native language or are not familiar with their culture.

In the large urban middle school where I have served as a literacy specialist for the past three years, the percentage of non-native English speakers in a classroom ranges from 15 to 50 percent. The major focus of my work in this school is to help teachers reflect on and revise their instruction in order to improve the academic skills of all students, including English learners. I support the teachers' work by observing, coaching, and modeling instruction in their classrooms. I also participate in weekly grade-level meetings held by mainstream, bilingual, and special education teachers. In these meetings we pose questions about teaching and learning in diverse classrooms, gather literacy data from students, look at student work, examine ways to address particular students' academic needs, read and discuss current literacy research, and share promising practices and strategies to improve reading and writing throughout the curriculum. A community of practitioners, we support one another's work as agents of literacy change in a changing student population.

While most of the second language learners in our school are from Latin American, Caribbean, and Asian countries, the number of students from Somalia has increased over the last decade. Some of these students have come from war-ridden areas in Somalia and have little or no prior schooling. Others have received instruction in refugee camps in Kenya, Ethiopia, and Yemen, but their education was frequently interrupted. Yet others are fully literate in their native language. Overall, most of the Somali students exhibit low English literacy skills on arrival in our school.

Our district has few certified bilingual specialists who are proficient in both Somali and English, and most of our mainstream and ESL teachers are unfamiliar with the religious and cultural customs of Somali students. We have been challenged to find effective ways to teach these students because it is clear to us that many have "a long road ahead of them to acquire grade-level academic skills" due to significant gaps in their prior education and lack of English skills (Farah, 2000, p. 62). This chapter details our work with one group of Somali students in a social studies class and presents the various pedagogical supports that helped these students improve their writing in English.[1]

Setting Schoolwide Standards for Good Writing

Writing across the curriculum was a concern to all teachers in grades six to eight. Consequently, weekly grade-level meetings focused on ways to improve student writing throughout the school. First we established standards for effective writing. After much discussion about the qualities of good writing, teachers went on to develop rubrics for evaluating student writing in sixth, seventh, and eighth grades. A rubric is a set of criteria that helps teachers and students evaluate student work. Rubrics provide students with clear expectations for performance and teachers with differentiated criteria to help them identify specific areas for improvement and reinforce successful areas of student writing. Our rubric identified four areas of focus in writing: content, organization, style and voice, and mechanics. Once rubrics were established for each grade, weekly meetings were devoted to sharing strategies for improving student writing in these four focus areas.

The content focus addresses how well a student responds to the question or completes the task; provides an effective topic or thesis statement; substantiates and elaborates a response with evidence, details, examples, and illustrations; and reflects written understanding of the content area. Organization captures how logically the writing is structured, reflecting inclusion of an effective beginning, middle, and end, appropriate sequencing of ideas, and use of transitions. Style and voice pertain to how clearly the writer states a point of view, shares insights and understanding, uses language to create pictures in the reader's mind, and shows interest in or even passion for the subject. The mechanics focus covers mastery of standard conventions of English grammar, punctuation, and spelling.

As part of our schoolwide literacy improvement plan, all students in grades six to eight completed on-demand writing samples in October, January, and June to evaluate writing needs, establish long- and short-term goals, and monitor student progress.[2] All writing samples were evaluated using a grade-level rubric; scores were compiled and analyzed and used to inform subsequent decisions about writing instruction. Establishing standards for good writing, assessing student work, revising instruction based on assessment results, and reassessing and reevaluating students' growth and our own growth as practitioners and as a community of learners were integral to our becoming effective agents of literacy change.

The Classroom Setting

One gifted teacher, Andra Freeman, who was certified as an ESL and English language arts teacher, invited me into her classroom. Although she did not speak Somali, Andra served about twenty Somali students each year in a self-contained classroom. Her students' ages and ESL skills (ESL I to ESL IV) were varied.[3] As her students' English skills improved, they started taking math and science classes in the mainstream program and English language arts and social studies with Andra.

During the 1999–2000 academic year, Andra had twenty students whose ages ranged from eleven to fourteen. The longest any one student had been in the United States was four years; most of her students had been in school for only one or two years. Before their arrival some students had received English instruction in refugee camps in Kenya.

Andra was an active member of our weekly grade-level meetings. As part of the grade-seven teacher team, she helped develop both the rubric used to evaluate writing performance of native English-speaking students and the ESL rubric based on citywide guidelines for ESL students (see Tables 1 and 2). Encouraged by district administrators, Andra used the ESL rubric to evaluate her students' writing performance in October 1999.

After one term, however, she changed to using the schoolwide grade-seven rubric for several reasons. First, most of her students were chronologically in grade seven during the intensive period of instruction in which we worked together. Furthermore, Andra believed that all students should be held to high standards regardless of linguistic differences, and that the focus of instruction should be to provide students with effective supports and ample practice so that they can reach and even exceed curricular standards. Based on her appraisal of student writing, the grade-seven rubric provided evaluative criteria that were attainable but established a high benchmark for these students. Additionally, she realized that many of her students would soon be completely mainstreamed, possibly in grade eight but definitely in high school, and would then be held to the same standards as all other students in mainstream classrooms. These students, like all public school students in Massachusetts, would also be required to pass the state-mandated Massachusetts Comprehensive Assessment System (MCAS) test in order to receive an academic diploma or to pursue higher education.[4] Thus, Andra thought that it was essential to establish higher standards for these students than those required by the citywide ESL guidelines.

Focus Students

This chapter describes the work we did in a six-week period with a group of five Somali students, Alia, Ahmed, Shadia, Mohamed, and Fatma. Although their ages and their English skills varied, they all had the experience of being uprooted, leaving their native land abruptly at a young age, living in another country and in refugee camps, having their education repeatedly interrupted, and arriving recently in the United States.

Table 1
Grade-7 RUBRIC

	4 *Pudding filled with lots of goodies and topped with whipped cream*	3 *Pudding filled with lots of goodies*	2 *Plain ol' pudding!*	1 *Pudding mix and milk*
Content	• Answers the question(s) or responds to the task completely • Provides all necessary information • Elaborates using accurate details, examples, reasons, illustrations, ideas, and other sources • Clearly states the purpose • Uses a format that suits the purpose and enhances the response	• Answers the question(s) or responds to the task completely • Provides most necessary information • Uses some accurate details, examples, reasons, and other sources • States the purpose • Uses a format that suits the purpose and response	• Answers the question(s) or responds to most of the task • Provides minimal information • Uses few accurate details, examples, and reasons • States the purpose but it is unclear • Uses a format that does not enhance the response or match the purpose	• Does not complete the task • Provides little or no information • Uses few accurate details or examples • States no purpose • Uses format that detracts from the purpose and response
Organization	• Stays focused on the topic • Has a clear and coherent beginning (topic sentence), middle (supporting sentences), and end (clincher sentence) • Uses transitions throughout • Is carefully organized, logical, and sequential	• Stays focused on the topic • Has a clear beginning (topic sentence), middle (supporting sentences), and end (clincher sentence) • Uses transitions occasionally • Is organized and logical	• Strays from the topic • Has a beginning, middle, and end • Is disorganized and confusing	• Strays from the topic • Is disorganized and confusing • Has a beginning and middle but no end
Style and Voice	• States a clear point of view and contrasts it with other points of view • Takes chances and tries something new or unexpected	• States a point of view that is appropriate for the task • Tries something original	• Changes the point of view throughout the piece	• Presents a point of view that is unclear

TABLE 1 *(continued)*
Grade-7 RUBRIC

	4 *Pudding filled with lots of goodies and topped with whipped cream*	3 *Pudding filled with lots of goodies*	2 *Plain ol' pudding!*	1 *Pudding mix and milk*
Style and Voice (cont.)	• Uses words in a concise and precise way that creates pictures in the reader's mind (simile, metaphor, figurative language) • Shows careful and complex thinking (synthesizes and analyzes) and reflects the writer's feelings or opinions • Grabs the reader's attention • Uses vocabulary above grade level • Uses tone that is appropriate for the purpose and the audience	• Uses words in a way that creates pictures in the reader's mind (colorful words, lots of action words) • The writing is interesting and draws the reader in • Uses grade-level vocabulary • Reflects the writer's feelings and/or opinions	• Uses little descriptive language or colorful words • Is somewhat interesting to the reader • Uses limited vocabulary	• Is not interesting enough to read • Uses very simple vocabulary
Mechanics	• Incorporates revisions • Is polished and in a legible and appropriate format • Follows rules of grammar, punctuation, and spelling without error • Uses a variety of sentences that are complete • Cites and integrates sources correctly	• Incorporates revisions • Is presented in a legible and appropriate format • Follows rules of grammar, punctuation, and spelling with few errors • Uses a variety of sentences that are complete • Integrates quotations correctly	• Incorporates few revisions • Has partially legible format • Has many errors in grammar, punctuation, and spelling • Uses many incomplete and run-on sentences	• Incorporates no revisions • Uses incorrect and illegible format • Has significant errors in grammar, punctuation, and spelling • Uses incomplete and run-on sentences throughout

TABLE 2
ESL-III Rubric

	4 OUTSTANDING!!!	3 GOOD!!!	2 NOT YET, BUT CLOSE!!!	1 LOTS OF WORK TO DO!!!
Content	• Answers the question(s) or describes the problem with some elaboration • Includes accurate information • Uses details, examples, and description • States a clear purpose • Shows understanding of content	• Answers the question • Includes some accurate information • States the purpose • Shows some understanding of the purpose	• Tries to answer the question • Provides little information • States the purpose but it is unclear • Uses some details	• Answer is vague • Uses no examples • States no purpose
Organization	• Stays on topic • Has a clear beginning, middle, and end • Is organized	• Stays on topic most of the time • Has a beginning but mostly a middle • Is organized most of the time	• Strays from the topic • Has a middle • Is confusing	• Strays from the topic • Has little or no organization
Style and Voice	• States a clear point of view • Uses descriptive words to show feeling and passion • Tries something new or unexpected • Uses descriptive words that create pictures in the reader's mind	• States a point of view most of the time • Uses simple words to show feeling • Uses some descriptive words	• States a point of view that is confusing • Presents opinions or feelings that are unclear	• Shows no feelings or opinions

These five students received direct instruction two or three times weekly for fifty minutes while the rest of the class was engaged in other classroom tasks. Each Tuesday, I joined Andra and the students; for the rest of the week, Andra continued our work. Here I share the process that we used to promote writing development in this group of Somali students. I illustrate the writing progress that each of the five students made by showing the first, second, fourth, and sixth drafts written by two focus students, Mohamed and Fatma.

Born in the southern part of Somalia in 1986, Mohamed immigrated to his father's farm in Yemen at age four and lived there with his aunts for four years. He worked on the farm but did not attend school. In 1995, he arrived in New York and moved to Boston shortly thereafter. Already ten years old, he did not enroll in school until September 1996. He received bilingual instruction for three years before entering middle school at the ESL II level. By the middle of grade seven Mohamed had attained an English literacy proficiency of ESL level III.

Fatma was born in 1986 in Mogadishu, Somalia, and left her country in 1994 for a refugee camp in Kenya, where she stayed one year. She arrived in Boston and began school in September 1995. She was placed in a mainstream classroom for one year and then moved to a bilingual classroom for grades three and four. After spending fifth grade in a mainstream classroom, she entered middle school at ESL level II. By the middle of seventh grade, her English literacy proficiency approached ESL III.

Writing in Social Studies

In January of grade seven, writing in the content area of social studies became the focus of small-group instruction for Mohamed, Fatma, Alia, Ahmed, and Shadia. Social studies content in this grade focused on American history, and students began by studying European exploration and exploitation of the New World. Since content textbooks are written significantly above the proficiency level of these students, we decided to introduce students to the unit by reading the children's story *Encounter*, by Jane Yolen (1992). Set in the West Indies, the story depicts revisionist history about Columbus's exploitation of the Arawak and Taino peoples. It tells of a Taino boy whose nightmare of being invaded by evil strangers comes true. Although he tries to warn his people, they do not listen to him because he is only a child. The tale ends with the boy, now an old man, examining the cultural, spiritual, and economic destruction of his people. The text is replete with figurative language and exquisite illustrations by David Shannon that offer readers detailed and often haunting visions of European exploration and exploitation. Furthermore, it offers an effective link between fiction and nonfiction, providing students with a text that is easier to understand.

Before reading the story, we focused on setting. First we looked at the chapter in the social studies text that related to Columbus and his encounters with the West Indies. Since all students were accountable for information found in the textbook, it was imperative to make connections to the text at every opportunity. We all walked over to the map, where I identified the West Indies. We then asked students to locate Somalia on the map and trace the route they took before arriving in our school. For a while we talked about their homeland, its geography and vegetation, and what a long journey it was for them to come to Boston. Then we found Italy, Portugal, and Spain, countries from which many of the explorers originated. We talked about Columbus and how, although he was Italian, it was Queen Isabella of Spain who gave him the money and ships to come to the so-called New World.

We then focused on the cover of the text, which depicts the boy touching the robe of an almost godlike man (presumably Christopher Columbus) looking down at the child. Students reacted to the picture, discussing what kind of man they thought he was, based on his dress and facial expressions. I wrote the word *encounter* on the board and asked for possible meanings. When none was given, I suggested the synonym *meeting* but cautioned that an encounter is a very special kind of meeting, not like hanging out with friends or shooting hoops after school. I said that the boy's encounter was with unfriendly people whose purpose was to gain power or control. Students suggested that an encounter might happen when gang members meet each other unexpectedly, for example, on the subway. It was clear that they understood the meaning of the word.

Before moving into the story, we revisited the social studies text, discussing what they already knew about Columbus and activating prior knowledge. After noting that Columbus was an explorer from Italy who accidentally landed in the West Indies, we began the story. I read the text aloud, modeling an interactive read-aloud process: asking probing questions about the story; noting language that denoted sequence, cause and effect, and comparison and contrast; identifying imagery; focusing on figurative language; and calling attention to what was powerful in the writing. At different points in the reading, I summarized what I had read and asked students to summarize or retell important events in the story. Andra and I also posed questions that required students to infer, predict, or evaluate. As I read aloud and focused on illustrations, I encouraged students to make connections between events in the story and their own lives, connections between this story and other stories or excerpts in the social studies text about the explorers that they might have read, and connections between events in this story and events in the world.

Having been forced to leave their native country of Somalia due to tribal wars, these students identified with the frustration and pain the young boy in the story experienced. Their prior knowledge enhanced their understanding of theme and characterization. Students easily made connections between the text, themselves, and their world. After my initial reading, Andra and each student reread and retold the story aloud several times, continued discussion, and followed up with a writing activity. Students were presented with the following prompt: What did the boy see and feel in *Encounter?* Students responded in a first draft.

FATMA'S FIRST DRAFT

The boy had a dream that one day that these strange people are going to come something bad is going to happen to the people. That dream came true. First he saw three ships then he saw man's with these havy clothes. When Columbus man's were being nice. So the Columbus people give the Taino people nackles and other stuff, so the Taino people tought Columbus people how to smoke. They boy ran and went to this palce and he was talk to sachew the boy said I have a feeling that something bad is going to happen. So the next day Columbus people took five Taino people on the boat. On there way to the boat the boy was sitting at the back he said something bad is going to happen to my people. I have to jump in the ocean and tell my people not to go but they didn't lissen.

MOHAMED'S FIRST DRAFT

The boy smiled trouble was coming but nobody listen to him because he was just a child. When trouble came the boy said that the strangers were going to take or land but nobody listen to him because he was just a child. The strangers started trouble and took some of the young man the boy was in it. So he escuped from the boat. The boy jumped from the boat. Then as the boy grew older he couldn't help his people or land because it was too late because the strangers were too powerfull and many. They took over the land and owned the people. I wish I could stop them but I wasn't born then I feel very unhappy for them.

Andra and I then evaluated the writing samples using the grade-seven rubric. Each draft received ratings for content, organization, style and voice, and mechanics, as well as an overall score.

First Drafts	Content	Organization	Style and Voice	Mechanics	Overall Rating
Mohamed's first draft	1	1	2	1	1
Fatma's first draft	1	1	1	1	1

Mohamed's first draft lacked a complete, appropriate, or detailed answer to the question and referred to only a few examples in the text. Because the focus of this sample was writing in social studies, students had to demonstrate a grasp of content and meaning. Although Mohamed may have understood what happened in the story, he did not communicate that understanding. His organization did show a beginning, a middle, and an end, but the structure and flow of the writing were weak. Mohamed's style and voice, however, were very engaging, including phrases like "smiled [smelled] trouble" and "owned the people." Furthermore, he used compound and complex sentence types and rather difficult vocabulary. Although his work contained errors in mechanics, sentences were generally complete and grammar was not poor enough to merit a score of 1. Overall, because of lack of content and poor organization, the sample earned a 1. Despite the low overall rating, we were confident that Mohamed's writing could be improved through focused revision and discussion.

Fatma's first draft communicated more events in the story but also lacked sufficient elaboration and details. The writing was a bit more organized, but parts of the middle and end were confusing. Like Mohamed, Fatma interjected a voice and presented the personal stance of the boy in her writing. Mechanics were very weak, including many run-on sentences. This piece earned a rating of 1, but we knew that with hard work and revisions Fatma could also improve her rating.

Our next step was to have students work together to help each other revise their first drafts. Because there were only five students in the small group, we decided to model a peer revising and editing protocol that involved reading and talking aloud, questioning, and rewriting. In the first step of the process, I asked each student to read his or her paper aloud and instructed them to stop and correct any confusing phrases, ideas, or details they discovered. The purpose of this strategy was to reinforce self-evaluation and self-correction. Although it would have been helpful for each of us to have a copy of each draft, Andra and I decided that it was important for students to practice and improve listening skills, and having only one draft copy would be less intimidating to the writer. Those not reading aloud were told to listen carefully and to be ready to offer at least two positive comments about the writing and to ask at least two questions that would illustrate for the writer what was not clear in the writing.

I began by modeling the protocol of praising and questioning. "Mohamed, I really liked the phrase you used in the first sentence: 'The boy smelled [smiled] that trouble was coming.' Smelling trouble is an unusual and interesting way to describe what the boy was feeling and sensing. I also liked the way you used the word *owned* in the sentence 'They took over the land and owned the people.' *Owned* is a strong word that shows how the explorers forced the people to be slaves." Asking him to explain more clearly in his next draft, I followed up with the questioning protocol: "Why did the boy think that strangers were coming to the island?" and "Why did the strangers come to the boy's land?"

Mohamed's peers then praised his work, commenting on his use of "smelled" and "owned" and how his words made them feel sad for the boy because no one would listen to him. Students also raised questions to help Mohamed improve his next draft. Noting that he was not explaining everything clearly, they asked, "Who were the strangers?" "Why did the strangers want the land?" "How did the strangers take over the land?" "When the boy escaped, where did he go?" and "Why couldn't the boy help his people?" "What made Columbus and his men so powerful?"

We followed the same protocol for Fatma. I modeled the process again. "Fatma, I like the way you mentioned the incident about the boy visiting his statue. I also like how you included the scene in the story when the explorers capture the boy." Seeking to elicit improvement in her writing, I asked, "What other details describe the boy's dream?" and "What else can you tell us about the statue?" Students offered positive comments and raised some questions: "Why did Columbus and his men come to this land? What happened to the people on the island at the end? What else did the boy see? What did he see and what clues did he have that made him think that something bad was going to happen to his people? Why did Columbus and his men give beads to the boy?" and "What other things did these men give the boy and his people?"

As each comment or question was offered, the writers were required to jot it down at the bottom of the draft. The writer's next job was to incorporate the answers to the questions in a new draft and to mark the responses to questions with a pink highlighting pen on the paper. The second drafts were read aloud to the group the following week.

In his second draft, Mohamed elaborated on his story by answering our questions and adding a few more details of his own. While Mohamed read, his peers listened for answers to their questions and noticed words, phrases, and ideas that needed more elaboration or clarification. They remarked that he had not answered all their questions; they still wanted to know why the boy thought that trouble was coming to his island and what made him "smell" it. They also were unclear on how the boy escaped in the boat and why the natives could not protect their land. After hearing their questions, I asked, "What phrase is repeated many times in the writing?" Unanimously, students responded, "Columbus's men." We spent the next few minutes brainstorming other words we could write instead. Students suggested *soldiers, explorers, Europeans, strangers,* and *Spaniards.*

After Fatma read her second draft, Mohamed and others suggested that Fatma's writing would be improved if she used the alternatives we had come up with for "Columbus's men [man]" — a phrase she also had used repeatedly in her essay. These students demonstrated that they were quick and competent learners. I suggested that we think of other words for the phrase "the boy's people." Together we suggested *the Taino people, islanders, natives, island people,* and *inhabitants.*

Each week students produced a new draft and read it aloud to the small group. The protocol was always the same: readers stopped each time they read something that sounded wrong and listeners inter-

---

MOHAMED'S SECOND DRAFT

The boy smiled trouble was coming but nobody listen to him because he was just a child. When trouble came the boy said strangers are headed to our land nobody believed him because he was just a child. Strangers were Columbus' man. The strangers started trouble they came to the land to get gold and people they took some of the young man and the boy was in it. They were traveling for days when everybody was asleep he jumped from the boat he was swimming for a long time finally he made it to his land. The boy's people couldn't help their land because they weren't ready for protecting their land they thought Columbus and his men were friendly but the man which are Columbus's man were ready if there was any trouble. The boy's people didn't know about these people and what they wanted. I think the boy's people didn't know they were main or would take some of the people to be slaves. The boy knew they had trouble because of what they had with them and the actions they made. What made Columbus' man powerful was they had things that would protect them if they was any trouble like guns, sharp saws, and other things. Columbus's man were ready to take over the land because they were ready which means they had things to scare the people if they wanted to fight back. When the boy was young he couldn't help his people and land their wasn't much people who would fight for their land because some were slaves and their wouldn't be a lot on the land because they took the people to Columbus' country.

FATMA'S SECOND DRAFT

The boy had a dream that these ships that looked like birds with sharp teath and strange people are going to come. Something bad is going to happen to my people. That dream came true. First he saw three ships then he saw man's with these havy clothes. Those man's were Columbus's man's. Columbus' man's were being nice. So Columbus' man's give the Taino people nackless and other stuff. So the Taino people tought Columbus people how to smoke. They boy ran and went to his Zemis and said some thing bad is going to happen to my people. The Zemis didn't blanck. So the next day, the boy told his perents and his people they didn't listen to him because he was still a child. So Columbus' men took five of the Taino's people and the boy was in the boat. So the boy said something bad is going to happen the boy jumped then swame back to his island and told his people not to go but they didn't listen. As the boy grow older there was nothing he could do about it because Columbus' people were to powerful and strong. They took over the land.

rupted the reader when they heard something that did not make sense. Each time the reader stopped we talked about changes that could be made; the writer immediately made the changes on the draft and reread the phrase or sentence with the changes. After a piece was read all the way through, teachers and peers offered positive comments and helpful questions. Writers were then responsible for incorporating responses to these questions into their next draft.

On days when drafts were not being read aloud, Andra had students practice writing complete sentences, developing paragraphs, and using correct verb tenses. Although everyone needed more practice in these areas, students were progressing daily. They reread or retold parts of the story to a partner to further elaborate and clarify their writing or they searched for answers to questions on their own. In this very tedious process, readers and listeners worked diligently to identify areas that did not make sense, run-on sentences, repeated words or phrases, places where new paragraphs should begin, and ideas that needed more elaboration and clarification. Writing multiple drafts was the most difficult part of the process, but it lies at the core of this literacy strategy and I believe had the greatest impact on improvement.

Mohamed's and Fatma's fourth drafts illustrate the significant improvements that resulted from peer and teacher support and student efforts while utilizing a structured peer revising and editing protocol.

As with every draft, Andra and I evaluated students' writing.

Fourth Drafts	Content	Organi-zation	Style and Voice	Mechan-ics	Overall Rating
Mohamed's fourth draft	3	2	3	2	2
Fatma's fourth draft	2	2	2	2	2

Mohamed had added content, detail, and elaboration to his writing. He responded to his peers' questions by further incorporating and explaining important events in the story. He had more to say and was able to organize the piece better. Additionally, Mohamed provided more description, added sentence variety, and used grade-level vocabulary. His mechanics also improved, with more complete sentences and corrected grammar and spelling. Fatma also had added content to her piece by providing more elaboration about important events in the story. Like Mohamed, she had more to say and she organized what she had to say better. Including more description and words that painted pictures in the reader's mind enhanced her style and voice and she had better command of mechanics, as reflected in fewer run-on sentences and errors in grammar. A fifth draft followed, and then we announced that students would now work on their sixth and final draft.

As part of their final week's work, Andra and I conferred with each student about his or her writing. Our conversations focused on clarity, verb tenses, elaboration, effective topic and clincher sentences, sentence structure and variety, grammar, and spelling. We referred back to the questions their peers had posed and encouraged Mohamed and Fatma to respond with further details and elaboration. For us this was the most challenging part of the process because we were determined

MOHAMED'S FOURTH DRAFT

The boy smelled trouble was coming but nobody listened to him because he was just a child. When trouble came the boy said strangers are headed to our land but nobody believed him. The strangers were Columbus and his men. Columbus and his soldiers started trouble because they came to the land to get gold and people.

The strangers took some of the young men and the boy. The Europeans and some of the young men that were taken were traveling for days to Spain. When everybody was asleep in the boat, the young boy jumped from the boat. He swam for a long time finally made it to his land.

The Tainos people couldn't help their land because they weren't ready for a fight. They didn't know about the other people. They thought the soldiers were friendly. When coming to the land because they saw that the islanders were easy and could be taken away. The Taino didn't know what was happening until they started trouble.

The Taino boy new they were starting trouble because of what they did to them and the actions they made. What made Columbus and his workers so powerful was they had things that would protect them if there was any trouble like guns, sharp saws, and other dangers weapons.

The visitors were ready to take over the land because they were ready which means they had things to scare the people that were being taken away if they wanted to fight back. When the boy was young he couldn't help his people or land because he was just a child because he was not strong enough to fight for his land.

When he got older it was too late because they already took over his land and people. There wasn't much people on the land who could fight for their land because some were slaves. There isn't a lot on the land because they took the Taino people to their country.

FATMA'S FOURTH DRAFT

The boy had a dream that ships that look like birds with sharp teeth and strange people are going to some. Something bad is going to happen to my people. That dream came true. First he saw three ships, then he saw mans with heavy clothing. Those mans were Columbus mans. When those mans came, they were being nice at first so they could take over the land. So when the invaders came they give them neckles and other stuff. The Taino people thought they were nice so they tought the mans how to smoke.

The boy ran to visit his statue he called Zemis and said something is going to happen to my people. The Zemis didn't blink. The next day the boy saw guns and nifs. The boy told his parents but they didn't listen because he was still a child.

Then the men took five of the Taino people and the boy. He was sitting on the back of the boat. So the boy said to himself that something bad is about to happen. The boy jumped from the boat and swame back to the island and told his people not to go but they didn't listen. As the boy grew older, there was nothing he could do about it because Columbus' men were too strong and powerful. They took over the land.

not to let students off the hook. We expected students to achieve the highest standards. These were the final drafts.

Andra and I evaluated Mohamed's and Fatma's final drafts.

Final Drafts	Content	Organi- zation	Style and Voice	Mechan- ics	Overall Rating
Mohamed's final draft	4	3	4	3	3
Fatma's final draft	3	3	3	3	3

Mohamed's final draft communicated accurate and elaborate understanding of content. He included rich detail and description and supported his ideas with textual support and personal inferences. Each paragraph began with a sentence that continued the flow of the story,

MOHAMED'S FINAL DRAFT

The boy smelled trouble was coming but nobody listened to him because he was just a child. When trouble came the boy said strangers are headed to our land but nobody believed him. The strangers were Columbus and his men. Columbus and his soldiers started trouble because they came to the land to get gold and people.

Trouble came again when the strangers kidnapped some of the young men and the boy. The Europeans and some of the young men that were taken as slaves traveled for days to Spain. They were afraid because they did not know where they were going. When everybody was asleep in the boat, the young boy jumped from the boat because he knew they were headed for slavery. He swam for a long time and finally made it to his homeland.

The Taino people couldn't protect their land because they weren't ready for a fight. They didn't know about the other people. They didn't know that the invaders would steal, kidnap, and kill. They thought the soldiers were friendly. When coming to the land because the Spaniards saw that the islanders were easy and could be taken away. The Taino didn't know what was happening until the Europeans started trouble.

The Taino boy knew that the Europeans were starting trouble because they brought guns that sounded like thunder, sharp silver sticks, and dangerous knives. They grabbed the Taino, stole gold, and killed them. What made Columbus and his workers so powerful was they had things that would protect them if there was any trouble like guns, sharp swords, and other dangerous weapons. The visitors were ready to take over the land because they had things to scare the people that were being taken away if they wanted to fight back.

When the boy was young he couldn't help his people or land because he was just a child. He was not strong enough to fight for his land. When he got older it was too late because they had already taken his land and his people. There weren't many people on the land who could fight for their land because they had become slaves in Spain. After the people and the land were destroyed Columbus traveled to other lands to start more trouble.

FATMA'S FINAL DRAFT

The boy had a dream. In his dream there were strange birds with sharp teeth that were flying to his island. When he woke up, he had a bad feeling that something terrible was going to happen to his people. That dream came true. First he saws three ships that looked like the birds in his dream. Then he saw men. Those men were Columbus' men. They were wearing heavy clothes that were many colors. They looked like parrots. His nightmare became real.

The boy senced trouble was coming. Then the invaders came and gave the Taino people necklaces, strings of beads, and hats. They gave the people this stuff so the island people would think that they are nice. So the inhabitants taught Columbus' people how to smoke. The boy was afraid and ran to his Zemis and said that something bad was about to happen to his people. The Zemis didn't blink.

The next day the boy told his parents and his people that the explorers were bad people because they boy saw their sharp knives and guns that sounded like thunder. Then the men took five of the Taino people. One of them was the boy. The invaders were taking them to Spain to be slaves. As the boy was sitting in the back of the boat, he said to himself that something bad is about to happen. Suddenly, he jumped out of the boat and swam back and told his people not to follow but they didn't listen because he was a child.

As the boy grew older there was nothing he could do because the invaders were too powerful and strong. So they took over the land.

and he made good use of transitions. Overall, the piece had a solid beginning and middle and incorporated a very strong voice. Repeating the motif of "smelling trouble," he created suspense and kept the reader engaged. The piece demonstrated a good command of mechanics despite errors in tense and grammar.

Although her final draft was not as engaging as Mohamed's, Fatma also had continued to improve her piece by adding detail, supporting examples from text, and description that communicated a solid understanding of the story. Beginning, middle, and ending paragraphs included effective transitions and sentence variety. She used similes and a repeated dream/nightmare motif. Despite continued errors in verb tense, Fatma clearly demonstrated improved grammar.

Overall, the improvement in Mohamed's and Fatma's drafts during this six-week study exemplified the growth that we observed in all five students' English writing. These students' improving literacy skills were evident in the independent writing samples they produced in the schoolwide assessment at the end of the school year. Even when they did not have the benefit of teacher and peer support and the time to produce six drafts, compared with their performance in October these students showed great progress in June. Seventh-grade teachers who rated student writing jointly did not give Andra's students any special consideration. Student writing indicated grade-level comprehension of the content and a growing sense of style and voice on a par with their native English-speaking peers. Based on their independent writing skills, these students were not ready to produce writing that could receive the highest rating since none had achieved excellent command of English grammar and vocabulary or organization in their writing. Yet it was clear that, with appropriate supports and consistent practice, they were making progress in the long and arduous process of gaining English writing skills.

Discussion

The encouraging results of Andra's teaching should inspire teachers of second language learners. The improvement witnessed in student writing in Andra's classroom resulted from many people working in concert to bring about literacy change.

Teachers and specialists participating in weekly grade-level meetings acted as agents of literacy change. As a community of practitioners, we enabled, challenged, and supported each other and contributed to one another's professional development (Schlumberger & Clymer, 1989). We established standards for good writing, assessed student writing, revised instruction based on assessment results, discussed successful teaching practices, and reassessed and reevaluated students' and our own growth as a community of learners. We discussed how to address each student's specific needs by looking at the student work produced in each other's classes. We began to break down the isolation that has for far too long left classroom teachers to struggle individually when the help or support that we need to improve our teaching often can often be found in our colleagues teaching next door (Berriz, 2000, this volume). We gained clarity and moved toward uniformity in our expectations of our students' writing. All these elements of the process were integral to our becoming effective agents of literacy change.

As a primary change agent, Andra held high expectations of student performance, and she communicated clearly and reinforced her expectations with appropriate teaching strategies. Through the regular use of the seventh-grade rubrics in her classroom, she helped her students internalize what was expected of them. Andra chose appropriate instructional strategies geared toward the particular needs of her students. In this particular classroom the appropriate instructional strategy was to teach "writing as a social process," with much discussion, revision of student writing, and a routine that children were comfortable with (McLane, 1990). Andra not only revealed the editing and revising strategies that good writers use (Elbow, 1973), she also structured classroom time to model and practice these strategies. Capitalizing on the many resources available to her, including the students' native language skills, varied levels of English skills, and world knowledge, she made sure that all students comprehended classroom content, made personal connections to the curriculum, and took responsibility for their own and others' writing development (Moll, 1989, 1990; Moll & Greenberg, 1990). She also created a safe and interactive classroom context that facilitated meaningful and purposeful student-student and student-teacher interactions (Au, 1992; Ramirez & Merino, 1990; Trueba & Delgado-Gaitan, 1983).

Andra and I acted as agents of literacy change during the six-week intervention in this positive classroom context. We implemented several strategies drawn from the literature on effective instruction for second language learners (Brisk & Harrington, 2000; Johnson & Roen, 1989; Keene & Zimmerman, 1997; Moll & Greenberg, 1990). For example, we built on Keene and Zimmerman's suggestion (1997) that students come to understand text by interrogating it at a variety of levels and finding text-to-self, text-to-text, and text-to-world connections. Andra and I tried to model all three levels of questioning and connection to text. For example, we activated text-to-self connections when we asked students to trace personal immigration routes on the world map and share stories about leaving Somalia. Students made connections not only to Columbus but, more important, also to the young boy in the story. Like the Taino people, these students had lost family, homes, land, and possessions and had been forced to accommodate to a strange culture. Andra and I also reinforced text-to-text connections as we moved between reading *Encounter* and their social studies textbook, noting similarities in content and differences in the kind of language used in each text. Some students remarked that they enjoyed Yolen's descriptive language and Shannon's engaging pictures but that the social studies text was boring and uninteresting. Text-to-world connections were elicited when Ahmed, the oldest and most introspective student, volunteered a comparison between the experiences of the Taino and the ethnic cleansing in Bosnia.

Students themselves acted as agents of literacy change as they learned to take responsibility for their own and their peers' writing improvement, using self-criticism and self-correction, and giving and receiving peer feedback in the process of revising and editing their own and one another's written work. Peer collaboration in Andra's classroom provided impetus for development in students' thinking and learning and in their ability to communicate what they are thinking and learning more effectively in writing (Rueda, 1990; Vygotsky, 1978; Wertsch, 1985). By participating in homogeneous and heterogeneous collaborative learning groups, each student had an opportunity to learn from and to support the others' English literacy skills and understanding (Kagan, 1986; Slavin, 1987). More proficient students helped the less proficient, and students who were more familiar with language and culture helped those who were less familiar by translating from English to Somali. As part of the peer editing process, students asked critical questions of one another.

Educators are professionally and morally responsible for helping students of diverse cultural, economic, and linguistic backgrounds to develop literacy skills and achieve academic excellence. Given the correct educational support, all children can learn. Of course, each classroom is different, as "there is no single recipe for good teaching" (Beykont, 2000, p. 55). Teachers must consider carefully what will and will not work in their particular classroom context with their students. An important piece of the work involves identifying and using various change agents in our classrooms and throughout the school and beyond. This chapter highlighted teachers, specialists, and students as agents of literacy change. Community members, families, and community-based organizations are also vital resources to draw upon (Berriz, 2000, this volume; Farah, 2000; Moll, 1989; Moll & Greenberg, 1990). It is our responsibility as educators to bring together varied supports and create conditions conducive to literacy change for all students.

Notes

1. I would like to thank ESL and regular education teacher Mrs. Andra Freeman, R. G. Shaw Middle School, West Roxbury, Massachusetts, for her cooperation.
2. All three prompts for sixth grade addressed a personal narrative focus. Prompts for seventh grade addressed a content area focus requiring students to write 3–5 paragraph expository essay responses pertaining to content areas. Specifically, the first sample addressed English language arts, the second social studies, and the third science. Eighth-grade students addressed a mix of narrative and content prompts to provide practice in both and to prepare students for the state-mandated MCAS assessment.
3. Students with low English skills are offered four levels of ESL support. If they have no English skills they are considered Step 1 and are offered ESL I classes. If they have some/limited English skills they are considered Step 2 and are offered ESL II and ESL III classes. If they are close to proficient in English, they are considered Step 3 and are offered ESL IV classes. Students who complete ESL IV classes are considered ready to be placed full-time in English monolingual mainstream classes.
4. The Massachusetts Comprehensive Assessment System, or MCAS, is a series of standardized tests that all Massachusetts public school students in fourth, eighth, and tenth grade are required to take. These tests are supposed to assess whether students are learning the statewide curricular frameworks. High school students must pass the tenth-grade test in order to graduate.

References

Au, K. (1992). Constructing the theme of a story. *Language Arts, 69,* 106–111.

Berriz, B. R. (2000). Raising children's cultural voices: Strategies for developing literacy in two languages. In Z. F. Beykont (Ed.), *Lifting every voice: Pedagogy and politics of bilingualism* (pp. 71–94). Cambridge, MA: Harvard Education Publishing Group.

Beykont, Z. F. (Ed.). (2000). *Lifting every voice: Pedagogy and politics of bilingualism.* Cambridge, MA: Harvard Education Publishing Group.

Brisk, M. E., & Harrington, M. M. (2000). *Literacy and bilingualism.* Mahwah, NJ: Lawrence Erlbaum.

Elbow, P. (1973). *Writing without teachers.* New York: Oxford University Press.

Faltis, C. J. (2001). *Joinfostering: Teaching and learning in multilingual classrooms*. Upper Saddle River, NJ: Merrill Prentice-Hall.

Farah, M. H. (2000). Reaping the benefits of bilingualism: The case of Somali refugee students. In Z. F. Beykont (Ed.), *Lifting every voice: Pedagogy and politics of bilingualism* (pp. 59–71). Cambridge, MA: Harvard Education Publishing Group.

Garcia, E. E. (1996). Preparing instructional professionals for linguistically and culturally diverse students. In J. Sikula (Ed.), *Handbook of research on teacher education* (pp. 802–813). New York: Simon & Schuster Macmillan.

Johnson, D. M., & Roen, D. H. (Eds.). (1989). *Richness in writing: Empowering ESL students*. New York: Longman.

Kagan, S. (1986). Cooperative learning and sociocultural factors in schooling. In California Department of Education, *Beyond language: Social and cultural factors in schooling language minority students* (pp. 231–299). Los Angeles: California State University, Evaluation, Dissemination, and Assessment Center.

Keene, E. O., & Zimmerman, S. (1997). *Mosaic of thought*. Portsmouth, NH: Heinemann.

McLane, J. B. (1990). Writing as a social process. In L. C. Moll (Ed.), *Vygotsky and education* (pp. 304–318). New York: Cambridge University Press.

Moll, L. C. (1989). Teaching second language students: A Vygotskian perspective. In D. M. Johnson & D. H. Roen (Eds.), *Richness in writing: Empowering ESL students* (pp. 55–70). New York: Longman.

Moll, L. C. (Ed.). (1990). *Vygotsky and education*. New York: Cambridge University Press.

Moll, L. C., & Greenberg, J. B. (1990). Creating zones of possibilities: Combining social contexts for instruction. In L. C. Moll (Ed.), *Vygotsky and education* (pp. 319–348). New York: Cambridge University Press.

Ramirez, J. D., & Merino, B. (1990). Classroom talk in English immersion, early-exit and late-exit transitional bilingual education programs. In R. Jacobson & C. Faltis (Eds.), *Language distribution issues in bilingual schooling* (pp. 61–103). Clevedon, Eng.: Multilingual Matters.

Rueda, R. (1990). Assisted performance in writing. In L. C. Moll (Ed.), *Vygotsky and education* (pp. 403–426). New York: Cambridge University Press.

Schlumberger, A., & Clymer, D. (1989). Teacher training for teacher collaboration. In D. M Johnson & D H. Roen (Eds.), *Richness in writing: Empowering ESL students* (pp. 146–161). New York: Longman.

Slavin, R. E. (1987). The developmental and motivational perspectives on cooperative learning: A reconciliation. *Child Development, 58*, 1161–1167.

Trueba, H. T., & Delgado-Gaitan, C. (1983). Socialization of Mexican children for cooperation and competition: Sharing and copying. *Journal of Educational Equity and Leadership, 5*, 189–204.

Vygotsky, L. S. (1978). *Mind in society: The development of higher psychological processes* (M. Cole, C. John-Steiner, S. Scribner, & E. Souberman, Eds.). Cambridge, MA: Harvard University Press.

Wertsch, J. V. (1985). *Vygotsky and social formation of the mind*. Cambridge, MA: Harvard University Press.

Yolen, J. (1992). *Encounter*. Orlando, FL: Harcourt Brace.

Connecting Classroom and Community through the Arts and Oral Narrative

BERTA ROSA BERRIZ

What I have been proposing is a profound respect for the cultural identity of students — a cultural identity that implies respect for the language of the other, the color of the other, the gender of the other, the class of the other, the sexual orientation of the other, the intellectual capacity of the other; that implies the ability to stimulate creativity of the other. (Freire, 1997)

Our mainstream classrooms include children with diverse family histories, languages, and cultures. Recently, the diversity of mainstream students has dramatically increased. A mainstream classroom of the new millennium may include Pakistani children; Asians from Chinese, Vietnamese, and Korean families; African, Polish, or Irish immigrants; children of mixed heritage and Latinos from the Caribbean, and South and Central America. A dramatic increase in transnational migration, economic polarization, the concentration of poverty in the nation's inner cities, and White flight from urban areas are having an impact on our city schools. Our nation's poorest and most culturally diverse students are in our inner-city classrooms.

For the most part, our schools are failing bicultural students — those whose home cultures are not supported in school.[1] Students of diverse cultural backgrounds are separated by an ever-widening gap in academic achievement from European American and native English-speaking students. Research in Texas, Massachusetts, and California shows that an overwhelming majority of bicultural students will not be able to pass the high-stakes tests required to graduate from high school (see Haney, this volume; Maxwell-Jolly & Gándara, this volume; Uriarte, this volume). According to the National Assessment of Educational Progress (1999), which has tested national samples of students for about thirty years, "Minorities are not performing nearly as well as White students early in the first grade and very large gaps develop rapidly during the first three years of school" (pp. 6–7).[2] I believe that many of these children do not succeed because, in the absence of school support for their home cultures, they do not have equal access to learning. For example, school staff may not reflect the demographics of the student group and may not know how to teach across cultural difference. The multiple languages of the community may not be included in school announcements, posted material, or parent meetings. Families may not feel welcome in a school where no one can speak to them in their own language or provide them with information about the school. The curriculum may only include Eurocentric history, literature, and ways of knowing. A recent report issued by the Applied Research Center (Gordon, Piana, & Keleher, 2000) provides compelling statistical evidence of discrimination against culturally and linguistically diverse students, as reflected in high dropout rates, high discipline referrals, and limited access to advance placement, as well as the unrepresentative racial makeup of the teaching corps.

Teachers must build culturally inclusive classroom communities in order to address these problems (Berriz, 2000). We must invite every child and all that he or she represents to enter the learning experience. All children and their families hold a wealth of cultural knowledge that intersects with academic content and curriculum. Creating a link to family culture can help students find a niche within the classroom environment. Teachers can strengthen the foundation for new learning by building on the experiences of a child and his or her family. In turn, each child's cultural knowledge and experience enriches everyone's learning.

A culturally inclusive classroom is a democratic space that provides equal access to all students by rooting learning in their communities (Berriz, 2000). By democratic I mean that students and teachers are cocreators of knowledge in the process of understanding how the curriculum relates to their communities and everyday lives. In the democratic classroom, everyone is able to speak and be heard. Demo-cratic practice challenges students to think critically and solve aca-demic problems while considering their peers' points of view. The challenge of considering the perspectives of their diverse peers ex-pands students' ways of thinking. Engaging family culture supports all learners, and teaching cross-cultural understanding is essential in our increasingly multicultural society.

Connecting the classroom to the community enriches the learn-ing environment for all students because it embeds school knowledge in the fiber of everyday lives (Berriz, 2000; Farah, 2000). The commu-nity-connected classroom supports rigorous academic learning while using the resources of the community. Students do not have to choose one over the other; instead, they experience how education enables them to learn from and contribute to their communities. The ways that teachers engage with a community's diverse histories, experi-ences, and points of view enriches the learning environment for all.

The groundbreaking work of Luis Moll and James Greenberg (1990) has inspired me to pay closer attention to the knowledge that families pass on to their children. As researchers in collaboration with classroom teachers, Moll and Greenberg reported on how families can enrich classrooms and support the connection between home and school by sharing funds of knowledge — that is, the abundant cultural knowledge families and communities have about topics ranging from agricultural practices and home remedies to institutional access and employment opportunities. Teachers in the study developed teaching strategies to tap family and community funds of knowledge. Parents became teachers and gained a place of prominence in the teaching and learning community.

Typically, schools do not effectively tap into these family treasure troves for curriculum development. What are engaging ways to tap these funds of knowledge and connect the classroom to the commu-nity? How can mainstream teachers recognize and use the resources of their students' family cultures to deepen the rigorous learning of aca-demic content? How can the arts and oral narrative be used to build a culturally inclusive classroom? In this chapter I report on several effec-tive ways that teachers in three settings are teaching across the cul-tural and linguistic divide. Each offers insights into ways to bring students' cultural and family knowledge into the classroom. First, I discuss specific strategies that a colleague used in her elementary school classroom to integrate academic content, the arts, and oral narrative through two projects: the Family Map and the Family Story Quilt. Next, I present my observations of a series of literacy workshops and bookmaking projects involving middle school students with limited formal education and their families. The final classroom example focuses on innovative efforts that connect classroom learning and community knowledge at the high school level.

Cultural Arts and Oral History Bring Cultural and Family Knowledge into Classrooms

The Family Map

The beginning of the school year is a fertile time to encourage student relationships with one another and with their own cultural backgrounds. Both of these connections support student learning. In a mainstream third-grade classroom, where I am making observations and conducting student interviews, my colleague Judy Wise is seeking ways to welcome students' cultures and family knowledge. For example, when students entered the classroom on the first day they found one wall covered by a blank world map. The Family Map project and the activities that arose from this project focused attention on where children came from and what they knew about the places they or their families have lived. For their first geography assignment, students took home an enlarged map of their state or country of origin to fill with locations associated with family stories, celebrations, and family members' memories of their first days of school. The students brought in photographs or drew pictures of their families. Family pictures soon framed the large world map. The exhibit visually intertwined the personal with the academic in the classroom community.

I remember the first year that I used this map project in my classroom. Listening to my students, I discovered that it was easier for some of my students to learn their home addresses when they saw the relationship of their new neighborhood to their old neighborhood on the world map (Berriz, 2000). It was as if the global helped to make sense of the local. This insight influenced me to revisit the way I taught other subjects. In mathematics, I started to introduce the whole number before I taught its parts. For example, I teach the concept of division by having twenty-eight students sit together at their desks, then asking them to move the desks around to make four equal groups. In science, I teach the concept of matter before getting into its different manifestations of solid, liquid, and gas. Over the years, responding to my students' different ways of learning has made my classroom more effective.

The Family Map project in Judy's classroom opened a year-long series of activities in which students collected oral narratives. Children interviewed family members on various topics: What are the names of rocks and minerals in your country or neighborhood? What advice would you give your child to keep for the future? What is your favorite story from your grandmother or other friend or family member? How does sound travel? The answers to these curricular questions brought family knowledge into the classroom. For example, José's father was an engineer. He could tell José that sound traveled in waves through matter. José gave an example from the experience of swimming in the ocean: "You know how you can hear your sister screaming at you even when you are under water at the beach?" Jamar gave an example from urban life: "You know how you can hear the neighbor's radio through your wall?" Both answers reflected ways of knowing embedded in the daily life of the students and their families. One answer incorporated knowledge of wind and waves from the island-based Caribbean experience; the other revealed knowledge derived from urban life. All students had heard sound travel in many different settings, and the echoes of their knowledge reverberated around the room.

Exploration of family funds of knowledge enriched student learning and teaching throughout the year. For example, to introduce a science unit on minerals, Judy asked children to bring in their favorite rocks. The resulting eclectic rock collection encouraged students to learn the names of rocks and minerals from many lands: Juanita brought in a crystal from the caves near Utuado in Puerto Rico; Kevonia told the story of puddingstone from Roxbury, a part of Boston; Kevin and Kaweisi brought in stones used in traditional games of China and Africa. Understanding sedimentary, igneous, and metamorphic rocks seemed easier with the personal connections to friends in the class. One of the assessments for measuring student learning in the rock unit was a city walk, during which children found samples and described in their own words the different types of rock formations. This unit, like all units tied to the Family Map project, began by tapping student and family knowledge and then tying this information to academic content. The Family Map and the projects that came from it created a place of prominence for the knowledge that students brought into the classroom.

The Family Story Quilt

Early in the school year, Judy also introduced the Family Story Quilt project as another means of inviting family funds of knowledge into the classroom and nurturing relationships among students.[3] This quilt project is a literacy-based integrated art experience that builds classroom community using art and oral history. To begin, students went home with the assignment of learning about important family history, such as births, weddings, and travel. Each student then created a paper collage about one or more of his or her family stories. The outcome was an artistic representation of identity portraits that included cultural words and phrases, as well as paragraphs written by students about every person in the classroom. Students assembled their collages on a background of bright mural paper to make a quilt. The collages were a visual reminder that enabled children to see how they were connected to one another. The family quilt further enhanced the panorama of a new classroom with familiar images of home.

Joanna created a paper collage with splashes of ocean blue framed in patterns of colorful flowers. She portrayed herself in the ocean in the Dominican Republic, swimming with her cousin. Tamika, an African American child, interviewed her partner Joanna about her collage and created a riddle to describe her partner: "Brown, and bright, a lover of colors, math and ocean waves. Who is she?" Riddles, poetry, and rhyme are commonly used in both Spanish-speaking Caribbean and African American traditions. Including riddles in the linguistic collage of the classroom encouraged children to listen for unique and shared cultural expressions.

Students' home languages came to life in the classroom with the inclusion of key words when students retold their family stories to their peers. Jerome told a story about visits to his grandmother's house on Saturdays. Much of the story revolved around a tree in her back yard and the word *tree* was central to the call and response that accompanied the presentation of his story. Idelina, a child from Cape Verde, knew the word *tree* in Cape Verdean Creole. In the oral retelling of Jerome's story, as he said the word *tree*, the class responded with the Creole word, *árvi*. The sounds of words from children's family stories

in many languages were a powerful affirmation that this classroom included everyone. The teacher acknowledged the value of speaking
more than one language by asking children who were learning English
to teach words in their native language to the whole class. The classroom community developed a common vocabulary from diverse family cultures and languages. This experience provided an opportunity
for members of the class to get to know one another and to understand that the group landscape included the languages of each child in
the classroom community.

The quilt project challenged students to express themselves effectively, both in art and language, in order to communicate their family
stories. The use of oral narrative encouraged communication among
students from varied ethnic, racial, and linguistic backgrounds. The
strategy of building bridges between the classroom and communities
by having students bring information and stories from home worked
well in this multicultural setting.

Family Literacy Workshops Bring Families into the Classroom

Tapping funds of knowledge by bringing parents into schools is another effective strategy. The Family Literacy initiative at the Neighborhood School in Boston recruited families to work with their middle
school literacy students on developing reading and writing through
joint bookmaking workshops. Literacy students are those who have
limited prior schooling experiences and who are not yet proficient
readers and writers in any language. Antonio Moreno, a middle school
classroom teacher and workshop leader, noted that respect for parents
as partners in teaching his students literacy is at the philosophical center of his work with families:

> As a teacher, I believe that my connection with the home needs
> to be close. Even before school starts, I call the families to intro-
> duce myself. I trust parents to do their best for the children.
> When good things happen, I call to praise, to invite, and to ask
> for help. When a parent arrives at my door, I attend to them. I see
> the children. I delight in them and praise them. Most of my par-
> ents participate in the school in some way. All of these workshops
> and extra events take time. I work hard with my respected col-
> leagues. It is the passion for our work that holds us.

One aspect of Antonio's literacy program was a series of three literacy workshops with families held during the school day. The workshops honored each family's language and knowledge base as a resource. Children and families worked in English and Spanish and workshop leaders supported the exchange of ideas by translating. Antonio invited me to observe this series of family literacy workshops, the first of which was called Love of Reading and Writing. All parents received invitations to participate in a reading-aloud experience based on the literacy model used throughout the school. The children of the parents who came to the workshop could sit with their families while a book was read aloud in Spanish and in English. The reading modeled appreciation of print by highlighting the title, author, and illustrator of the book. Families and students then participated in a dialogue that demonstrated strategies for engagement in the reading, such as anticipating outcomes. Afterward, students returned to their classrooms and parents asked questions about the approach. Parents and teachers worked together in an academic environment that encouraged exchange of information. At the end of the workshop, parents received a book in the language of their choice to take home and read with their children.

The second workshop was titled Folklore, Poems, Songs, Rhymes, and the Oral Tradition. The workshop began with parents and children sitting together and presenting poems, songs, and rhymes from their cultures. Antonio observed, "It was delightful for families to find out that many of the rhymes exist in various forms throughout our diverse international cultures." In the second half of the workshop, parents made books of poems together with their children and with the support of teachers. Families then took home their handmade books that were filled with poetry from the group's various literary traditions and were representative of everyone's culture. Parents also brought home a blank book to fill in with their children. Antonio began to see results with the children of the families who participated: they seemed more confident and motivated to be in school, and their reading improved. The family literacy program unfolded along with the experiences and the needs of the group.

Family Experiences with Overcoming Hardship was the most intense of the three family literacy workshops. This workshop also involved bookmaking and focused on childhood memories and the challenges of adult life. Parents' childhood memories were colorful, joyful, and nostalgic, but later memories often included stories of hardships, such as tough economic times, discrimination, and the challenges of learning a new language, which tarnished beautiful childhood memories. After hearing their parents' stories, the literacy students became the teachers. They sat in a circle inside the circle of parents — fishbowl style — and held a conversation with their teacher about what makes a good story.[4]

The children said that a good story begins by setting the scene and introducing the most important characters, then there must be a problem or a mystery to solve. The best endings are the ones that surprise. Children, who were just learning about the qualities of good writing, inspired the creation of books from their parents' personal stories. Work on turning oral narrative into written text began in the workshop and continued over the coming weeks. This workshop helped to create trust between families and the school through the respectful way that sensitive stories of overcoming hardship were placed in beautifully illustrated and written books and shared with the group members. The following is one of the stories composed by a parent and her child.

FAMILY STRUGGLE FOR A BRIGHT FUTURE

In a small barrio, there lived a large family made up of the mother and father with eight children. They lived in a tiny and humble home made of wood with a beautiful orange Flamboyant tree in front of the porch.

Though the family was poor, the humble father, who was called Tono or Nato, never stopped working. Nato was a farmer by day and a factory worker at night. All of this work enabled him to support his eight young children.

The children slept two to a bed. The youngest girl was affectionately called Caculo or "Cachón." She was the brightest, always winning with cunning games and tricks. Cachón was often in trouble at school. Before the school bell rang in the morning Cachón already had scraped knees and dirty clothes from climbing and jumping.

Cachón was happy. She loved business. In the evenings, she would sell sweets to her cousins and neighbors. Her parents were

always calling her name because she loved to roam the country-
side picking fruits and crossing the dangerous stream behind her
house.

The day of the Three Kings arrived. Cachón was sad because
she could not receive all that she would like. She screamed and
cried furiously because there was nothing for her under her bed.

After listening to his daughter cry for a while, Nato went to a
store to buy Cachón a black rag doll with arms made of rubber.
When Cachón saw the doll, she continued to cry desperately.
She did not want to touch the rag doll.

The years passed quickly. The children grew and the parents
struggled so that each one would have a brighter future. Five of
the children went to college and the other three finished high
school. They all decided to work and live independently.

Today, Cachón is a grown woman. She closes her eyes and
recalls the days when papá Nato did not have a car to go to
church or to visit their grandparents. Today, Cachón is a happy
mother of three children. When they are mischievous, she imag-
ines that she is paying for all of the prankish deeds of her youth.
Sometimes, Cachón thinks of giving to her children all of the
things that she did not have as a child. Then, she reconsiders,
thinking that not all that is material gives happiness. She knows
that she owes a great deal to her father.

Today, Cachón's mother and father live in a stronger house
on that same lot. Cachón lives far away from her parents, culture, and traditions. This is a story of a girl who had next to nothing but grew up surrounded by beautiful nature and a loving
family. Cachón lives always happily.

The momentum of Antonio's family literacy work gained the support of other professionals in the school, including the parent center
director and the literacy specialist. These professionals recruited parents to become directly involved in the classroom. Mrs. Estefan was a
parent who participated in the family literacy workshops and later volunteered in the fourth-grade math class with Mrs. Bernard. I asked
Mrs. Estefan what kept her interested in the work of the classroom.

She replied, "I am fascinated with the wonder of learning. Intellectually, I am trying to understand what goes on with the children. It seems that they are saying to me, 'If you are willing to help me, I am willing to learn.' I would like teachers to never turn any parent away, neither in gestures or in words." As a teacher, Elaine Bernard is also learning from having a parent volunteer in her classroom: "Rosa Estefan is like having a mother in the classroom. She mothers the children. This reminds me of the nurturing part of teaching and learning. She will let me know when one of the students has an issue. At the same time, she cuts less slack to parents. Rosa believes that there is no excuse for parents not accepting responsibilities of parenting. She has helped me keep my expectations of parents high."

Antonio's work with literacy students has been effective because it recognized the prominent role that parents play in the development of children's reading and writing skills. It capitalized on prior experiences, tapped family funds of knowledge, and relied on the fact that parents want the best for their children and will eagerly and courageously participate in school when teachers welcome them and honor what they bring. Children's literacy flourished. In turn, literacy became a tool for children to learn from families, their own and others', about effective ways of dealing with the challenges of everyday life. Interaction among family members reinforced family bonds while nurturing family-school relations. The Family Literacy Program valued families as cocreators of knowledge.

Drama and Action Research Bring Community Knowledge into the Classroom

Community knowledge can enrich learning and teaching at all levels of education. One effective example that I have observed at the high school level involved students in the health career academy at John F. Kennedy High School. Students at the health career academy were fulfilling their world language requirement by studying Spanish as a second language with a specific focus on health issues. During my weekly observations, I saw that students studied academic content related to health careers, collected oral narratives through research projects in their communities, examined community health concerns, developed skits and role-plays to present what they had learned, and learned Spanish in a meaningful manner.

Students in Mr. Angel Ortega's language class first discussed specific qualities of a healthy community in order to establish baseline expectations for health care. Reviewing a list of the eleven qualities of a healthy community developed by the World Health Organization, the students were surprised to find out that these included a clean environment, adequate housing, and other basic needs, in addition to access to high-quality health care. Students then worked in pairs, sharing personal experiences in health care as a way of developing some questions about their concerns. The students came up with two simple questions to take to the community members that they interviewed: What do you think is most important for a healthy community? What do you think is the major obstacle to quality health care for you?

Mr. Ortega's students then went out to interview family and community members and returned with a wide range of answers. Some came with stories of serious problems, such as long waits in the emergency room and disrespectful treatment by medical institutions and personnel. Students from varied language groups told stories about missing school so that they could translate for their parents at the clinic. By engaging in this process, students discovered that their diverse families and communities shared many of the same health issues.

In small cooperative groups, students then created dramatic skits using their findings. The students used both languages while composing scripts and making decisions about their presentation, but their skits had to be in Spanish. Using native Spanish-speaking students as resources, students wrote skits that included family and community experiences as well as new vocabulary and concepts from the curriculum. The community stories heightened students' concern for the rights of patients. Students' desire to represent real-life health issues through the dramatic arts energized both language and content learning. Building on this successful experience, future classes mobilized students to collect information from families and community members pertaining to nutrition and environmental pollution issues. The class successfully made the bridge to community knowledge and experiences through action research and drama.

This project also increased the value that students placed on one another. Although their language and cultural backgrounds differed, their professional aspirations and their communities' health concerns connected them. The project created authentic reasons for students to work together. As students created skits in small groups, they came to value one anothers' family and community experiences and knowledge. Spanish-speaking students became a valuable linguistic resource for the whole class. In addition, it became clear to students that their studies and planned careers were of vital importance to the future health of their families and communities.

Reflections on Strategies in Culturally Inclusive Classrooms

Across the varied school settings and the elementary, middle, and high school classrooms described in this chapter, teachers have endeavored to connect their classrooms to the community. They built on student strengths, tapping funds of family knowledge to enrich and enliven the learning of academic content. The Family Map project in Judy's classroom and the activities that followed from it let students know that each individual in the classroom can contribute to the learning process. This geography-based project taught students that knowing about their family geography is both valuable and valued. The Family Map called on students to enrich classroom knowledge with family knowledge, and the exchange among students gave a place of prominence to the familiar. Using family knowledge to initiate academic content, the classroom became an intellectual home away from home. The Family Map made a connection between family geography and school geography, thus making social studies instruction relevant to the students' lives. I believe that this type of culturally relevant instruction contributes to equal access to learning and greater school success for culturally and linguistically diverse students (Heath, 1983).

Culturally inclusive pedagogy ensures that each child in a classroom has an opportunity to speak and be heard. The Family Story Quilt project added the dimension of family stories to Judy's classroom. The quilt became a catalyst for students to explore the meaning of family stories in various ways: by creating a collage of stories, telling a story, and writing about a classmate's story. It encouraged youngsters to learn words in their classmates' languages and think about their own story in relation to others' stories. The quilt was a meaningful literacy challenge that required students to learn about their peers while developing listening, speaking, writing, reading, and oral self-expression.

Antonio's family literacy project was effective because it recognized the crucial role that families play in the development of the literacy skills of middle school students who had not had an opportunity to develop literacy skills in a language. Bookmaking and reading projects led by the students themselves opened the doors of the school, inviting families to join in the school's efforts to support literacy instruction. Family stories were respectfully heard and artistically represented in books that honored them and reflected the value of the partnership between school and home.

The use of theater in Angel's classroom at the Kennedy High School also connected classrooms and community. Another powerful result of this project was that the students realized that the academic work of school not only connects to their lives but also shows them how they can make a difference in their communities. Students involved in socially relevant projects, such as creating skits focused on community health issues, are more motivated to participate in school. Extending the curriculum to the community and integrating students' extended social circles into the curriculum ignited students' interest in schooling.

The family map, quilt, and literacy workshops and the popular theater all make use of the arts. The arts are key to cultural inclusion because they move children to imagine and create meaning from their realities (Greene, 1995). In the process of making cultural art in the classroom, young people are encouraged to articulate their own voices in relation to others. The arts develop voice by actively requiring students to participate in the world of school (Giroux, 1988). The reciprocity required of students in projects like the family quilt enhances skills that are essential for building community in the culturally inclusive classroom.

Weaving relationships among families, school, and community is essential for creating a culturally rich, challenging, and respectful context for learning. As educators in mainstream classrooms, we are blessed with the bicultural students (Darder, 1991) that we need to make our curriculum culturally responsive. Despite changes in demographics and diversity, as teachers we have control in our own classrooms and influence in our schools (Tatum, 1997). Therefore, we also have an ethical and moral responsibility to work toward changes that ensure equal access to learning for our culturally and linguistically diverse students. Each setting requires particular solutions: students bringing cultural information from home, workshops bringing families into schools, or students going out into the community to ask questions and collect data. Teachers committed to making a difference will find ways to tap funds of knowledge and create more culturally inclusive classrooms. Teachers can actively develop solutions in concert with colleagues, families, and students.

We must find ways to honor the experiences of children, families, and communities as a way to enrich the learning for all students in our classrooms. Recognizing the resources that children already have creates a fruitful environment for learning and challenges students to experience other cultures with open minds. That is, in a culturally inclusive classroom, all students are encouraged to contribute to learning and create culture anew from a position of strength. Capitalizing on the beauty and strength of children and their families is an important and enlivening project for student and teacher alike. While building cross-cultural understanding, teachers can play a crucial role in preparing students to interact effectively as global citizens without having to sacrifice their family cultural identities.

Epilogue

The effective practices that I presented in this chapter were born out of a few teachers' declaration of war against teacher isolation and their taking charge of their own professional development. Judy Wise, Antonio Moreno, Angel Ortega, and I have taught in the same school district. Though we came from different ethnic and linguistic backgrounds, we shared the common experience of entering the teaching profession lacking adequate preparation for the challenges presented by the changing student demographics and structural barriers to equitable education. Over the years, we turned to each other for professional support; we held regular meetings; we read together; we observed each other teaching; we gave each other feedback; we learned from one another.

Our conversations became an important location for reflection as each one of us sought ways to connect to our own identities and to those of our students as a means of overcoming obstacles to learning in our classrooms. "I find our many similarities striking," Judy observed. "We share a need to understand our relationship to the many cultures that make up our individual identities and place similar importance on understanding and validating the cultures of our students." She added, "We also support the critical need for curricula that integrate who our students are with the skills and values needed to be lifelong learners and positive contributors in an ever-changing world community."

In addition to participating in our group, Judy maintains a writer's journal that she shares with a group of fellow teachers. She belongs to several networks in which teachers exchange alternative approaches to educational challenges, including the use of oral histories and experiential learning techniques that are part of her current teaching repertoire. She also participates in a teacher-led team working toward creating a respectful school environment through classroom-based and school-community projects. After thirty years of teaching, Judy says that she continues to grow with her students and her fellow teachers.

Teacher study groups, anchored by a sense of shared needs and mutual respect, are a source of authentic accountability for teachers' best work. By creating spaces for collective inquiry, mutual support and encouragement, and respectful debate, urban educators can challenge the solitary role of classroom teaching in the midst of a dramatic and constantly changing educational context. In turning to one another, teachers can directly challenge the restrictions imposed by traditional educational hierarchies. Action research, reflective practice, and teacher study groups challenge the paradigm of the "outside expert" and capitalize on the rich and diverse experiences and accumulated practical knowledge of teachers.

The things that Judy, Antonio, and Angel do in their classrooms flow directly from the courage that they have derived from joining forces with one another and with other activist teachers. Affirming the value of critical professional networks, educator Beverly Tatum writes, "We all need community to give us energy, to strengthen our voices and to offer constructive criticism when we stray off course" (1997, p. 205). In the process of tearing down the walls of isolation surrounding our classrooms and pursuing our ethical and political commitment to create educational equity, our colleagues and our students are an enduring source of professional development, inspiration, and spiritual sustenance.

Notes

1. I use the term *bicultural student* (Darder, 1991) to honor the experience of navigating two cultural worlds of community and school. If we use culturally responsive pedagogy, children can learn the school culture while maintaining the family culture.
2. *Reaching the Top: A Report on the National Task Force on Minority High Achievement* (1999) shows that, using traditional measures of academic achievement

such as grades and class rank, African American, Native American, and Latino students were severely underrepresented among high achievers.

3. The quilt is an adaptation of the Oral History Center curriculum, Studying Life Stories in the Classroom. The Oral History Center in Cambridge, Massachusetts, has used oral narrative as a means of celebrating community history and culture since 1982.

4. "Fish bowl" is a popular education technique that structures participation for group problem-solving. In this case, the inner circle — literacy students — led a literary conversation. The audience — parents — sitting in the outer circle first listened to the characteristics of a good story and then engaged in the bookmaking activity.

References

Berriz, B. R. (2000). Raising children's cultural voices: Strategies for developing literacy in two languages. In Z. F. Beykont (Ed.), *Lifting every voice: Pedagogy and politics of bilingualism* (pp. 71–95). Cambridge, MA: Harvard Education Publishing Group.

Darder, A. (1991). *Culture and power in the classroom.* Westport, CT: Bergin & Garvey.

Farah, M. H. (2000). Reaping the benefits of bilingualism: The case of Somali refugee students. In Z. F. Beykont (Ed.), *Lifting every voice: Pedagogy and politics of bilingualism* (pp. 59–70). Cambridge, MA: Harvard Education Publishing Group

Freire, P. (1997). A response. In P. Freire, J. W. Fraser, D. Macedo, T. McKinnon, & W. T. Stokes (Eds.), *Mentoring the mentor: A critical dialogue with Paulo Freire* (pp. 303–329). New York: Peter Lang.

Giroux, H. (1988). *Teachers as intellectuals.* New York: Bergin & Garvey.

Gordon, R., Piana, L. D., & Keleher, T. (2000). Facing the consequences: An examination of racial discrimination in U.S. public schools. Oakland, CA: ERASE, Applied Research Center. Available on-line at http://www.arc.org/erase/reports.html

Greene, M. (1995). *Releasing the imagination: Essays on education, the arts, and social change.* San Francisco: Jossey-Bass.

Heath, S. B. (1983). *Ways with words: Language, life, and work in communities and classrooms.* New York: Cambridge University Press.

Moll, L., & Greenberg, J. (1990). Creating zones of possibilities: Combining social contexts for instruction. In L. Moll (Ed.), *Vygotsky and education: Instructional implications and applications of sociohistorical psychology* (pp. 319–348). Cambridge, Eng.: Cambridge University Press.

National Assessment of Educational Progress. (1999). *Reaching the top: A report on the National Task Force on Minority High Achievement* [On-line]. Available: http://www.doe.k12.gov.us/sla/ret/naep.html

Tatum, B. (1997). *Why are all the Black kids sitting together in the cafeteria? and other conversations about race.* New York: Basic Books.

PART THREE

Preparing Teachers to Teach Across Language Difference

Creating an Equal Playing Field: Teachers as Advocates, Border Crossers, and Cultural Brokers[1]

LILIA I. BARTOLOMÉ

Much of the discussion about preparing teachers of language minority students focuses on the best strategies to address students' academic and linguistic development. Although this focus is necessary, it is equally important to examine the important role of teacher political and ideological clarity in working with language minority and other subordinated minority student groups.[2] In this chapter, I argue that, in addition to pedagogical techniques that are responsive to the needs of language minority students, teachers need to gain both political clarity and ideological clarity in order to increase the chances of academic success for their language minority students and subordinated minority students.[3]

The dramatic increase in low-income, non-White, and language minority students in U.S. public schools signals an urgent need to understand and challenge the ideological orientations of prospective teachers in teacher education programs. One current challenge is the adequate preparation of the overwhelmingly White, female, and middle-class preservice teacher population to work with subordinated students, who are quickly becoming the majority in many of the largest urban public schools in the country (Gomez, 1994). Although the nation's school population is made up of approximately 40 percent minority children, nearly 90 percent of teachers are White (National Center for Education Statistics, 1992). The social-class differences between teachers and students also continue to widen. For example, 44 percent of African American children and 36 percent of Latino children live in poverty, but most teachers come from White, lower-middle- and middle-class homes in rural and suburban communities (Zimpher, 1989). There are also significant differences between teacher and student language backgrounds: most teachers are English monolingual, whereas there are approximately 5 to 7.5 million non-native English-speaking students in the public schools (McLeod, 1994, p. iv)).

Given these changing student demographics, it is evident that all teachers, not just bilingual and ESL teachers, are responsible for preparing language minority students (Gebhard, Austin, Nieto, & Willett, this volume; Maxwell-Jolly & Gándara, this volume; Nieto, 2000b). The social-class, cultural, and language gaps between teachers and students call for teachers to critically understand their own ideological orientations about cultural, linguistic, and class differences, and to comprehend that teaching is not a politically or ideologically neutral undertaking.

The chapter is organized in three sections. First, I explain why it is important to recognize and better understand the ideological dimensions of teachers' beliefs and attitudes toward subordinated minority students. Second, I discuss the results of an exploratory interview study on teacher ideology conducted at Riverview High School in southern California. In conclusion, I briefly discuss how these teachers' beliefs and life experiences can inform teacher preparation efforts.

Teachers' Ideological Orientations

Increasing one's ideological awareness requires comparing one's personal explanations of the wider social order with those propagated by the dominant society. Evidence is growing of the relationship between the process and outcome of language minority education and educators' beliefs and attitudes regarding the legitimacy of the dominant social order, which creates unequal power relations among cultural groups. Previous research suggests that prospective teachers tend to regard the existing social order uncritically and, often, unconsciously (Bloom, 1991; Davis, 1995; Freire, 1997, 1998a, 1998b; Gomez, 1994; Haberman, 1991; Macedo, 1994; Sleeter, 1992). For example, it is my experience that prospective teachers often come into teacher education programs subscribing to deficit views of minority students and believing that the solution to their academic underachievement lies in assimilating them, that is, making them more like middle-class White students.

Preservice teachers tend to see the social order as a fair and just one. Farley (2000) explains that the dominant ideological belief that Blacks and Latinos are responsible for their own disadvantages "appears deeply rooted in an American ideology of individualism, a belief that each individual determines his or her own situation" (p. 66). When people believe that the system is fair, that is, that African Americans and Latinos have the same opportunities as White Americans, they usually do two things: blame the minorities themselves for any disadvantages they experience rather than blaming White discrimination or an unfair system, and oppose policies designed to increase minority opportunities (e.g., bilingual education, affirmative action). As Farley points out:

> In one regard, such reasoning seems to make sense: if the system is fair and everyone has equal opportunities, then such programs would amount to an unfair advantage for minority groups. *The problem, however, is that the system is not fair: numerous discriminatory processes make it harder for some groups to get ahead in American society.* (2000, p. 66, author's emphasis)

Prospective teachers and practicing teachers often resent having to take courses that challenge some of the dominant-culture ideologies they unconsciously hold (Gonzalves, 1996). It is interesting that even when prospective teachers recognize that certain minority groups have historically been poorer, have underachieved academically, and have had higher mortality rates than Whites, their explanations for such inequalities are usually underdeveloped or nonexistent (Bartolomé, 1998; King, 1991).

Unfortunately, this reproduction of the dominant ideology and lack of political clarity often translates into uncritical acceptance of the status quo as natural, and of assimilationist and deficit-based views of non-White and language minority students. Educators who do not identify and interrogate their negative, racist, and classist ideological orientations often work to reproduce the existing social order (Bartolomé, 1998; Bloom, 1991). Even teachers who subscribe to the latest teaching methodologies and learning theories can unknowingly end up perverting their work because of unacknowledged racism (King, 1991). Recent literature on effective teachers' beliefs and atti-tudes about teaching minority students describes these teachers as knowledgeable and skilled practitioners, calling attention to their abil-ity to recognize the subordinate status accorded to minority students of low socioeconomic status (SES) and take steps to validate these stu-dents in school (Beauboeuf, 1997; Garcia, 1991; Howard, 2000; Lad-son-Billings, 2000; Nieto, 2000a, 2000b).

In this chapter, I describe the beliefs and reflections of four educa-tors regarding best ways to educate their working-class minority stu-dents. These four educators were identified by their colleagues and school administrators as successful and exemplary in their work with language minority and subordinated minority students.

In an effort to tap into their political and ideological orientations, these teachers were asked to describe their beliefs about effectively pre-paring low-SES, language minority high school students in general, and Mexicanos/Latinos in particular.[4] In the interviews, these educa-tors shared their counter-hegemonic beliefs, their strong sense of stu-dent advocacy, and their commitment to creating a more just and equal playing field for their students. Their definitions of student suc-cess included academic success (passing courses, graduating from high school, and going on to college), social integration in the high school culture (feeling a sense of belonging and comfort in school), and the self-confidence and life skills to navigate their current lives. It is inter-esting that they did not focus solely on academic definitions of success in their discussions, but also recognized the significance of the social and cultural dimensions of effective schooling.

I show how these successful educators appear to understand that teaching is a political undertaking and how they question common cultural views of minority students. They all pointed out that language minority students often, through no fault of their own, are viewed and treated as low status in the greater society and in school settings. The teachers also understood the important socializing role that schools assume. Although the teachers varied in their personal political orien-tations (they self-identified across the conservative-liberal spectrum), they all questioned dominant-culture explanations of the existing so-cial order, rejected deficit views of their students, and reported aggres-sively working to equalize what they perceive to be an unequal play-ing field for their students.

The Study

Riverview High School

The educators interviewed work at Riverview High School (a pseud-onym). This 100-year-old school is located in the southern California coastal community of Rancho Nacional, approximately eighteen miles north of the Mexican border. Riverside High School has a recent his-tory of impressive success: in 1994, *Redbook* magazine recognized it as a Best High School. In 1996, the school was named a California Distin-guished School, and approximately 70 percent of each graduating class attend either community or four-year colleges and receive mil-lions of dollars in scholarship money. Past research on effective schools has included Riverview in its sample of schools (see Lucas, Henze, & Donato, 1990).

The school is culturally and linguistically diverse and serves stu-dents from low-SES homes. The student enrollment is 70 percent La-tino and 8 percent Filipino American; the remainder consists of smaller numbers of Whites, African Americans, and Pacific Islanders. Sixty-two percent of all Riverview students come from homes where a language other than English is spoken, the majority being Spanish speakers. According to school records, non-English-speaking and lim-ited English proficient students comprise 23 percent of the current en-rollment (Riverview High School Profile Information, 1996). The school offers regular- and honors-level courses in bilingual (English/ Spanish) and sheltered English instructional settings, as well as bilin-gual counseling services (English, Spanish, and Tagalog) for students not deemed proficient in English. The majority of Riverview students come from low-income homes that receive Aid for Families with De-pendent Children and are thus eligible to receive free nutrition and lunch services.

The Four Exemplary Educators

Four Riverview high school educators, identified as exemplary by ad-ministrators and colleagues, discussed their experiences with Mexi-cano/Latino students and other language minority students and effec-tive ways to teach them. My strategy was to begin with experienced educators who were perceived by their peers to be particularly strong in their work with Riverview students. I hoped that these educators would serve as key informants who were knowledgeable and confident about sharing their beliefs and experiences.

A total of ten educators were interviewed during one academic year, but data analyses have been conducted on four individuals thus far. These four educators had from eight to twenty-five years' experience and consisted of the White female principal, Dr. Peabody; a Chicano history teacher, Mr. Tijerina; a White female English teacher, Mrs. Cortland; and a White male math teacher, Mr. Broadbent (all teacher names are pseudonyms). The educators were similar in age (mid to late fifties). Two of the teachers taught exclusively or primarily in English, and Mr. Tijerina had experience in both English mainstream and English-Spanish classroom settings.

The interview protocol consisted of open-ended questions intended to elicit teacher views about their own experiences with Latino students and other language minority students and factors related to educating them. Teachers also discussed their personal histories and the life journeys that led them to teaching. They described their own experiences as students and their early experiences with non-White people. Other interview topics were their teacher preparation experiences, conceptions of effective teaching, and their explanations of Riverview's touted effectiveness with Mexicano/Latino students.

The Findings: Common Ideological Beliefs about and Experiences with Asymmetrical Power Relations

The educators interviewed attributed their students' academic and social success to the school personnel's ability to create and sustain a caring, just, and equal playing field for students, such as Mexicano/Latino students, who have not often been treated well in school or in the greater society. The teachers appeared to question particular dominant-culture beliefs, specifically, the meritocratic explanations of the existing social order. They also rejected deficit views of Mexicano/Latino students and resisted romanticized views of the White middle-class (mainstream) culture as superior. These teachers reported having engaged in social or cultural border-crossing experiences, in which they personally felt the attribution of low status or witnessed someone else's subordination.[5] The educators also saw themselves as cultural brokers or advocates for their students and perceived this to be a key aspect of their work in helping their students to figure out the school culture and to succeed.

Questioning Meritocratic Explanations of the Social Order

These four educators questioned the validity of a "meritocratic" explanation of the existing social order, which places Mexicano/Latino and other minority groups at the bottom and Whites at the top of the socioeconomic and political ladder. Mr. Broadbent, for example, explained that Mexican American academic failure could be countered if teachers could give their working-class students "a taste of the better life" or let them see "how the other half lives." He pointed out that often such opportunities are not based on merit or ability but on sheer luck. Had his own father not been moved up from enlisted man to officer despite the fact that he was not a college graduate, Mr. Broadbent too might not "have been pushed by someone who had seen it." His father's level of employment and status provided his father with a taste of a better life and made him push his two sons to go to college. In Mr. Broadbent's view, life is not fair, and people who are highly capable, because of working-class limitations, often are not exposed to the broader world and therefore rarely feel confident enough to "grab for it." He felt that working-class children, through no fault of their own, often are put into a disadvantaged position unless concerted efforts are made to equalize the playing field. As a math teacher, he frequently talked to students about college and careers that require mathematical expertise so that they could think about opportunities beyond high school. He also encouraged students to leave the Rancho Nacional community to see other lifestyles and places.

Mrs. Cortland also questioned the meritocratic notion of success by the "most able," particularly as it is commonly subscribed to in schools. She remembered that the choir she advises was almost eliminated from a competition because "they couldn't afford to compete." Mrs. Cortland explained that her student group, An International Affair (self-named because of their diverse makeup), received high scores at local and county competitions. Based on these scores, the group was invited to compete in a festival held in Las Vegas, but in order to compete the students had to raise funds. In a more affluent part of the district, parents had held a golf tournament and raised more than $30,000 for their children's trip to Australia. She juxtaposed that reality with the obstacles faced by her working-class Riverview students:

As we began to do the fundraising, I noticed that the kids a month before it was time to go knew we were nowhere near the [needed] amount of money. Then I thought, "Well, we're going! It doesn't matter, we're going because we said we were going!" But they began to come up with all these excuses, "Well, my mom doesn't really want me to go" or "I have to work." So I said, "No! Money is not the issue. I will find sponsors for all these kids." And so that sunk in, that we were not going to be limited because we live in the 13th poorest city in the United States. And for the majority of these kids, I mean $100 — is that's the groceries for the month for the entire family! So when I took the burden away so we could just concentrate on doing it, not only did we go, we won first place. We won the Spirit of Las Vegas Award!

She questioned the blind belief in a meritocratic view of success and pointed out that "the level of excellence can only be assessed to the direct tie it has to the pocket book":

Am I supposed to tell these kids, "You're as good as you can get but we can't test your excellence or allow you to evolve any farther because we don't have the money?" No, we shouldn't have to worry about that if the charge in the curriculum is to create students who meet or exceed the [standards]. Then it can't be tied to the economy, it can't be tied to the color of their skin and it can't be tied to whether or not they've had this experience before in their lives.

Dr. Peabody also did not believe in a merit system when racism was such a reality in the lives of her students of color. She reported reminding White teachers and peers of the students' difficulties:

Even if you were oppressed as an Anglo, being poor or whatever . . . what I know is that the worst day or the worst part of all of that is never as challenging as [that encountered by] a Black person or Brown person. That whole color issue brings in a whole different thing.

She admitted that a big part of her job is trying to change the racist lenses of some of her teachers. Although there were not many teachers she would consider purposely racist and she avoided using the term *racist* in the school context because "it isn't that they're deliberately that way," Dr. Peabody said that racism is a fact that must be dealt with aggressively. As an example, she related an incident in which the

California Scholarship Federation (CSF) Honor Society adviser did not encourage her students to compete in a districtwide CSF scholarship competition because the adviser did not believe that her minority students were qualified to compete against White students from more affluent schools:

> I mean every flag in my head just went off. . . . I just went through the ceiling . . . that's a deficit model, that is, "How could these kids compete with anybody else?"

She confronted the teacher and used CSF alumni college graduation information to prove to this teacher just how qualified and outstanding her minority CSF students were.

These four educators articulated their belief that other factors, such as racism and economic restrictions, often assume greater importance in their students' lives than pure merit and ability. They relate this reality in a matter-of-fact tone, yet they do not fall into negative or deterministic views of their students' life chances. Instead, by taking this more comprehensive and realistic view of the social order and its potential negative manifestations at the school level, they can take action strategically to assist their students in school.

Rejection of the Dominant White Culture as Superior

Another belief common to these educators is their rejection of deficit views of Mexicano/Latino students and a refusal of blind acceptance of dominant White culture as superior or highly desirable for their students. Many of the teachers voiced their belief that cultures in contact (such as Mexican Americans and Anglo Americans in contact in the Southwest) should inform and transform each other, with each cultural group taking the best from the other culture and discarding the worst from their respective cultures. Mr. Broadbent said, "I wonder whether or not we're throwing away the best parts [of Mexican culture]. It's as if they throw away the best parts and have assimilated the worst parts of American culture."

The many positive aspects of Mexican culture, such as demonstrating respect for elders (a practice Mr. Broadbent saw as becoming uncommon in mainstream American culture) was one he believed students should maintain. Interestingly, when he discussed the importance of helping his students learn about mainstream culture in an effort to better themselves, Mr. Broadbent deemphasized issues of ethnicity and race and focused on social class. He believed that educators should not try to assimilate students into the White mainstream but should introduce them to middle-class culture. Because of his own experience growing up as a working-class youth, he identified with and felt comfortable teaching and mentoring working-class Riverview students. Mr. Tijerina also discussed numerous positive aspects of Mexican culture, for example, that Mexicano/Latino students and other minority students tend to be more accepting of diversity than White students are. He provided as proof the fact that Riverview houses the district special education program and explained that students have positively and affectionately received their special education peers into the school.

In contrast to Mr. Broadbent's sole focus on SES, Mr. Tijerina discussed issues of ethnicity, race, and racism when discussing prevalent deficit views of Mexicano/Latino students. He maintained that effective teachers of Mexicano/Latino students and other minorities have to be conscious of cultural differences and wary of their own tendencies to view the kids as inferior and of trying to make them like White students. He explained that to be effective teachers of Mexicano/Latinos, you must discard deficit notions and "you have to like people of color — you have to authentically like dark colors, you have to love brown!"

> I think we have the feeling here [at Riverview] that minorities aren't inferior. I think there's a difference between patronizing in some schools where they really think a person is inferior to some degree, but "Hey, you can make it if you try harder." The White people here — I don't think they feel that here. I think that they feel that our kids are equal — they have the same brains as kids in [more affluent, predominantly White schools, such as] Playa Dorada or Buena Vista or any place else. They do have the same brains — only the background is definitively disadvantaged — for lots of reasons.

In short, Mr. Broadbent emphasized socioeconomic class and Mr. Tijerina focused on race and ethnicity in their arguments against deficit perspectives of non-White students, but they share the belief that the disproportionate academic problems among Mexicano/Latino students are not a result of their culture or language. They draw a clear distinction between the restrictive life circumstances of their students and the students' innate potential. They believe that their students "do have the same brains" but that, through no fault of their own, they have experienced difficult life conditions that are often the direct result of living in poverty. They see their students' chief problem as not having money, but they do not restrict their students' academic potential because of their ethnicity or low socioeconomic standing.

The Educators: Cultural Border Crossers and Witnesses of Subordination

All four educators in the study reported personally experiencing or witnessing someone else's unfair treatment and arbitrary subordination. Mrs. Cortland, for example, grew up as a lower-middle-class girl in an affluent White community and learned early on to discern social-class and status differences. She shared her experiences of marginalization and explained that more affluent peers never fully accepted her and her sister. She described a particularly hurtful memory of her father not being able to afford to buy her sister the popular shoes (also the most expensive) worn by her peers at school. Mrs. Cortland recalled the discomfort of belonging to a lower class and being viewed as inferior despite her superior academic performance. Although this example might not seem to be an example of serious subordination, the important point is that she learned at an early age that her lower SES marked her as socially less valuable than her more affluent peers, despite her strong intellectual abilities.

Mr. Tijerina spoke of being a working-class Chicano who grew up in Rancho Nacional and attended Riverview High School approximately thirty-five years ago. As a working-class minority, he was forced to cross social and cultural borders in order to survive a middle-class, White school culture. During his years at Riverview High School (1960–1964), Mexican Americans constituted approximately 30 percent of the student body. Despite their numbers, they generally were not visible in the mainstream high school culture. He remembered vividly the second-class citizenship to which most Mexican American students were relegated, the condescending (at best) attitude directed at Mexicans, and the outright disrespect (at worst) that he and his peers experienced. The worst insult was to be called a dirty Mexican and told to go back to Mexico. He explained that these derogatory comments lay just under the surface of Mexican and White interactions and were frequently heard from White students at the slightest real or perceived provocation.

Mr. Tijerina explained that throughout his young life he was conscious of the low status ascribed to his working-class roots and Mexican ethnicity. He attributed his resilience to the strong pride he felt in being Mexicano (a value his father inculcated in him) and to his increasing understanding of racism and its manifestations. His later experiences with progressive community-based organizations in the 1970s and 1980s provided him with opportunities for formal study of White supremacist ideology and colonialization models.

The high school principal, Mrs. Peabody, attributed her early cultural border-crossing experiences to growing up as one of a few Whites in inner-city, predominantly African American Pittsburgh. As a working-class White girl growing up in an African American community, she explained that she learned about the advantages of cultural pluralism early on:

> Essentially my own story is that I grew up in a Black inner-city ghetto in Pittsburgh. To be a White person in a Black inner-city ghetto is a whole other interesting thing. At the time I didn't think much about it because I was there, but it turned out later to be a real strength. I learned about different people and different cultures. I did not think it was unusual to have Black friends and eat in their house, or Jewish friends, or Puerto Ricans because I did it all the time.

Although she also experienced firsthand what it means to be relegated to low status, as a "minority" White person in her predominantly African American community, she recognized the lifelong privilege and preferential treatment she received by virtue of being White. Her exposure to racism and discrimination was chiefly a result of her close work with people of color:

> These experiences have shown me that if you are a person of color, usually it is more difficult for you to achieve. . . . You know, being poor, disadvantaged and if you're going to add on top of that, Black or Brown or Red or something else, it becomes a greater challenge.

She shared her belief in allowing people of color to "use" her position as a White person (who is, therefore, perceived by other Whites as a more legitimate spokesperson) to carry their messages (e.g., support for bilingual education, allowing students to demonstrate against an anti-immigrant proposition). Dr. Peabody shared her conscious decision to use her privileged position as a White woman to become an agent for change in school settings:

When I started in Riverview School District, they [the Latinos] used me. I allowed myself to be used. So they used me to be the carrier of their messages. . . . I have a lot of credibility [as perceived by others because of her Whiteness] and because I am a very strong personality, I [cannot] be swayed off course.

Her own working-class background helped her understand Riverview High School and the surrounding community. She stated, "Rancho Nacional is a much higher-income area than the one I grew up in. It's also a much safer place . . . so I am very sensitive to these issues." Her identification with and feelings of solidarity with working-class Mexican culture were also evident in her relationship with a parent she met during her first principalship in the district. This parent became a real advocate for her, and she came to a startling realization: "Oh my God, she's more like my grandmother than most White [middle-class] women!" Dr. Peabody's feelings of solidarity with working-class Mexicano/Latino students have led her to assume the role of advocate and cultural broker for these students, parents, and communities.

The cultural border-crossing experiences of the educators in this study varied from typical "tourist" or "voyeur" White border-crossing in that the educators either personally experienced subordination or witnessed someone else's subordination. For various reasons, the reality of asymmetrical power relations among cultural groups became evident to them and left a permanent impression. They learned early on that some people are seen and treated as low status simply by virtue of their race, ethnicity, and social class. Given their "baptism of fire" during their border-crossing experiences, these educators apparently learned to more clearly discern and understand unequal power relations among cultural groups and work toward reducing and preventing their reproduction at Riverview High School.

Educators as Aggressive Cultural Brokers

All the educators mentioned the need to mentor and show students the way to a better life as part of their professional responsibility as teachers and administrators. Given their clarity in understanding the arbitrariness of social status and the asymmetry of power and economic relations, they shared their commitment to helping their low-SES students of color, typically depicted as low status and deficient by the greater society, to overcome their marginalization in order to better understand school culture. Although they did not use the term *cultural broker,* they all spoke about their role in helping students more effectively navigate school and mainstream cultures.

Mr. Broadbent seemed particularly preoccupied with the students' inability to see beyond their experiences in Riverview High School and the Rancho Nacional community. He spoke often of the need for students to see "how the other half lives" as motivation to do well in school. One of his greatest frustrations was his perceived inability to help students see their high school experience as a stepping-stone toward college or a well-paying job. He helped students see the bigger picture and assumed control over their learning process, which has been to teach them "the rules of the game" in very explicit ways. When teaching math and computer technology courses, for example, he often explicitly links the skills and knowledge bases taught with job opportunities in an effort to help students demystify "high-tech" jobs, see the immediate relevance of the classes, and view these employment opportunities as feasible for them.

Mr. Broadbent repeatedly spoke of the importance of not withholding information from students. Because his subject matter, math and computer technology, can easily be mystified, he made conscious efforts to teach the courses in accessible and student-friendly ways. He offered the Navy as a good example of an institution in which power is maintained by a select few precisely by withholding information from the majority. As part of his strategy for establishing honest, caring, and trusting relations with students, he highlighted his ability to communicate with his students:

> I think for the most part I've been able to talk to the kids. I don't talk down and I don't, like in the Navy where people were trying to hide something from you just so that they could have power, I tell the kids straight out what I think [and expect in class] and I don't hide anything from them.

He saw his job not only as imparting strong mathematics knowledge for immediate and later use, but also as mentoring students. He likened his role as teacher to his own father's role as parent: "I'm like a stepfather for many of my kids, especially the boys who don't have a dad at home." In this parent-mentor role he exhibited authentic concern and caring for students, but he recognized that simply caring for students is not enough. Teachers need to back up their caring with real action in the form of solid content instruction and honest teacher-student communication.

Mr. Tijerina also emphasized the importance of teachers' assuming a mentoring role for their students. In his opinion, most Riverview students were "good kids" who, because of their unfamiliarity with school culture, required teacher guidance in figuring out the rules of the game in school and beyond. He mentioned that students receive help not only from teachers but also from top-quality counselors at Riverview, who provide assistance and counseling in English, Spanish, and Tagalog. Their outstanding record of getting students into college has relied on their practice of demystifying college, for example, by taking students (and parents) on college visits and inviting former Riverview graduates to share their college experiences. Counselors also help students fill out applications, write statements of purpose, and practice interviewing strategies.

Mr. Tijerina shared his own techniques for helping students demystify school culture, such as talking students through the grading process. He explicitly discusses his class rules and even role-plays with students so that they clearly understand class academic and behavioral expectations. He is particularly explicit when it comes to grading procedure:

> I tell them, "You can see your grades whenever you want" — we have folders on all the students' work. I say, "Hey, you can see them whenever you want, you know, here's your total. I grade you on the curve or on a class scale, or on a standard scale, whichever is best for you." . . . I treat them like adults, [letting them know,] "I'm not trying to cheat you. I'm not trying to trick you."

He is adamant in his belief that as teachers of young people, particularly young people who don't understand the school culture clearly, it is important that teachers be open, sincere, and honest, as well as encouraging:

> [As a teacher], you're not here to put down students or to give them F's. You're not here to confuse them. You're not here to threaten them. You're not here to be dishonest with them. You're here to encourage them, to make them feel good, to help them, to help them go to college, to help them do all those good things — that's what you're here for.

The educators in this study articulated the importance of explicitly helping their students to better understand both school and societal mainstream cultures. They reported that in school they consciously work to help students effectively deal with both explicit and hidden aspects of the curriculum. In general, the educators claimed to treat their students as partners in the simultaneous acquisition of academic and social content and processes during learning experiences. These teachers mentioned the importance of demystifying grading and evaluation procedures and the college application process as strategies for helping their students become confident, empowered learners. They reported striving to provide their students with the practices and knowledge bases that many middle-class and more privileged parents regularly give their own children to ensure their competitive advantage, which are typically unavailable to working-class youth (Stanton-Salazar, Vásquez, & Mehan, 2000; Stanton-Salazar, 1997).

Implications for Teacher Education

It is evident that the four educators in the study understand at some level that teaching is not an apolitical undertaking. These educators question dominant-culture explanations of the existing social order. They also say they reject deficit ideologies and respect and value Mexicano/Latino and working-class cultures. They resist romanticizing White, middle-class, mainstream culture and reject uncritical assimilation as a goal for their students. Furthermore, because they also perceive that their students are not operating on an equal playing field, these teachers are willing to act as advocates and cultural brokers for their students. These findings suggest the power that teachers and other educators have as change agents to create more just and democratic schools and learning opportunities (see Friedman, this volume).

I believe that there are lessons to be learned from these experienced educators of language minority students. In this section, my comments focus on teacher education course work and practicum experiences. The target educators in the study questioned three common dominant-culture myths about the social order: meritocracy, deficit views of minority students, and uncritical, romanticized views of White mainstream culture. One potential implication includes incorporating into the teacher-preparation curriculum learning experiences that promote or, at a minimum, challenge prospective teachers to consider many of the counter-hegemonic beliefs articulated here.

It is therefore imperative that students in schools of education formally and explicitly study ideology to identify both dominant and counter-hegemonic ideologies. Areas for critical study include alternative explanations for the historical academic underachievement of minorities, meritocracy theories for explaining the existing social (dis)order, and assimilationist models for understanding current race and ethnic-group relations. I am suggesting that the teacher education curriculum (course work and practicum experiences) be deliberately designed and carried out to expose prospective teachers to a variety of ideological postures so that they can begin to perceive their own ideologies in relation to others' and critically examine the inequalities and injustices present in schools and in the society as a whole. While the end result, hopefully, will be the preparation of teachers who, like the educators in my study, are not afraid to assume counter-hegemonic positions in an effort to better understand and change current conditions of inequality in schools, the means for bringing about awareness of ideological and political issues can, and should, vary from program to program (see Friedman, this volume; Gebhard et al., this volume).

Additionally, the border-crossing experiences of these teachers, in which they personally experienced or witnessed someone else's subordination, should be replicated or simulated in course work and practicum experiences. These curricular experiences should be organized in ways that increase the likelihood that prospective teachers learn the arbitrariness of subordination and marginalization (similar to what the educators learned via their cultural border-crossing experiences). I am in no way suggesting that teacher educators brainwash their students to think in an ideologically uniform way, nor am I suggesting that prospective teachers be mistreated so they can experience subordination firsthand and thus grasp the concept of asymmetrical power relations.

Numerous teacher-preparation programs provide learning experiences with the potential to cross borders and help prospective teachers increase their political and ideological clarity (see Gebhard et al., this volume). For example, some teacher education programs require students learn a second language so that they can better communicate with language minority students (see Maxwell-Jolly & Gándara, this volume, for further discussion). Other programs require prospective teachers to visit, observe, and student teach in low-income and culturally diverse schools in order to learn about "cultural differences" (see Friedman, this volume; Gebhard et al., this volume). A few innovative programs actually go as far as presenting their students with opportunities to study abroad (e.g., Mexico, Spain) in order to develop bilingual and bicultural competency, as well as cross-cultural sensitivity. However, most teacher-preparation programs do not offer courses and practicum experiences that enable students to identify and understand the role of ideology (hegemonic and counter-hegemonic) in teaching (Bartolomé, 2000). Few programs are deliberately structured to ensure that prospective teachers study alternative ideological positions regarding the low social status and academic achievement of subordinated populations.

Despite good intentions on the part of teacher educators and the tremendous potential of many of these learning activities to increase political and ideological clarity, prospective teachers are generally left to make sense of these cross-cultural and cross-socioeconomic class experiences on their own. The unanticipated result of many of these learning experiences is that students emerge more bound to their unquestioned ethnocentric ideologies precisely because they go into these learning situations without explicitly identifying and questioning the ideological lenses that filter their perceptions. For example, I have had student teachers who completed part of their student teaching in Mexico. While there, they witnessed poverty and mistreatment of indigenous people and of the poor. A common reaction has been to denounce those practices in Mexico and to rejoice on their return to the United States, "where these things don't happen." A well-conceptualized teacher education program would foresee and plan for this type of student reaction. At a minimum, debriefing sessions designed to deal with dominant ideologies and resulting social hierarchies here and in Mexico would serve to clarify students' ideologies.

Interestingly, during cross-cultural learning experiences like those described above, I have observed a small minority of participating students undergoing, on their own, cultural border-crossings similar to those described by the four target educators in my study. Some prospective teachers have described how learning a second language placed them in a position of vulnerability that allowed them to see the world from the eyes of a second language learner. They felt the vulnerability in attempting to acquire a new language and understood the difficulty of learning a second language. Similarly, after working in low-income schools in this country and abroad, many students have approached me irate and indignant about the life and school conditions of low-SES, non-White students. Their anger and indignation

served as a catalyst that propelled them to question what they previously considered a fair social order and to take some type of action to
subvert the system and do right by their students.

The concept of subverting the system brings to mind a young
woman I worked with years ago in a public university teacher education program. Like many students in teacher education programs, this
young woman entered the program with unconscious beliefs about
the social order and status quo. With her unexamined ideological orientation and rather sheltered life experiences, she demonstrated little
comprehension of the very real inequities confronting low-SES language minority students and other subordinated students.

I distinctly remember her initial discomfort with Freire and other
critical pedagogues' writings and, in particular, her rejection of the notion that teachers of subordinated students often have to work in ways
that go against the grain in order to do right by the children. The young
woman voiced her disbelief and discomfort with this critical notion
and argued that it was not necessary for teachers to resort to subversive
behavior since the key function of schools, as institutions, is precisely
to help students. The student recalled her own experience as a middle-
class White public school student and maintained that school systems
were fair places and that students who failed to succeed did not take full
advantage of the opportunities afforded them. However, later in the
semester, while completing her student-teaching experience in a predominantly African American and Mexicano/Latino urban elementary
school, she told me one day that she had engaged in her first act of conscious resistance against school rules that seemed to hurt and further
subordinate her students. The urban elementary school in which she
did her student teaching had very few green areas; she found the lack of
grass and vegetation to be unacceptable for young children. One area of
the school had a small tree and grass area, but it was off-limits to students. On a particularly warm day, she decided to read a story to her
students in the shade of that small tree. Although she was well aware
that students were not allowed in this area, she consciously broke the
rule in order to, as she explained, provide her students with an optimal
storybook-reading experience. She angrily pointed out that White students in middle-class and suburban schools take for granted learning
opportunities such as sitting on the grass and having a story read to
them, whereas her children were prohibited from sitting on the only
patch of green available at the school! Although this student's act of

subversion was not particularly radical or extreme, it is precisely this outrage and sense of student advocacy — reflective of increased political and ideological clarity — I believe all teachers must possess in order to serve their students well.

Some preservice teachers, like the target educators in the study, surmise on their own that their previously held ideological explanations for the existing social order (e.g., that the social order is fair and based on ability and merit, that if people work hard enough they can overcome oppression) were not adequate for explaining the grave inequities, injustice, and subordination they witnessed. Unfortunately, in my experience as a teacher educator, most prospective teachers are not quite perceptive or flexible enough to consider alternative ideological explanations without assistance from teacher education personnel.

To help students consciously develop their own ideological postures, prospective teachers must be exposed to a course of study that includes the ideological and critical theoretical frameworks on dominance and subordination. As Howard (2000) explains, a constant challenge is to help prospective teachers, particularly White individuals, to identify and critically examine the status quo, especially in terms of race. He believes that it is important to understand social dominance history and current patterns in our society, as members of other societies also must understand their own particular brands of social dominance. His challenge to teacher educators and prospective teachers is that we become anti-domination and anti-racist without becoming anti-White. I believe that one possible solution for not confusing anti-domination with being anti-White is to ensure that theories and practices of social domination are examined in a comparative manner across course work and practical experiences. Many of my White prospective teachers lower their defenses and their feelings of guilt when confronted with literature that examines the experiences of subordinated groups around the world (Cummins, 1996; Lee, 1991; Ogbu, 1987, 1990, 1991; Shimahara & Konno, 1991). In addition, literature that chronicles the historical resistance of righteous White people to the oppression of non-White and poor people helps students understand that it is not a teacher's ethnicity or social-class standing but, rather, the teacher's political and ideological clarity and solidarity with students that can make the difference in the schooling of subordinated students.

Therefore, although the curriculum should reflect an anti-domination and not a blind anti-White stance, it is nevertheless crucial to deromanticize middle-class White culture in much the same way that this study's target educators do. In my language arts methods courses at the University of Massachusetts Boston, for example, we critically examine the phenomenon of minority student language and literacy underachievement in an ideological and social-dominance framework so as to better understand why and how subordinated cultural groups seldom do well in dominant-culture schools in any society. In addition, I use course readings that demystify the touted superiority of White middle-class students' language and literacy skills (see Courts, 1991, for an example of this type of critical reading). However, one should never stop at critiquing and deconstructing; one should also begin to address ways in which educators can work strategically to help students, much as this study's target teachers do via their work as cultural brokers, advocates, and mentors.

After the deconstruction process, teacher educators can share with prospective teachers instructional approaches, methods, and techniques and other "best" practices. The benefit of teaching methods within larger theoretical frameworks is that prospective teachers will begin to identify key underlying principles that render particular methods effective in particular sociocultural and political contexts (Bartolomé, 1994).

Concluding Thoughts

This study's results suggest that prospective and current teachers must begin to develop the ideological and political clarity that will guide them in denouncing a discriminatory school and classroom context so as to instruct, protect, and advocate for their students. According to Freire (1998a, 1998b), besides technical skills, teachers should also be equipped with a full understanding of what it means to have courage, that is, to denounce the inequities that directly cripple certain populations of students and effectively create psychologically harmless educational contexts. Freire challenges us to see through the dense fog of ideology and become courageous in our commitment to defend subordinated student populations, even when it is easier not to take a stand. Like the four realistic yet hopeful educators in this study, Freire reminds us of the importance of clearly identifying obstacles in order to come up with clear and realistic strategies for overcoming them:

> What keeps a person, a teacher able as a liberatory educator is the political clarity to understand the ideological manipulations that disconfirm human beings as such, the political clarity that would tell us that it is ethically wrong to allow human beings to be de-humanized. . . . One has to believe that if men and women created the ugly world that we are denouncing, then men and women can create a world that is less discriminating and more humane. (Freire, 1997, p. 315)

Notes

1. This chapter is expanded from Bartolomé and Balderrama (2001). Parts of the chapter are reprinted with permission from Columbia University Press.
2. "Political clarity" refers to the ongoing process by which individuals achieve ever-deepening consciousness of the sociopolitical and economic realities that shape their lives and their capacity to transform their lives. It also refers to the processes by which individuals come to understand better the possible linkages between macro-level political, economic, and social variables and subordinated groups' academic performance in the micro-level classroom. Thus, it invariably requires educators to struggle to link sociocultural structures and schooling. "Ideology" refers to the framework of thought used by members of a society to justify or rationalize an existing social (dis)order. "Ideological clarity" refers to the process by which individuals struggle to identify both the dominant society's explanations for the existing societal socioeconomic and political hierarchy and their own explanations. Ideological clarity requires that teachers' individual explanations be compared and contrasted with those presented by the dominant society. The juxtaposing of ideologies should force teachers to understand better if, when, and how their belief systems uncritically reflect those of the dominant society and support inequitable conditions in schools.
3. Subordinated minority groups are cultural groups that historically have been politically, socially, and economically disempowered in the greater society. Although individual members of these groups may not consider themselves subordinate in any manner to the White "mainstream," they nevertheless are members of a group that historically has been perceived and treated as subordinate and inferior by the dominant society.
4. "Mexicano/Latino" is used to describe the student population at Riverview High School. Historically and currently the Latino population has been of Mexican ancestry, but I want to acknowledge Latino students who are not of Mexican ancestry. The term *Mexicano* is used instead of the more common *Mexican American* or *Chicano* because a significant number of the Latino students are first-generation or immigrant Mexicanos.

5. "Border crosser" refers to an individual who is able and willing to develop empathy with the cultural "other" and to view as equal the values of the other while conscious of that cultural group's subordinated social status in the greater society. A border crosser will critically consider the positive cultural traits of the other and simultaneously critique the discriminatory practices of his or her own culture that may have contributed to the creation of the cultural other in the first place. In other words, a border crosser, while embracing the cultural other, must also divest from his or her cultural privilege, which in itself often functions as a cultural border. The educators in this sample crossed ethnic and socioeconomic cultural borders and came to the realization that some cultural groups, through no fault of their own, occupy positions of low social status and are marginalized and mistreated by members of higher status groups. This realization enabled the educators not only to empathize with the cultural other but also to take some form of action to equalize unequal power relations and arbitrary attributions of low status.

My definition of a cultural border crosser differs from more conventional definitions that merely focus on a person's ability to successfully interact and exist in an alternative social economic or ethnic cultural reality without dealing with the real issues of asymmetrical power relations and compromising their position of cultural and social privilege. This type of border crosser can travel the world and study the other in a detached and curious manner without ever recognizing that cultural groups occupy different positions of power and status and that many cultural perceptions and practices result from such power asymmetries. These types of ideologically and politically "blind" border crossers assume tourist or voyeur perspectives that are very much tainted by their unconscious deficit and White supremacist ideologies.

References

Bartolomé, L. I. (1994). Beyond the methods fetish: Toward a humanizing pedagogy. *Harvard Educational Review, 64,* 173–194.

Bartolomé, L. I. (1998). *The misteaching of academic discourses: The politics of language in the classroom.* Boulder, CO: Westview Press.

Bartolomé, L. I. (2000). Democratizing bilingualism: The role of critical teacher education. In Z. F. Beykont (Ed.), *Lifting every voice: Pedagogy and politics of bilingualism* (pp. 167–186). Cambridge, MA: Harvard Education Publishing Group.

Bartolomé, L. I., & Balderrama, M. (2001). The need for educators with political and ideological clarity: Providing our children with "the best." In M. Reyes & J. Halcón (Eds.), *The best for our children: Latina/Latino views on literacy* (pp. 48–65). New York: Teachers College Press.

Beauboeuf, T. (1997). *Politicized mothering among African American women teachers: A qualitative inquiry.* Unpublished doctoral dissertation, Harvard Graduate School of Education, Cambridge, MA.

Bloom, G. M. (1991). *The effects of speech style and skin color on bilingual teaching candidates' and bilingual teachers' attitudes toward Mexican American pupils.* Unpublished doctoral dissertation, Stanford University.

Courts, P. L. (1991). *Literacies and empowerment: The meaning makers.* South Hadley, MA: Bergin & Garvey.

Cummins, J. (1996). *Negotiating identities: Education for empowerment in a diverse society.* Ontario, CA: California Association of Bilingual Education.

Davis, K. A. (1995). Multicultural classrooms and cultural communities of teachers. *Teaching and Teacher Education, 11,* 553–563.

Farley, J. E. (2000). *Minority-majority relations* (4th ed.). Upper Saddle River, NJ: Prentice Hall.

Freire, P. (1998a). *Pedagogy of freedom: Ethics, democracy, and civic courage.* Lanham, MD: Rowman & Littlefield.

Freire, P. (1998b). *Teachers as cultural workers.* Boulder, CO: Westview Press.

Freire, P. (Ed.). (1997). *Mentoring the mentor: A critical dialogue with Paulo Freire.* New York: Peter Lang.

García, E. (1991). Effective instruction for language minority students: The teacher. *Boston University Journal of Education, 173,* 130–141.

Gomez, M. L. (1994). Teacher education reform and prospective teachers' perspectives on teaching "other people's children." *Teaching and Teacher Education, 10,* 319–334.

Gonzalves, R. (1996). *Resistance in the multicultural education classroom.* Unpublished manuscript, Harvard Graduate School of Education, Cambridge, MA.

Haberman, M. (1991). Can culture awareness be taught in teacher education programs? *Teacher Education, 4,* 25–31.

Howard, G. R. (2000). *We can't teach what we don't know: White teachers, multiracial schools.* New York.: Teachers College Press.

King, J. E. (1991). Dysconscious racism: Ideology, identity, and the miseducation of teachers. *Journal of Negro Education 60,* 133–157.

Ladson-Billings, G. (2000). Fighting for our lives: Preparing teachers to teach African American students. *Journal of Teacher Education, 51,* 206–214.

Lee, Y. (1991). Koreans in Japan and the United States. In M. A. Gibson & J. Ogbu, *Minority status and schooling* (pp. 131–167). New York: Garland.

Lucas, T., Henze, R., & Donato, R. (1990). Promoting the success of Latino language-minority students: An exploratory study of six high schools. *Harvard Educational Review, 60,* 315–340.

Macedo, D. (1994). *Literacies of power: What Americans are not allowed to know.* Boulder, CO: Westview Press.

McLeod, B. (1994). Introduction. In B. McLeod (Ed.), *Language and learning: Educating linguistically diverse students* (p. iv). Albany: State University of New York Press.

National Center for Education Statistics. (1992). *American Education at a glance.* Washington, DC: Office of Education Research and Improvement.

Nieto, S. (2000a). Placing equity front and center: Some thoughts on transforming teacher education for a new century. *Journal of Teacher Education, 51,* 180–187.

Nieto, S. (2000b). Bringing bilingual education out of the basement, and other imperatives for teacher education. In Z. F. Beykont (Ed.), *Lifting every voice: Pedagogy and politics of bilingualism* (pp. 187–208). Cambridge, MA: Harvard Education Publishing Group.

Ogbu, J. U. (1987). Variability in minority responses to schooling: Nonimmigrants vs. immigrants. In G. Spindler & L. Spindler (Eds.), *Interpretive ethnography of education* (pp. 255–278). Mahwah, NJ: Lawrence Erlbaum Associates.

Ogbu, J. (1990). Minority education in comparative perspective. *Journal of Negro Education, 59*, 45–55.

Ogbu, J. (1991). Low school performance as an adaptation. In M. Gibson & J. Ogbu (Eds.), *Minority status and schooling* (pp. 249–285). New York: Garland Press.

Shimahara, N. K., & Konno, T. (1991). Social mobility and education: Burakumin in Japan. In M. A. Gibson & J. U. Ogbu (Eds.), *Minority status and schooling* (pp. 327–353). New York: Garland.

Sleeter, C. (1992). Restructuring schools for multicultural education. *Journal of Teacher Education, 43*, 141–148.

Stanton-Salazar, R. D. (1997). A social capital framework for understanding the socialization of racial minority children and youths. *Harvard Educational Review, 67*, 1–40.

Stanton-Salazar, R. D., Vásquez, O. A., & Mehan, H. (2000). Re-engineering academic success through institutional support. In S. T. Gregory (Ed.), *The academic achievement of minority students: Perspectives, practices, and prescriptions* (pp. 213–247). Lanham, MD: University Press of America.

Zimpher, N. (1989). The RATE Project: A profile of teacher education students. *Journal of Teacher Education, 40*, 27–30.

What We Would Have Liked to Know: Preservice Teachers' Perspectives on Effective Teacher Preparation

AUDREY A. FRIEDMAN

I have had all the privileges of an upper-middle-class upbringing and a suburban public education. Why should they [the students] listen or care about what I have to say? (Lisa, a preservice teacher)

You know what's weird? The first impression [I had] when I walked in there. My high school [had been] all White, and it was like a weird awakening. I noticed that my environment had totally changed physically; there was a huge spectrum of colors around me and a huge spectrum of abilities in just one class. (Sandra, a preservice teacher)

Sandra's and Lisa's reflections echo many of my own feelings as a first-year teacher thirty years ago. Not much has changed; who I was then is not so different from who they are now. In the United States, our teaching force continues to be predominantly White, middle-class, monolingual, and unprepared to teach a diverse student population (see Maxwell-Jolly & Gándara, this volume, for a review). What has changed is the students we serve: today's public schools present an increasing diversity of culture, language, and ethnicity (Beykont, 2000). Teacher education programs must be redesigned to prepare preservice teachers to address the needs of all students (Gebhard, Austin, Nieto, & Willett, this volume; Nieto, 2000).

In this chapter I report on one such effort to improve the secondary teacher education program at the Lynch School of Education at

Boston College. This effort has been informed by our philosophy, the literature on effective teacher preparation, and an interview study that I conducted with eight preservice teachers enrolled in our program.[1] The interviews focused on our students' experiences teaching in their full-time placement in an urban high school. In these interviews I sought (a) to identify ways I can improve my practice as a teacher educator in order to prepare my students to excel as urban educators; and (b) to gather data and generate insights that will inform our teacher education program. Specifically, I asked two research questions: How effective is our teacher education program in preparing preservice teachers to meet the diverse needs of students in mainstream urban classrooms? What changes are needed to improve our program?

During several semistructured, open-ended interviews that extended throughout their sixteen-week placements, these preservice teachers identified the successes, failures, needs, and struggles they experienced. Our students' responses emphasized that neither their personal background nor their teacher education experiences adequately prepared them to teach effectively in this setting. They felt that they needed more training in meeting the needs of linguistically and academically diverse learners. They identified a significant lack of resources in the urban classrooms. They asked for support in learning how and when to negotiate a school culture that does not accommodate a diverse population. The interviews revealed all too clearly that there are areas in which we have yet to achieve our goals in our teacher preparation program. Although we are making headway, we still have a long way to go.

I first discuss the unique elements of our teacher preparation program in secondary education. I then introduce the eight preservice teachers in our program who participated in my exploratory study and the urban high school in which they were placed. Pervasive themes that emerged during the interviews concerning what is needed to improve their teacher preparation follow. In the final part of the chapter, I present changes in our teacher preparation program that have been implemented, modifications that are in progress, and recommendations for further change.

Our Teacher Education Program

The Lynch School of Education philosophy, mission statement, and course work seek to prepare teachers who will accommodate diversity, implement a constructivist approach to teaching and learning, collaborate with all stakeholders in the school community, inquire and reflect about practice, and teach for social justice. These five themes inform all teaching and learning, field experiences, and course work, including curriculum design, instructional content, assessment, and evaluation. Our students are predominantly monolingual, White, and middle- to upper-middle-class. In our program we rely on collaborative inquiry and reflective practice to prepare them to address the needs of a diverse student population and to effect instruction that provides equitable access to educational opportunity for all learners.

All preservice teachers in mainstream education, special education, and bilingual education experience similar course work; there are no substantially separate teacher preparation programs, except for the differentiation between elementary and secondary levels. All students in the secondary track complete a major in the content area, and also take classes from the course offerings on the social contexts of teaching and learning, standard and alternative assessment, methods of curriculum and instruction, issues of social policy and the purposes of schooling, and theory and pedagogy for teaching literacy to linguistically, academically, and culturally diverse learners within mainstream classrooms. Instruction in our classes does not focus on teaching the right or best method, but emphasizes the dynamic, reflective, and constructivist nature of teaching and learning. Essentially, preservice teachers learn that effective teaching is student centered. One methodology does not, should not, and will not fit all. Practices are promising at best, because a so-called best practice may not be best for all students. It is the needs of students that should dictate curricular and instructional decisions.

Before entering full-time student teaching, preservice teachers complete three prepracticum experiences. Each experience is ten weeks long in each of three settings: urban, suburban, and private or parochial. During each ten-week experience, our preservice teachers observe teaching in different classrooms, collaborate with different teachers, work with students, and prepare and deliver several lessons. An important element of our teacher education program is that during one of the three prepracticum placements, which is usually in an urban school, preservice teachers are required to observe, collaborate, prepare, and deliver instruction in a bilingual classroom regardless of their abilities in the native language of their students. They subsequently select one of the prepracticum experiences as the site for full-time student teaching. During their full-time student teaching experience, preservice teachers also participate in a weekly teacher-as-researcher seminar in which they inquire into practice and identify a classroom-based research question around teaching, learning, school culture, and so on. They use their classroom as a research site, collect and analyze data, and share their findings in a culminating paper and oral presentation.

Another unique element of our teacher education program is that at many of the placement schools, preservice teachers receive onsite mentoring from one of our faculty members. Onsite mentoring enhances collaboration and trust between preservice and veteran teachers at varied levels of expertise and experience, and thereby improves teaching and learning for everyone. For example, as an onsite mentor I collaborate with preservice teachers and teachers at one high school. Being familiar with the bilingual, special education, and mainstream education faculty and administrators, I am able to help our students understand, establish relationships, and cooperate with the staff more effectively. These trusting relationships enable preservice teachers to make use of effective teacher development tools such as videotaping of classroom instruction for reflection and discussion, and peer coaching. For example, on several occasions, preservice teachers identified a focus or question around teaching literacy in mainstream classrooms and then were videotaped. Cooperating teachers, the literacy specialists, other preservice teachers, the supervisor, and administrators viewed the tape, shared observations, provided feedback, and offered support. The preservice teacher reflected on and incorporated appropriate suggestions and a follow-up lesson was videotaped to note changes, or to elaborate further on the focus or question.

The combination of repeated practicum opportunities, field-site mentoring, and theoretical grounding in course work aims to provide the necessary supports to preservice teachers in our program.

The Preservice Teachers

The eight preservice teachers that I interviewed are similar to the majority of those who will enter the urban teaching force in the next decade: predominantly female, White, and from the suburbs. Alyssa, a preservice English teacher, was the only Latina (Mexican American) in a monolingual, White student body at her own upper-middle-class suburban Catholic high school. Alyssa learned Spanish as part of her high school curriculum. The social context of her college was similar to that of her high school: predominantly upper middle class and White. Alyssa originally wanted to become an elementary school-teacher, but during her first prepracticum she decided that "[she] did not want to spend the day holding children's hands and wiping their noses" and so she changed to secondary teaching. After working in the high school, she observed that "even in high school a teacher is a mother to children."

Sandra, a White preservice English teacher, attended an affluent, monolingual, suburban public high school that was 90 percent White and 10 percent Asian. The school had "pretty much everything you could ever want to have in a public high school." She became fluent in Spanish during high school. Her college environment was very similar to the high school she attended. Sandra enjoyed high school and English and so decided to teach English in a high school.

Jennifer, another White preservice English teacher, also attended an upper-middle-class, monolingual, suburban public high school; she remembers that there were three African American and a few Asian students in her school. Her college experience was also primarily White and affluent. Jennifer studied Spanish in high school; she speaks and understands Spanish but is not proficient. Jennifer always wanted to become a teacher, she says, because "I wanted to help students feel the same way I felt during my [own] education."

Lisa and Heather attended the same suburban high school. In-spired by her mother, a special education teacher and middle school administrator, Lisa was eager to fulfill her goal of becoming a high school English teacher. She had already completed a full-time preser-vice teaching experience in a suburban school, but she wanted addi-tional experience in teaching. She studied French in high school but does not have a good command of it; several times she commented that she wished she had studied Spanish so she could work more effec-tively with her Latino students. Heather is a White preservice Spanish teacher. She studied French and Spanish in high school and Spanish in college. Both Heather and Lisa noted that their peers in college were from predominantly well-to-do families.

John, a White preservice history teacher, attended an urban public high school during freshman year but then transferred to a private Catholic high school. He remarked that his mom got a job so she [could] send him to a Catholic school, "which was a much safer, nicer place to be." John enjoyed both settings, but observed that the Catholic school was more focused on preparing students for college. John also became fluent in Spanish and French in high school and was considering certification in bilingual education. He decided to teach because he "truly enjoyed learning and working with kids."

Mary, another White preservice history teacher, attended a large urban public high school. She observed that her high school was diverse: "50 percent Asian (Chinese, Korean, and Japanese), a few Latinos, and 50 percent White." Because of her passion for history, she had always wanted to be a teacher and identified teaching as a major early on in the program. "I had such a great experience with my [high school] teachers,"she said. "They were very motivational, very inspiring. And that kind of urged me [on]." She was not fluent in a foreign language.

Angela, a lawyer, entered teaching because of her work with juvenile offenders and social services. As a lawyer she had often felt powerless: "I wanted to have a direct impact on urban school reform — I wanted to do whatever I needed to do to give these kids a level playing field." Angela attended a White, monolingual, upper-middle-class suburban high school. She did not find college and graduate school much different in terms of student enrollment. She was not fluent in a second language.

Of the eight preservice teachers (seven White, one Latina, seven female, and one male), five had attended suburban public high schools, one had attended an urban high school, and two had attended suburban Catholic high schools. All but one had attended predominantly White high schools, and only one school had an ESL program. Of the eight, five majored in English, two in history, and one in Spanish. Four identified themselves as proficient in a second language.

These preservice teachers all fulfilled their student teaching requirement at the same urban high school. The racial and ethnic breakdown of the thousand-member student body is 50 percent African American and Black (Haitian, Cape Verdean, Jamaican, etc.), 34 percent Latino, 9 percent Asian, and 7 percent White. Fifty percent of the students come from other countries, including parts of Central and South America, the West Indies, Cape Verde, Cambodia, Laos, Thailand, China, Korea, Japan, Vietnam, and Russia, and 20 percent are in the bilingual program.[2]

Mainstream classrooms in this high school are diverse in every sense of the word. Each class, ranging from twenty-five to thirty students, includes at least three and as many as ten bilingual students. Classes also contain students who speak only English but whose parents are non-native English speakers. All classrooms are heterogeneous and inclusive, reflecting special education, linguistically different, and advanced learners. Each classroom has students who display different learning styles, needs, and attitudes; who espouse varied religious and social values and beliefs; who reflect several chronological and developmental ages; and who represent a variety of cultures, ethnicities, and languages. Some students care for siblings and extended family at the end of the school day, and others work three to five hours after school or participate in extracurricular activities. Still others are juvenile offenders and teenage mothers.

The Challenges Facing Preservice Teachers

The following pages elucidate themes that were common to the experiences of our eight preservice teachers in this urban placement. Many of these themes are well substantiated in the research about teaching in urban schools, with clear implications for teacher education. These common themes emphasize preservice teachers' need for systematic inquiry into their personal beliefs about students of color and their need for more culturally relevant pedagogy in accommodating the academic requirements of culturally and linguistically different learners. Another recurring theme is the significant lack of resources in urban classrooms. New themes also emerged. Our preservice teachers noted the need for more collaboration between faculty in the arts and sciences and those in education, not only for mediating theory and practice but also for developing and implementing instruction that prepares high school students to reach standards and pass the high-stakes standardized tests. Finally, preservice teachers recognized that school policy sometimes conflicts with effective teaching. They wished that they had more opportunities to think about the political culture of schools and to learn how and when to negotiate or subvert policies that undermine student learning.

Challenging Personal Beliefs

Upon placement in this urban high school, the student teachers quickly realized that they had not critically examined their own privi-

leges, nor their personal beliefs and prejudices about racially and linguistically different students. As Sandra explained:

> I knew that suburban kids, whether or not they wanted to be in
> school, worked to get A's and go to college. I believed all the stuff
> about urban kids: that they don't want to be here, they didn't
> care about graduating.

After three weeks in the classroom, Sandra was forced to acknowledge
her biases and preconceived notions about her students:

> It was like a weird awakening. I noticed that there were physically
> different colored people around me, but at the same time they
> were not that different. I walked into this classroom and I was
> teaching these kids that I had heard would not be doing quite as
> well [as White kids] or that would be giving me behavior prob-
> lems . . . and I noticed that at the top of the class are three Blacks.
> I wanted to hit myself for believing the myths I had heard or even
> created myself.

For Sandra, acknowledging her personal prejudices about urban students was humbling and revealing. She noted that she needed to tell
others that they had "to confront what they believed" and then "let it
go" in order to arrive at the truth so they "could do what was right in
the classroom."

Jennifer said that during her freshman year she wanted to teach in
an urban school because she believed that if she could succeed there,
she could succeed anywhere. Then she became fearful that the challenge would be too great. "I gave in to the stereotypes you hear about
urban schools [from] other people, the media, news about the violence
in some of the schools. I even heard that I should not respect kids, [I
should not] be overly polite, and that I should walk through the hall-
ways as if I had a purpose, otherwise it will be dangerous." On the job,
Jennifer learned that she had to weigh and consider others' truths
carefully. "I wanted to establish a relationship of trust with my students, but in order to do this, I need to know more and understand
about their lives, cultures, and beliefs."

Mary remembered that there were separate ESL classes for Asian
students at the high school from which she graduated and assumed
that students in all schools were not mainstreamed until they were

proficient in English. Her inference was that being bilingual is an impediment that requires special instruction. In her urban placement, she learned that many students were not fully proficient in English and that, although instruction was difficult, "Bilingual students brought richness to the already diverse classroom." These students were intelligent even though language issues masked their true abilities. Mary commented, "A lot of my students were brilliant, they just didn't have the skills or the motivation to do the work."

The issue of respect was brought up repeatedly among the eight preservice teachers. Lisa worried that students would not respect her because she was new, young, and White and came from a privileged background. All had anticipated that they would feel "out of place" in their classrooms and not be taken seriously for varied reasons. Lisa summarized: "I have had all the privileges of an upper-middle-class, upbringing and a suburban public education. Why should they [the students] listen or care about what I have to say?" After beginning her urban placement, Heather observed, "Being fair is the key, treating them equal every day, you know, starting new every day." Angela concluded, "Students know when you're afraid, know if you respect them, know if you care."

Firsthand experience forced these preservice teachers to examine, challenge, and change their own beliefs and prejudices. Identifying and confronting biased and preconceived notions about race, ethnicity, language, and ability was essential as they entered the field. They became more sympathetic to the issues and problems that students and teachers face in urban schools. They recognized that their expectations about urban classrooms were informed by experiences in predominantly monolingual, White suburban high schools, and by assumptions and biases that were racist and inaccurate. They also had never thought about the many privileges they enjoyed. Mary noted that although her history methods course demonstrated some ways to teach diverse students, she did not recognize her misconceptions about urban students until she began talking and listening to them and getting to know them. Confronting these issues of bias, personal privilege, and mistaken assumptions about students of color earlier in their teacher preparation would have prepared Mary and her peers for a more effective transition into urban schools and improved their ability to accommodate the cultural diversity of urban mainstream students.

Accommodating Diverse Learners

Linguistically Different Learners

> In working with Sam I realized that there was only so much I could do. I did not know the appropriate strategies to work with him. (Lisa)

Our preservice teachers often found themselves struggling to meet the academic needs of linguistically different learners. Jennifer's classes contained a large percentage of Asian students. She observed that they were not disruptive, but she never really knew if they understood what she was teaching. "I need more strategies for helping these kids learn. I sometimes find myself ignoring them because they are not disruptive, and this is wrong. I need strategies to help them." These preservice teachers requested more accurate ways to diagnose the specific academic needs of bilingual students in order to address them effectively.

These teachers also consistently voiced the need for teaching strategies and ways to modify instruction that facilitated learning for all students. Sam, an Asian student in Lisa's ninth-grade class, demonstrated limited English proficiency, but he received no additional language support. Because she could not understand him, communication was a major issue and he proved to be a real challenge for Lisa:

> I learned to listen very carefully to him and, much to my embarrassment, had to ask him to repeat himself numerous times. Students who spoke with Spanish accents were much easier to understand, but his dialect was really difficult. After a while, I understood the intonation and inflection of his dialect and I could tune in. I also learned to speak slowly and carefully.

There were other Asian students in the class, but none of them spoke Chinese. It was very clear to Lisa that Sam wanted to learn, to fit in, and to be part of the class, so she encouraged him at every opportunity. As she worked with him, she discovered he was very bright and found it was frustrating not to be able to help him. "He got a C–. I know he could have gotten a B+ if someone who knew the right strategies had worked with him."

Alyssa encountered similar issues in teaching writing to bilingual students in mainstream classrooms. She used Spanish during instruction, explaining difficult concepts in literature and the writing process to her Spanish-speaking students. Alyssa felt that conversing in Spanish enhanced students' understanding of the material, as well as their emotional comfort in the classroom. Since most of her bilingual students were from Spanish-speaking homes, her Spanish skills made teaching writing a bit easier for her, but it wasn't enough:

> I wished I were aware of new teaching strategies that have a strong focus on oral communication coupled with effective written communication, especially for those students who don't speak English at home. New teachers must accept that teaching writing is a long, hard process and that there will be much frustration and that success will take longer with bilingual and special education students.

Lisa found teaching her Latino students academic English writing challenging: "In their expository writing, I noticed a great deal of repetition of ideas and lots of run-on sentences. I sensed that they repeated ideas and phrases because they were not confident in expressing other thoughts they might have had."

Heather's beginning Spanish classes spoke Haitian Creole or several dialects of Spanish. She suggested that potential foreign language teachers should learn how to teach a foreign language to students who are bilingual. She complained that methods courses in foreign language teaching never distinguished between different types of learners. She recognized her own personal need for additional training in teaching foreign languages to non-native English speakers.

Heather and the other preservice teachers talked about feeling uncomfortable at first when students spoke in their native language during class. After a while they acknowledged that linguistically different students must feel similarly when they hear proficient English speakers converse. They recognized that the shoe was on the other foot and that speaking in one's own language is necessary for comfort and even survival in an environment that demands proficiency in a non-native language. All agreed that proficiency in more than one language is an advantage for students and teachers alike.

The student teachers who spoke Spanish found that fluency in Spanish was invaluable in their placement. They emphasized the need for a language requirement in their undergraduate preparation. Several suggested that a Spanish-English dictionary should be included in the survival kit for urban high school teachers, or at least "a sheet of common phrases or how-to's in Spanish and Haitian Creole and other languages." Preservice teachers proficient in Spanish used it daily in their classrooms, finding that it was invaluable not only in facilitating instruction but also in establishing a personal connection with their students. They wished that they could communicate with students from other language backgrounds as well.

Academically Diverse Learners

Preservice teachers were discouraged by the range of students' academic skills and felt unprepared to modify instruction to promote learning for all students. Lisa noted, "We all took courses like 'Working with Diverse Learners' and 'Reading in the Content Area,' but these are not enough. I would have liked to learn more about everyday learning problems I see in my classroom." Frustrated, Heather observed, "Here [in college] we learn how to teach to the perfect classroom, the perfect student. I need to know how to teach in this world." One common concern was how to teach writing across the curriculum. In Massachusetts, state-mandated standardized tests require that students demonstrate ability in writing five-paragraph expository essays in response to open-ended questions. Students are required to read and analyze text and synthesize a reasonably articulate response in writing in order to graduate with an academic diploma.

John was astounded by the low level of writing skills many of his students demonstrated in history classes. He found himself researching ways to teach students how to write via graphic organizers and process writing strategies, and by providing extensive practice in a variety of writing tasks. A good writer himself, he believed that "there is plenty of room for writing in history class. I gave them writing assignments where they expressed their point of view, tasks where they assumed the persona of any person living during World War I and wrote a letter about how the war affected their life, where they evaluated the Progressive Era and wrote a five-paragraph expository essay about the Harlem Renaissance." John developed rubrics that articulated the expectations and criteria for evaluating each writing assignment, required and responded to multiple student drafts, and constantly reinforced the need to speak and write evaluatively. Students complained about how they had to do *it* (writing essays) in their English classes. Chuckling, he responded, "You have to do *it* in history class *too*." He wished he had received far more practice and strategies for teaching writing. Alyssa also expressed the need for better strategies in teaching writing: "Students can tell me orally but they cannot or choose not to write things down." She noted that bilingual students presented language problems, native English speakers had writing problems, and advanced students complained about multiple drafts of essays. In sum, teaching writing "was a constant struggle" for her.

Another area of concern for these preservice teachers involved assessment and identification of the varied learning challenges of their students. All of the teachers agreed that they were not prepared to diagnose and effectively instruct students who spoke English as a second language and had special learning needs:

> I can't really pick out a special needs student here. When they're integrated into a classroom, I don't know how to differentiate between a lazy student, a bilingual student, a special needs student, or a student who is bilingual and has special needs. (Heather)

None of the eight teachers had taken any courses on alternative assessment and instruction for bilingual learners and they believed that systematic training would have enhanced their instruction. They requested course work and training in instructional strategies that would help them more effectively enable diverse students to understand the general curriculum and perform at statewide standards. Lisa commented that her friends who were elementary education majors had room for additional course work and could even minor in special education. Course work for secondary education majors included a complete major in the content area, which used up electives for additional study in special education. Disconcerted, Lisa said, "I'm definitely not equipped to deal with a lot of the learning disabilities in the classroom." These teachers consistently identified a need for more effective assessment strategies for diagnosing learning problems and better strategies for mediating instruction for all students; one or two courses is not enough.

The preservice teachers I interviewed spoke of the pressure that high-stakes testing and standards-based educational reform placed on their instruction. They all observed that they had not received appropriate preparation in their content areas. Although student teachers valued the variety and flexibility allowed in the content courses they studied, they noted that course work generally did not parallel mandated high school curriculum. It wasn't until they had completed their prepracticum experiences that these preservice teachers had a clearer idea of the specific curriculum they would need to implement. They thought that, in addition to being uninformed about standards-based curricula, arts and sciences faculty teaching undergraduate content courses were not informed about teaching diverse students in high school.

Our student teachers voiced a need for more culturally relevant content. Enhanced and earlier awareness about urban teachers' need for curricula relevant to culturally diverse and linguistically different learners would have prompted them to take different courses in their undergraduate preparation. History teachers identified gaps in American and ancient history. English teachers wished they had taken more courses in the teaching of multicultural literature. As Heather explained:

> Most of the kids here are Latino. I took a lot of Spanish literature. I am only now taking twentieth century Latin American literature [so] that I can relate and make that real connection to students. If I had known, then I would have taken Latin American literature and said, "Hey, this guy is from your country. You should know him. Let's study him." And make that real connection.

All these teachers spent extra time researching at the college library or downloading information about authors, literary periods, related curricula, primary sources, and other useful documents that were not part of their undergraduate education but were relevant to instruction. A broader range of culturally relevant course work that was more congruent with school curriculum would have improved their preparation.

A Lack of Resources

These preservice teachers were disheartened by the lack of certain human resources at this urban high school: most veteran teachers in this school were not prepared to address their students' academic needs effectively. "My inability to serve these kids [bilingual students] effectively has really bothered me, but what is more troublesome is that I think back and [realize that] students like Sam and the Latino students in my class had no one they could go to for help. I know with the correct help, all of them would have done so much better in my English classes," said Lisa. This shortage was partly due to inadequate teacher preparation. Reflecting back on their own course work, Angela, Jennifer, and Alyssa argued that there was too much of "let's just talk about theoretical cases and theoretical ideas," and "the theory of schools is very different from the reality of schools," and that all teachers (veteran and novice teachers alike) needed skills to work effectively with bilingual learners.

Another reason for the inadequacy was the current hiring practices. In general, literacy and reading specialists at their site did not have particular training in addressing the needs of bilingual learners and therefore could not provide support to mainstream teachers. Conversely, the expertise of those who did have the skills and experience (bilingual and ESL teachers) was not readily available because of the way common planning time was organized in the school. Bilingual teachers often met separately from the mainstream teachers. It seemed as if the school system was only beginning to change their hiring practices in recognition of the need for specialists and teachers that are trained and knowledgeable in working with diverse populations in general and teaching bilingual students in mainstream classrooms in particular.

The student teachers also complained about the scarcity and quality of material resources at this urban high school. Heather commented that there was no language laboratory for high school students to hear other people or themselves speaking Spanish:

> In Spanish methods class, I learned to do all these wonderful things, but obviously, if you don't have them [resources], you can't use them.

At the end of her experience, Heather remarked that what was most attractive about suburban schools were the resources. "I feel like I could do a better job if I had a proper language lab, proper books and materials for teaching a foreign language." Sandra observed, "It's not the teaching that's difficult, but it is the resources, not being able to get a smaller paperback versus a textbook, or not even to be able to get a student a textbook. I think that really hurts the students."

Textbook quality and availability was another problem. John was "shocked" by the quality of the history textbooks. Some of the history books that John had to use were outdated, but he found that even the newer texts were poorly organized and contained incorrect, confusing, and ethnocentric historical information. John gathered primary source documents that related to the historical periods and people that they were studying. He felt strongly that higher quality and a greater variety of texts needed to be used in teaching history in order to show varied perspectives on the same subject. Angela and Alyssa were frustrated that students could not take home textbooks and that often there were not enough classroom sets of textbooks or paperback books. Heather searched for resources she could use to augment her classroom:

> Even the educational resource library at school [the university] had only a small section that dealt with foreign language teaching. I scrounged every corner of the high school and found stuff from the seventies. Fortunately, teachers shared newer materials with me that they had bought themselves.

Lisa, Alyssa, Angela, Jennifer, John, and Heather spent hours on the Internet finding and downloading biographical, historical, and contextual information about authors, periods, and works they were teaching. Our preservice teachers experienced firsthand how urban students were hurt by the scarcity and poor quality of reading materials available to them. They responded creatively by working extra hours to find teaching resources that would enrich their students' learning.

Negotiating the School Rules

Preservice teachers spoke at length about how the reality of their urban school sometimes demanded teacher subversion and disobedience so they could do what was right for their students. Jennifer, John, Lisa, Sandra, Alyssa, and Mary shared numerous incidents in which they learned to bend or even break the school rules because official school policies had conflicted with effective teaching. They tried to handle disruptive students on their own, even though they knew that the official policy required more serious disciplinary consequences for students' misbehavior.

Heather learned to subvert the system by not reporting students when they acted out or did not complete their work. She entered her placement assuming that "I had to be strict and totally in control." After a while, however, she engaged in a battle for control that resulted in a cycle of disruption, detention, in-house suspension, missed work, and more disruption. "I learned to be more open and fair with students. I am still strict but a bit more relaxed," Alyssa commented. "When students are physically in the classroom, there is an opportunity for them to learn. On suspension, in a lock-up somewhere or at home, there is no chance." Although both Heather and Alyssa voiced concern about their actions that had subverted school policies, they believed that keeping their students in class was the only way they could help students for whom the public school could not provide effective alternative support.

These student teachers learned quickly that urban schools are not willing to serve all students, especially those who move in and out of the criminal justice system. Jennifer perceived that school policy inadvertently facilitated recidivism. When a paroled bilingual student re-entered the classroom from a detention center, school disciplinary policy held him to more rigorous standards. Failure to pass in homework, tardiness, and even minimally disruptive behavior required her to "write him up":

> I learned to be more tolerant because writing him up was counterproductive. Writing him up resulted in in-house suspension or return to prison. I needed him to be in class learning. It was a vicious cycle. He was in prison because somewhere down the line he didn't get what he needed.

On one such occasion, another paroled bilingual student was not completing his work and was being disruptive in class. When Jennifer reminded him that he would fail if he didn't change his behavior, he pleaded with her that every course failure would add three months to his parole. She made a deal that if he cooperated in class, came prepared, completed missing assignments, and tried to learn, he would pass. The next day he came in prepared with homework but displayed inappropriate behavior. She reminded him about the deal. When she recounted what he had said in class to her cooperating teacher, the teacher warned her that she must report the incident. "I agonized about this all day. I did not want to report him and decided not to. I called his mother and told her about the deal we had made. He came to class the next day prepared, [with] his work completed." By the end of the day, the dean of discipline had approached her and required her to write up the incident. "I started to cry. I had begun to establish a relationship of trust [with the student] and now this." The dean was supportive but reminded her that school policy enforced strict disciplinary action for students who had been incarcerated. "I had no choice and wished I had never confided in my cooperating teacher. The next day the student came to my class, angry and hostile, reminding me that I had broken a promise. I made a deal and did not keep my end of the bargain. He was right and I was ashamed. Next time, I would keep quiet." Several days later, Jennifer learned that this incident had triggered several others and that deporting the student to the Dominican

Republic was the next step. The realities of schools sometimes demanded that teachers subvert the system. These eight teachers wished that teacher preparation had taught them about the culture of schools and effective ways to negotiate within that culture when school policies conflict with effective teaching and learning.

Changes in Our Teacher Education Program

The challenge of teacher preparation programs is to prepare a predominantly White, female, middle-class population to teach a racially, culturally, and linguistically diverse population of students (Chisolm, 1994; Weiner, 1993, 1999; Zeichner, 1993). At the Lynch School of Education, we take this challenge seriously. Based on the results of this exploratory study, our teacher education program has begun to make changes to enhance preservice teachers' ability to provide effective instruction for diverse learners in mainstream classrooms.

In line with the literature, the comments of the eight preservice teachers in my study revealed that they found urban teaching difficult (Bartolomé, this volume; Faltis, 2001; Gomez, 1993; Gonzalez & Darling-Hammond, 1997; Nevarez, Sanford, & Parker, 1997; Weiner, 1993, 1999). As Sandra observed, the first impression of her classroom was very different from what she had experienced in her own high school and college. She and her peers initially felt out of place. In addition to the usual feelings of inadequacy associated with being novice teachers, they realized that they held unexamined assumptions and beliefs about students of color.

As indicated in previous studies, successful teaching in urban schools depended in part on how effectively teachers make sense of their own beliefs, predispositions, and attitudes about student diversity in their classrooms and unlearn their biases about particular groups of students (Bartolomé, this volume; Cochran-Smith, 2000; Gebhard et al., this volume; Ladson-Billings, 1999; Nieto, 2000; Shultz, Neyhart, & Reck, 1996). Effective teachers constantly reflect on and mediate acquired knowledge about multicultural issues with the realities of these schools (Ahlquist, 1991; Brisk, 1998; Carlson, 1992; Futrell & Witty, 1997; Nieto & Rolon, 1997). These preservice teachers concurred that confronting their own prejudices, being culturally responsive, and doing what is right for students were essential factors in becoming good teachers in urban classrooms.

As a response to preservice teachers' need to systematically and critically examine personal beliefs about race, culture, and language, our faculty developed a pilot program in cooperation with the field placement office. In both the undergraduate and graduate teacher education program at Boston College, preservice teachers are now being exposed early on to strategies for challenging beliefs about diversity, in addition to inquiry and reflective practice. During the freshman development seminar and three prepracticum experiences in the sophomore and junior years, preservice teachers examine the five themes integral to our school's educational mission and philosophy and identify their own biases and beliefs about diverse students. Readings and seminar content draw from work on culturally relevant pedagogy and critical theory, as well as methodologies of qualitative research. Students learn to question their assumptions about diversity and to differentiate between observations, assumptions, inferences, and value judgments. Through focused journal entries related to classroom observations and experiences, they are forced to question observations they make about their own students, teachers, and school culture, and to consider how their predominantly White experiences strongly color their assumptions, inferences, and value judgments about mainstream students in urban classrooms.

In breakout groups facilitated by on-site supervisors and experienced teachers, preservice teachers discuss classroom experiences as they relate to their readings, question and challenge personal and external knowledge claims, and share problems and promising strategies about teaching and learning. During the full-time student teaching experience, preservice teachers present a fully developed research project and presentation around a research question framed in the context of their classroom. This project is the culminating event that demonstrates synthesis and implementation of the five themes of our educational philosophy and mission, an investigation of school culture, and an understanding of the social, political, and cultural issues that influence effective instruction. Journal entries, final self-evaluations, and school culture projects collected during the first semester of the pilot program have demonstrated how preservice teachers have challenged personal biases about race, culture, and linguistic diversity. Our hope is that these experiences will help our students examine and discard preconceived notions that urban students are not interested in succeeding in school or in going to college and urge them to have high academic expectations for students of color. We are continuing to search for additional and more effective means of ensuring that all of our students are assisted in examining and challenging their personal beliefs and attitudes as part of their teacher preparation at Boston College.

As high-stakes testing and standards-based educational reform loom large in public education, the focus on teaching content may demand more prescribed preparation in the content-area for secondary school teachers. Preservice teachers in the study felt unprepared to teach because the content courses that they had taken did not parallel the prescribed curriculum. They felt that a closer collaboration between faculty in the arts and sciences and in education would have mediated content knowledge and teaching practice. Mary remarked, "It would have been nice to have a history person to give you a real in-depth understanding of the content, side-by-side with a methods person." Our students noted that "arts and sciences faculty are not informed about teaching in urban schools or schools in general" and that collaboration between faculty of education and of arts and sciences would have provided better guidance on the variety of courses needed to become effective teachers of diverse student populations.

Taking into consideration their recommendation, we are now piloting a course entitled "Theory and Pedagogy in the English Language Arts Classroom" that was codeveloped and is cotaught by arts and science and education faculty. The goal of the course is to help preservice teachers develop curriculum and instruction that helps bilingual and special education students understand and apply different kinds of formal literary criticism to selected canon and multicultural literature. The English department has also added several courses that emphasize the teaching of specific content rather than just the content itself to both our undergraduate and graduate students. Similar collaborations are developing among the history, world language, and science departments at the Lynch School of Education.

Our eight preservice teachers consistently voiced the need for more strategies to meet the needs of linguistically diverse learners in their classrooms. They were discouraged by their own and their colleagues' lack of knowledge and skills in working with bilingual learners. Lisa remarked that systematic training in providing effective instruction to linguistically different learners would have dramatically affected how she worked with Sam. "I know if I had the right strategies, I could have helped him become a better writer and receive better grades." To address these needs and suggestions, our teacher education program is developing a minor in bilingual/ESL education as an option for all preservice teachers in our program. Although issues in bilingual education had been integrated into methods courses, we realized that a systematic and extended study of theory and pedagogy was needed for students interested in teaching in urban and changing suburban environments. A minor in bilingual education will provide focused and additional course work for students interested in honing their skills as they develop into more effective urban practitioners.

Change is also occurring at the placement site in response to our students' requests. During weekly planning meetings, mainstream, special education, bilingual education, and college faculty are sharing promising practices and strategies that enhance teaching and learning for English language learners and special needs students. Bilingual specialists are meeting with mainstream classroom teachers instead of meeting separately. In addition, we are looking at student work to help us not only develop more effective teaching strategies but also more appropriate assessments and evaluation tools. These improved models and opportunities for collaboration among veteran and novice teachers at the field site are important factors in the quality of preservice preparation that our students receive.

As faculty members at the Lynch School of Education, we have generated the changes detailed above based on our own observations and knowledge of the literature and on the responses of the students I interviewed. We have been encouraged by the apparent effectiveness of much of our program. Our preservice teachers' demonstrated ability to identify problems in their classrooms and teaching as well as gaps in their professional preparation and skills spurred us to institute important changes, but also made us proud of the extent to which our students had learned and could exercise the essential teacher skills of critical reflection on self, classroom context, and classroom practice. We were also encouraged by the resourcefulness of our students, for example, when they identified a lack of adequate texts and materials in their classrooms, they took the initiative, exercised professional responsibility, and searched for these items.

More Change Is Needed

As individuals and as faculty members we continue to consider such questions as whether to require preservice teachers to learn a second language and how best to assist preservice teachers in learning to negotiate school cultures and advocate for students. Our preservice teachers found even minimal proficiency in Spanish invaluable as they developed and implemented instruction for mainstream classrooms; they were glad that they had continued to study Spanish in college and suggested that a second language be required in their preparation as teachers. Alyssa remarked that knowing Spanish immediately elicited respect from mainstreamed Latino students. It showed that she not only understood the language difficulties they experienced, but that she also valued their language and admired their bilingual ability. Learning a second language enhances teachers' understanding of the challenges faced by bilingual learners and provides preservice teachers with another meaningful connection to the students they teach. Proficiency in a second language can enhance teacher effectiveness in mainstream classrooms, and I believe should be required of teachers who wish to teach in public schools.

Teaching is a political endeavor (Ahlquist, 1991; Banks, 1993; Delpit, 1995, 1998; Bartolomé, 2000; Cochran-Smith, 2000; Freire, 1998; Irvine, 1991; Macedo, 1994; Ladson-Billings, 1994, 1995, 1999, 2000; Stanton-Salazar, 1997). Our preservice teachers were confronted with personal experiences that illuminated how unaccommodating public schools were in meeting the needs of the students they served. Reflection and study of the sociopolitical structure of schools and school systems is essential in helping preservice teachers negotiate the political context of field placements. These preservice teachers shared numerous incidents during which they learned to bend or even break the rules and handle disruptive students on their own even though they knew student behaviors called for more serious consequences. Although they voiced concern about their actions, these preservice teachers believed that this was the only way they could help students for whom the public schools could not provide effective alternatives. The realities of schools sometimes demanded teacher subversion and disobedience. I believe that it is my responsibility to assist preservice teachers as they encounter and learn to understand and negotiate school cultures and the difficult ethical questions that confront teachers in urban schools every day. In teaching for social justice, teacher subversion, teacher advocacy, and teacher activism are essential (Bartolomé, 2000, this volume; Lima, 2000). Preservice teachers need to learn how to be subversive, which rules to break and when. They need to develop confidence to teach "against the grain" (Cochran-Smith, 2000), even when colleagues and the status quo regard such action as inappropriate.

Concluding Thoughts

For the past three decades, I have witnessed and experienced the challenges, struggles, and obstacles of urban classroom teaching that are illuminated by the voices of these preservice teachers. Neither they now, nor I thirty years ago, were adequately prepared for the reality of teaching in urban schools. There is so much we would have liked to know before stepping into these classrooms. Urban schools offer rigorous challenges: students come from a variety of cultural, ethnic, and socioeconomic backgrounds; many speak English as a second or even a third language; classrooms pose a plethora of academic and learning challenges; school policies are rigid and unaccommodating; material resources are unavailable; teachers are not prepared to teach the diverse student body. However, I believe that urban schools are places where teachers can (and do) make a difference. Urban schools offer teacher educators a context to intervene for educational equity and social justice. As a teacher educator, I am sustained by the belief that if I can change one preservice teacher's perception of culturally or linguistically different learners and nurture his or her development as a culturally and linguistically competent professional, then I will have made a significant difference in the lives of urban students.

Notes

1. This research was funded by a Title II Grant: The Massachusetts Coalition for Teacher Quality and Student Achievement. The Coalition involves seven school/college/community partnerships located in Boston, Springfield, and Worcester, Massachusetts, whose goal is to enhance teacher preparation and student achievement in urban schools.
2. This high school has declared that its mission is to provide all students with the highest-quality education, one focused on effective oral and written communication in more than one language and on problem-solving. The school culture emphasizes enhancing self-esteem and developing respect for other individuals and cultures in a climate that is conducive to learning. A primary goal of the school is to prepare students for postsecondary education, the world of work, and the responsibilities of adults in a diverse society. Within the high school there are five smaller learning communities: Business and Technology; Health

Professions; Law, Government, and Public Service; Media, Arts, and Communication; and the Grade Nine Academy. Each community focuses on a career theme that provides a context for competency and learning. The Grade Nine Academy is a rigorous academic program that facilitates the successful transition from middle school to high school. Like most urban public schools, this school has identified literacy in English language arts and mathematics as the primary focus of instruction. The Instructional Leadership Team is composed of at least one teacher per grade, bilingual, literacy, and special education specialists, the headmaster, assistant headmasters, guidance counselor, and a university partner. The ILT has articulated "revising instruction to enhance the performance of all students" as the major goal of the team's yearly planning, collaboration, and professional development. As a leadership team, participants share promising practices that improve literacy instruction and use evaluative assessment data to inform and revise instructional goals throughout the year. Pathway facilitators share promising practices with colleagues during weekly meetings, who then integrate them into their own instruction. The school and its faculty are committed to helping all children learn.

References

Ahlquist, R. (1991). Position and imposition: Power relations in a multicultural foundations class. *Journal of Negro Education, 60,* 158–169.

Banks, C. M. (1993). Restructuring schools for equity: What we have learned in two decades. *Phi Delta Kappan, 75,* 42–48.

Bartolomé, L. I. (2000). Democratizing bilingualism: The role of critical teacher education. In Z. F. Beykont (Ed.), *Lifting every voice: Pedagogy and politics of bilingualism* (pp. 167–187). Cambridge, MA: Harvard Education Publishing Group.

Beykont, Z. F. (2000). Introduction. In Z. F. Beykont (Ed.), *Lifting every voice: Pedagogy and politics of bilingualism* (pp. vii–xix). Cambridge, MA: Harvard Education Publishing Group.

Brisk, M. E. (1998). *Bilingual education: From compensatory to quality schooling.* Mahwah, NJ: Erlbaum Associates.

Carlson, D. (1992). *Teachers and crisis: Urban school reform and teachers' work culture.* New York: Routledge.

Chisolm, I. (1994). Preparing teachers for multicultural classrooms. *Journal of Educational Issues of Language Minority Students, 14,* 43–67.

Cochran-Smith, M. (2000). Blind vision: Unlearning racism in teacher education. *Harvard Educational Review, 70,* 157–190.

Delpit, L. (1988). The silenced dialogue: Power and pedagogy in teaching other people's children. *Harvard Educational Review, 58,* 280–298.

Delpit, L. (1995). *Other people's children: Cultural conflict in the classroom.* New York: New Press.

Faltis, C. J. (2001). *Joinfostering: Teaching and learning in multilingual classrooms.* Upper Saddle River, NJ: Merrill Prentice-Hall.

Freire, P. (1998). *Pedagogy of freedom: Ethics, democracy, and civic courage.* Lanham, MD: Rowman & Littlefield.

Futrell, M., & Witty, E. (1997). Preparation and professional development of teachers for culturally diverse schools: Perspectives from the standards movement.
In J. J. Irvine (Ed.), *Critical knowledge for diverse teachers and learners* (pp. 189–
216). Washington, DC: AACTE Publications.

Gomez, M. L. (1993). Prospective teachers' perspectives on teaching diverse children: A review with implications for teacher education and practice. *Journal of
Negro Education, 62,* 459–474.

Gonzáles, J. M., & Darling-Hammond, L. (1997). *New concepts for new challenges:
Professional development for teachers of immigrant youth.* McHenry, IL: Center for
Applied Linguistics and Delta Systems.

Irvine, J. J. (1991). Beyond role models: An examination of cultural influences on
the pedagogical perspectives of Black teachers. *Peabody Journal of Education,*
6(4), 51–63.

Ladson-Billings, G. (1994). *The dreamkeepers: Successful teachers of African-American
children.* San Francisco, CA: Jossey-Bass.

Ladson-Billings, G. (1995). Toward a theory of culturally relevant pedagogy. *American Educational Research Journal, 32,* 465–591.

Ladson-Billings, G. J. (1999). Preparing teachers for diverse student populations: A
critical race theory perspective. In A. Iran-Nejad & P. D. Pearson (Eds.), *Review
of research in education* (vol. 24, pp. 247–261). Washington, DC: American Educational Research Association.

Ladson-Billings, G. (2000). Fighting for our lives: Preparing teachers to teach African American students. *Journal of Teacher Education, 51,* 206–214.

Macedo, D. (1994). *Literacies of power: What Americans are not allowed to know.* Boulder, CO: Westview Press.

Nevarez, A., Sanford, J., & Parker, L. (1997). Do the right thing: Transformative
multicultural education in teacher preparation. *Journal for a Just and Caring Education, 3,* 160–179.

Nieto, S. (2000). Bringing bilingual education out of the basement, and other imperatives for teacher education. In Z. F. Beykont (Ed.), *Lifting every voice: Pedagogy and politics of bilingualism* (pp. 187–208). Cambridge, MA: Harvard
Educational Publishing Group.

Nieto, S., & Rolon, C. (1997). Preparation and professional development of teachers: A perspective from two Latinas. In J. J. Irvine (Ed.), *Critical knowledge for diverse teachers and learners* (pp. 89–124). Washington, DC: AACTE Publications.

Shultz, E. L., Neyhart, T. K., & Reck, U. M. (1996). Swimming against the tide: A
study of prospective teachers' attitudes regarding cultural diversity and urban
teaching. *Western Journal of Black Studies, 20,* 1–7.

Stanton-Salazar, R. D. (1997). A social capital framework for understanding the socialization of racial minority children and youths. *Harvard Educational Review,
67,* 1–40.

Weiner, L. (1993). *Preparing teachers for urban schools: Lessons from thirty years of
school reform.* New York: Teachers College Press.

Weiner, L. (1999). *Urban teaching.* New York: Teachers College Press.

Zeichner, K. (1993). *Educating teachers for diversity: NCTRL special report.* East Lan-
sing, MI: National Center for Research of Teacher Learning.

"You Can't Step on Someone Else's Words": Preparing All Teachers to Teach Language Minority Students

MEG GEBHARD, THERESA AUSTIN, SONIA NIETO, AND JERRI WILLETT

At [my undergraduate college], I was in the majority. That was mostly who was in the program: White women who were native speakers of English. [But] in the [BEM] summer program, out of thirty students, there were a handful of native English speakers. And no matter what language you brought to the program, you were constantly having to do things outside your language. It really made me relate to the experience of what it must be like to be a second language learner in a classroom. Every day, I came home with language exhaustion: just doing exercises and activities in other languages for even part of the day made me realize how challenging it must be. I'd had that feeling of language exhaustion from other experiences, but being in the program that summer increased my respect for people with multiple languages. When I went into the classroom in September, I was very sensitive to that feeling of language exhaustion. (Mary Cowhey)

Mary Cowhey is a first- and second-grade "mainstream" teacher in a combined bilingual/monolingual English classroom. At the time she was interviewed, she was also a master's student in the Bilingual/ESL/Multicultural Education (BEM) Practitioner Program in the School of Education at the University of Massachusetts Amherst. Mary's sentiments capture the essence of what the BEM faculty members want all teachers to know and understand about their work with language minority students. In our program, we grapple with such questions as: "What is the responsibility of schools and colleges of education that prepare teachers to work with students who are native speakers of languages other than English?" "What should all teachers, whether they plan to work in second language settings or not, know about language minority students?" "How can all teacher education programs, not just those that focus on language minority students, provide all prospective teachers with the skills and experiences they need to be prepared for the tremendous linguistic and cultural diversity they are bound to encounter in their classrooms?"

In this chapter, we report on the BEM Practitioner Program, a teacher education program that is attempting to address some of these questions. In designing our program, we are guided by a set of principles. First, we believe that all teachers, not just ESL and bilingual specialists, must be prepared to teach students of all backgrounds, including the growing number of language minority students (e.g., Olsen, 1991, 1994). Second, we feel that all teachers must make decisions within a pedagogical framework that critically focuses on issues of equity and social justice (Nieto, 2000b). Our commitment to these two principles has been shaped by our experience that most schools and colleges of education fail to prepare teachers to work effectively with students of diverse linguistic and cultural backgrounds (e.g., Ladson-Billings, 1995). It is certainly true that there are a number of high-quality teacher education programs with specializations in bilingual education and English as a Second Language (e.g., González & Darling-Hammond, 1997). However, in teacher education programs without these strands, sustained attention to issues of language and culture is often missing. It seems that too many teacher education programs are still guided by the erroneous assumption that their job is to train teachers to work in "regular" (monolingual English) settings, when in reality all classrooms have, or will soon have, students whose first language is not English.

The master's-level BEM Practitioner Program has been developed to respond to this problem. The four authors of this chapter are the core faculty members in the program, and we have thought long and hard about developing the kind of program that prepares both specialists (i.e., those preparing to work in bilingual and ESL settings) and nonspecialists (i.e., those who plan to work in "mainstream" class-rooms) to be equally capable of teaching language minority and language majority students. In this chapter, we provide a rationale for our program and describe its key components. In addition, to find out how nonspecialists in the BEM program approach their work with language learners, one of us, Meg Gebhard, interviewed a number of current and past BEM teachers because we wanted to hear how the BEM program helped these teachers think about the education of language minority students in their classrooms. We include our analysis of these interviews as a way of reflecting on our efforts to bring a linguistically and culturally responsive focus to the preparation of all teachers in our program.

The Need to Reconceptualize Teacher Preparation

Federal mandates from the late 1960s and early 1970s, partly as a response to community activism, required that schools better serve children of all backgrounds. Many of the mandates were specifically targeted to students of linguistically diverse backgrounds, most of whom had historically been poorly served by U.S. public schools (García, 1995; Minami & Ovando, 1995). At this time, there was also a clear mandate for schools of education to prepare teachers, school personnel, and researchers to take leadership roles in educating students from diverse linguistic and cultural backgrounds. During this period the call for bilingual and ESL education increased (Ovando & Collier, 1998). A decade later, multicultural education also gained increased acceptance in schools of education and opened the door to transforming the assimilationist positions held by mainstream teacher education programs.

In spite of these changes, teacher education programs have not kept pace with the unprecedented demand for teachers who know how to work effectively with students of linguistically and culturally diverse backgrounds. At the dawn of the new millennium, there is still a critical shortage of bilingual and ESL teachers due to many factors. These factors include the combined effects of competing economic conditions, inadequate support for bilingual and foreign language education in the past, the reduced role of the federal government in language minority education, conservative political movements, and numerous legal challenges to bilingual education. Consequently, there is a shortage of specialists in bilingual education precisely at the time of greatest student need (Maxwell-Jolly & Gándara, this volume; Olsen, 1991, 1994). To make matters worse, a recent study conducted by the American Association of Colleges for Teacher Education (AACTE) found that only one-fourth of all teacher education programs in the United States have bilingual and ESL teacher education programs (Yasin, 2000). According to David Imig, president of the AACTE, "The writing is on the wall. [Schools of education] are going to have to accelerate their efforts to keep pace with the changing needs of the student population" (Yasin, 2000, p. 1).

Given the lack of trained ESL and bilingual teachers in the nation's schools, it is now widely acknowledged that these specialists can no longer be the only teachers who are responsible for educating linguistically diverse students. As the population of language minority students grows, as more language minority families move from cities to suburbs and small towns, and as bilingual programs are reduced to transitional and ESL programs, mainstream teachers more than ever will be teaching language minority students. As a result, there is a growing need to prepare all new and practicing teachers to understand what it takes to teach language minority students successfully while respecting the children's linguistic and cultural heritage. This need is keenly felt in Massachusetts, a state that has a growing population of language minority students. The BEM program was designed to respond to this need.

The BEM Practitioner Program

The BEM program is located in the School of Education at the University of Massachusetts Amherst. Western Massachusetts is a predominantly rural area whose patchwork landscape is knitted into mostly towns and small cities. Besides the occasional old textile mill, silo, or paper mill smokestack, the university's buildings form the only high-rises that one can see for miles. The university has a mission to serve the Commonwealth of Massachusetts, a region that as of the 1990 Census had about six million people. Each year, about 18,000 undergraduates and 6,000 graduate students attend the Amherst campus. Many teachers in our program come from the four counties surrounding the campus. We also accept teachers in our program from the other forty-nine states, Puerto Rico, and other countries around the world (e.g., Peru, Korea, Japan, and China).

The BEM Practitioner Program prepares educators to work with culturally and linguistically diverse learners in a variety of instructional settings (e.g., mainstream classrooms, dual language programs, sheltered content classes, and ESL/bilingual team-teaching configurations). Our program resides in the Department of Teacher Education and Curriculum Studies, one of three departments in the School of Education. Annually, more than forty student practitioners, mostly post-bachelor's, are enrolled in Master's of Education or Certificate of Advanced Graduate Studies degree programs. Some may be simultaneously seeking either provisional or professional state certification in early childhood education or in a particular subject matter area. The BEM program introduces both specialists (bilingual and ESL teachers) and nonspecialists to issues of additive bilingualism, second language acquisition theory, and critical multiculturalism. Students in the program do not all take the same set of courses, but we try to incorporate our philosophy in all courses, field placements, and other program activities. Consequently, throughout the program, we hope all teachers will come to understand the following:

- Diversity is a resource, not a problem.
- Elementary and secondary students with previous schooling experiences need more than language instruction to help them meet the challenges of negotiating classroom interactions and expectations in academic subject matter.
- Students do not have to be separated from same-language peers to develop English language skills.
- Parents, other family members, and the community should be involved in the education of their children.
- Teachers must examine their own assumptions regarding students and their families to understand fully how racism and other biases operate within schools.
- Teachers must have high academic standards while simultaneously affirming student diversity.

Specifically, we try to help teachers puzzle through complex issues of equity and excellence, particularly as they relate to language minority students in both mainstream and specialized classes. Although we pay careful attention to issues of pedagogy, we do not focus on pat answers, such as prescribing specific classroom routines or pedagogical techniques as the magic cures to the problems of teaching and learning (Bartolomé, 2000). Rather, we want teachers to see themselves as cultural mediators by taking leadership roles in critically assessing taken-for-granted assumptions about the nature of language, learning, and diversity, particularly as these issues relate to learning English as a world language (Pennycook, 1994, 1998). By doing so, we hope teachers will be able to negotiate differences within their classrooms and school communities as a way of constructing a more democratic, culturally responsive context for student learning.

We believe that our program's approach to preparing educators to work with culturally and linguistically diverse learners is unique in several ways as we strive toward these goals. First, we do not assume that classrooms are monolingual/monocultural places. Rather, we believe that it is to the benefit of all learners, including native English speakers, to develop more than one language. How effectively this occurs depends on a number of factors, including age, opportunities to learn a second language, how well the first language is developed when instruction in the second language begins, the nature of the community in which the program is housed, and the institutional contexts in which teaching and learning take place (Gebhard, 2000; Olsen, 1994; Portes & Rumbaut, 1996). Nevertheless, even in contexts where it may be difficult to develop two languages (e.g., where there is minimal institutional support or encouragement for bilingualism), teachers can learn to base their curricular and instructional decisions on the assumption that bilingualism and biculturalism are worthy goals. For example, rather than focusing simply on ways of teaching English, we encourage teachers to ask, "How do we support and encourage learners who are in the process of 'becoming bilingual' despite practices and attitudes that make it difficult for them to do so?"[1] Similarly, we encourage teachers to think about how schools need to change to accommodate cultural differences, rather than concentrating on how schools can assimilate students who are culturally different.

Second, we do not segregate mainstream teachers (both preservice and in-service) from specialists (ESL, bilingual, and multicultural teachers) and grade-level teachers (early childhood, elementary, secondary, and adult) as other teacher preparation programs often do. Rather, all teachers take classes and have other experiences together to support the formation of sustaining professional communities of practice (Louis & Kruse, 1995; Thiessen, Bascia, & Goodson, 1996) and learn from one another's work in diverse settings by collaborating on common challenges, such as ensuring that the content of their instruction is age appropriate and meaningful to linguistically and culturally diverse learners while supporting second language development. Other challenges include finding ways to organize instruction around powerful learning principles and strategies (e.g., cooperative learning) and adapting curriculum to meet the mandated standards established by regulating state bodies while furthering the goals of social justice.

Finally, our program does not transmit an authoritative body of knowledge that we expect teachers to consume without question. Instead, through the design of individual programs of study and collaborative work in our courses, we aim to provide opportunities for teachers to explore their identities as *transformative intellectuals,* a term coined by Henry Giroux (1988) to describe educators who contribute deliberately and critically to the discourses and practices that constitute schools and society. Giroux contrasts teachers who are transformative intellectuals with educators who take on identities as producers and consumers of dominant discourses and practices.

To give readers a better understanding of our approach to preparing teachers, we describe some practices of the BEM program. Undergirding these practices are three key concepts that are incorporated into the program: a social-justice perspective, a dialogic stance, and a praxis orientation. These concepts are all integral to the process of preparing new educators.

A Social-Justice Perspective

A social-justice perspective is the foundation of the BEM Practitioner Program; it is infused into all program practices, beginning with selecting teachers who will create a vibrant learning community. We select individuals for the program who are committed to social justice and whose strengths and experiences will help our entire community better understand social justice: those who are "border-crossers" (Giroux, 1992; see also Bartolomé, this volume, note 5) and who speak languages and dialects other than standard English; those who have experienced poverty, immigration, culture shock, oppression, and prejudice; those who respect differences and want to work for a better world; and those willing to critically examine their own ideologies and assumptions. We recruit individuals who have shown us in various ways, not always through traditional tests or grades, that they can think critically, gather evidence, analyze complex problems, develop arguments, and articulate the philosophies underpinning their practices.

Naturally, having a diverse community does not automatically result in creating a just community. As Beykont (1997) observes, people who experience oppression in one aspect of their lives do not necessarily understand other kinds of oppression or see beyond their own oppression. A White female teacher may understand gender-based discrimination, for example, but not color-based discrimination (Beykont, 1997). These issues are constantly brought out in our courses and other program activities, resulting in negotiations that are often as difficult as they are necessary. Although we try to create the conditions in which differences of opinion and experience can be hashed out respectfully, we understand that consensus is not always possible or desirable (Willett, Solsken, & Wilson-Keenan, 1998). Nonetheless, we attempt to organize class discussions so that all voices can be heard and learned from.

Another way that we introduce a social-justice perspective into the program is through nurturing the leadership qualities of participants as a way of helping them develop the strength and experiences they need to meet the many challenges they will face in their schools and communities. The primary means of promoting this kind of leadership is through the courses we offer and the pedagogy we use. In many courses, teachers work collaboratively on authentic and practical problems concerning social justice, such as infusing the state-mandated curriculum with an inclusive perspective or drawing on language acquisition theory to articulate the reasons for proposing a new practice to benefit English language learners. These course-based projects later develop into what we call "Leadership Projects," which are vehicles for engaging with issues of diversity and equity in a public forum that extends beyond the university. These projects may be collaborative or individual and are developed in consultation with faculty members. Projects have included making a video about the Latino community for new families, staff, and students in a school; developing a series of workshops about how mainstream teachers can support learners who are becoming bilingual; giving a presentation to a school committee about the problem of using Native Americans as sports mascots; and writing a bilingual handbook for ESL newcomers collaboratively with a school's ESL and mainstream children.

We also support the development of a social justice perspective by helping teachers understand that their profession is inherently political (Freire, 1970). In other words, they need to understand that every educational decision, whether related to pedagogy or policy, is political and that their decisions reflect their values and beliefs about students and students' families. Furthermore, the social-justice perspective carries over into school settings and beyond, as we encourage teachers to ask questions such as, "Is the bilingual program in the basement?" (Nieto, 2000a). When asked, this question forces teachers to think about the location of bilingual and ESL programs on school campuses and how this physical location influences students' access to sociolinguistic and material resources required for an equitable academic education.

A Dialogic Rather Than Monologic Stance

Although our social-justice perspective is explicit, we take a dialogic rather than monologic stance toward our cultural productions (Bakhtin, 1981, 1986); that is, we try to create the conditions in which diverse voices can be heard and provisional ideas and conclusions can emerge from dialogue across our differences. These conditions are created primarily through our efforts to recruit and retain a diverse group of teachers in our program, but diversity alone does not result in understanding. Without critical awareness about one's own cultural beliefs, dialogue too often validates rather than critiques taken-for-granted assumptions. Other practices in the program also encourage dialogue. For example, by putting teachers with varied teaching experiences and professional goals into the same classes (e.g., language specialists and general classroom teachers, preservice and in-service teachers) and not sequencing courses (e.g., so that the content of all courses can become part of the dialogue), we increase the possibility that teachers in our program will see one another as resources. Within these cross-discipline, cross-cultural, multilingual groups, it is possible for us to engage in the hard work of developing a social-justice perspective by confronting our own biases. For example, in the course "Foundations of BEM Education," we encourage and support teachers in exploring and confronting the privileges they have enjoyed as a result of institutional racism and the other biases that exist in our society. In one course assignment, teachers use Peggy McIntosh's (1988) article on White privilege as the model for writing about what it means in concrete terms to have the privilege of being native speakers of English. In other courses, teachers tape, transcribe, and analyze their own collaborative interactions so that they see how easy it is for those who speak, act, or believe differently to become marginalized, even in their own project-based groups.

Dialogue in our courses also occurs around real-life educational problems and tasks that teachers work on in their heterogeneous and collaborative groups. In the process of working through these tasks, the ideologies, identities, and meanings that individuals bring to the group become part of the dialogue. For example, in a course on language analysis, teachers work in groups to analyze the structure and ideology of texts used in actual classrooms. Teachers make predictions about the kinds of difficulties learners might have in using these texts and then design ways to help learners make better sense of written materials. English-language learners in the schools serve as informants regarding their understanding of these texts; when insights from ESL students become part of class discussion, it soon becomes evident that many teachers' assumptions about students do not hold up. This situation helps teachers realize that they must constantly seek input from their students rather than rely solely on either standardized tests or authoritative assumptions about what makes a text difficult for different learners.

A Praxis Orientation

The notion of praxis, inspired by the work of the late Paulo Freire (1970), is another theme that permeates all aspects of the program. Praxis means taking action on the world in order to change it and also critically reflecting on these actions and changes. In a course called "Assessment, Testing, and Evaluation," preservice teachers collaborate with practicing teachers to develop culturally responsive and critically challenging ways to prepare linguistically diverse students for the mandated statewide standardized test. Although taking action in the BEM learning community is one important way to change the world, we also design activities that support how teachers think about and take action outside their classrooms. For instance, a few years ago an elementary teacher at a local school developed a collaborative project with a graduate of the BEM program who taught Cambodian students. The purpose of this project was to address the academic and social problems of many of their Cambodian students. These problems were making it difficult for the students to engage successfully in academic work, and the teachers assumed that if a group of teachers and students worked collaboratively on the problems, school life might become more engaging. More recently, another teacher developed a unit about the Underground Railroad, in which elementary school students demonstrated how they might have supported people attempting to escape from bondage and discussed how these skills could be used today.

Another example of a praxis orientation is evident in a course entitled "Teaching Heterogeneous Classes." This course draws together in-service and preservice teachers from many subject areas and teaching levels so that those who are majoring in ESL, bilingual, and multicultural education interact with the mainstream content teachers they must work with in schools if they are to advocate effectively for their second language learners. Teachers work in teams to design curriculum for heterogeneous classes. A cooperating teacher from a school or agency brings in a particular learning issue that he or she has encountered in a heterogeneous class. The teams explore the issue proposed by their cooperating teachers, often reframing it based on their readings and dialogue, and then design an interdisciplinary curriculum that is more responsive to the learners and reflective of transformative practice. The interdisciplinary curriculum enables all members of the team to contribute their expertise and experience to the curriculum. The kinds of projects teachers have developed in this course in the past include the following:

1. A project for an ESL and Hmong literacy program for adults, funded by a grant and taught by two public school teachers who had Hmong children in their classrooms. Inspired by books written by people in other Hmong communities around the country, the Hmong women and their teachers decided to research and write about traditions and experiences in their local community and produce a bilingual book, for which they would seek a publisher. For the book, the children in the public school classes wrote and illustrated stories that they had heard in the community. The goals of the project were to (a) help the community preserve and pass on their traditions to the younger generation; (b) share their rich culture with people outside the Hmong community; (c) learn about dominant literacy practices; and (d) develop biliteracy skills.

2. An interdisciplinary and problem-based project for a middle school that served a growing Russian immigrant community. The project engaged the middle school students in researching, designing, and proposing a gathering place for teenagers in the community. The team struggled with how to include the Russian students, whose parents wanted them at home studying after school rather than congregating with other teenagers. A goal that emerged as a result of dialogue in the class was how to work with the Russian bilingual teachers more equitably and collaboratively.

3. A project that aimed to work with parents as curriculum partners in a transitional bilingual elementary classroom. The team visited the family of each child in the classroom to brainstorm themes and ideas for helping their children develop biliteracy. The members of the group presented their work at our annual Curriculum Fair and it inspired other teachers, several of whom chose to do something similar for their teacher-research projects the next semester.

4. A curriculum for a new two-way Spanish/English bilingual program at the kindergarten level. The group struggled with issues such as how to handle the enormous power that English and mainstream culture has in schools. This diverse team discovered that some of the same hegemonic notions were operating in very subtle ways in their own curriculum deliberations. This issue surfaced when the group grappled with the theme of their project, "All about Me," a mandated theme for the kindergarten curriculum in the school. The Latino teachers in the class, for example, felt that the theme was too individualistic, preferring instead a community-based perspective that was more congruent with their cultural orientation. As a result, the team first had to understand their classmates' objections to the theme and then figure out how to wed the mandated curriculum theme with a more culturally appropriate perspective.

5. A project centered around "Current Issues," a course in the social studies department of a local high school for "non–college bound" students. Having unpacked widely held assumptions about students who are not college bound, the team's project eventually focused on an issue that emerged in dialogue with the high school students, namely, disciplinary policies and practices that are disrespectful to students. The high school students decided to make suggestions on how to revise the school's student handbook to make it more respectful. The curriculum team helped the high school students formulate writ-

ten and oral arguments that would make sense to the administrators and faculty in ways that would enable the team to incorporate standards from the state's curriculum frameworks. It was not good enough for students to say, "School sucks"; the high school students also needed to put forth the reasons why and how they believed school was unresponsive to their needs and then frame their revisions in a way that the administrators and faculty could take seriously. By doing this, the team helped students develop strategic competence in the dominant discourse while supporting them in their effort to transform the school practices they found oppressive.

A third example of a praxis orientation is a course on policy, in which teachers undertake projects that examine policy issues that may negatively affect a local, national, or international community, and they propose innovative responses to address the problem. One such project included a review of the impact of the Massachusetts teacher certification examinations on candidates with second language backgrounds. Other projects have involved an analysis of policy initiatives concerning indigenous education and dual-immersion programs in China, Mexico, and the United States.

BEM in Action: Teachers' Voices

To provide the reader with a sense of teachers' perspectives of the BEM program, Meg Gebhard, the first author and a new faculty member, interviewed three current and two former BEM students.[2] These interviews were conducted to incorporate the teachers' voices in this chapter and to understand more fully how teachers experience the program's approach to professional development. The perspectives of these five teachers stand in contrast to previous studies on the socialization of teachers in general (Darling-Hammond, 1994; Little, 1990). Lortie's (1975) landmark study, for example, describes how the work of teachers is often compromised by a weak knowledge base, high norms of autonomy, and a sense of profound isolation. In contrast, as the following discussion illustrates, these BEM teachers described their work as intellectual, collegial, and collaborative.

The program graduates who were interviewed included Patty Bode, an art teacher at a local middle school; Beth Wohlleb, a social studies teacher at the same school; and Mary Ginley, a second-grade teacher in a nearby community. The two currently enrolled teachers included Shakira Alvarez Ferrer and Mary Cowhey. Shakira Alvarez Ferrer had previously taught both introductory Spanish and English composition courses at the university level, and Mary Cowhey was coteaching in a mixed first- and second-grade bilingual/mainstream classroom. These teachers did not come into the BEM program seeking certification as either bilingual or ESL specialists.[3] We selected these teachers because we wanted to focus on people working in mainstream monolingual classrooms rather than specialists such as bilingual and ESL teachers who are more likely to have prior experience working across linguistic and cultural boundaries. Moreover, we focused on European American mainstream classroom teachers because they are the vast majority of teachers and the most likely to teach the growing number of language minority students in our nation's schools.

Each teacher was interviewed for about an hour, and the interviews were audiotaped and transcribed. The questions focused on their backgrounds, their expectations of the program, and their experiences in the program. The teachers were also asked to describe the guiding principles that shaped their work and to relate a moment or event when they recognized or witnessed these principles "coming alive" in their classroom practices. In thinking about what these interviews might offer, we expected that they would reveal an orientation that differs from teachers who have studied in more traditional programs, as suggested by the professional development literature (Darling-Hammond, 1994; Little, 1990). However, the level of clarity, sense of purpose, and insights these teachers offered pleasantly surprised us. Specifically, four salient themes emerged. The first of these themes relates to the awareness BEM teachers have of their own biographies, their race, and their class; second, the teachers defined their work in political and ethical terms; third, they described themselves as cultural mediators between students' home worlds and school worlds; and last, they characterized teaching as a collaborative activity conducted in solidarity with others.

Teachers' Biographies and Their Awareness of Race and Social Class in Their Work

The White BEM teachers had a great deal of awareness and were comfortable talking about their race and social class. Mary Ginley, for instance, described her motivation to return to school and pursue a graduate degree in this way: "I'm a White middle-class woman who grew up in a White middle-class neighborhood and went to a White middle-class college. I knew if I was really going to teach today's kids, I had a lot to learn." She gave a concrete example of how teachers often do not even consider how race and social class come into the picture:

> I went to a conference and this teacher said to me, "I don't understand you! What is all this multicultural stuff? Why can't we talk about how we are the same?" And I said to her, "The problem is when we do that, we are talking about how everybody is like us — White, middle-class, and monolingual." I know she didn't get it, but you have to step outside of yourself . . . and it takes a lot of energy to bridge that cultural gap.

Beth Wohlleb gave a specific example of how a "tight group" of Latino boys in the hallway could be a "red flag" for White teachers. She said she had learned to handle this kind of situation by "having an awareness of the racism that White teachers sometimes bring to that situation and to be able to catch yourself and realize that this is an important way for Latino boys to make school their own place." She tried, she said, "to recognize my impulses as a White teacher and to push myself to think deeper about why I make certain kinds of decisions."

Teaching as Political and Ethical Work

In all the interviews, these BEM teachers talked about their work in political and ethical terms. For example, they viewed their roles as teachers in ways that went beyond their classroom and the school and into the community. It was striking how many times these teachers talked about working not just with parents, but with extended families. As such, these teachers constructed the location and object of their work in a broader and less bounded way than teachers who limit their focus to the classroom and the mandated curriculum. Shakira Alvarez Ferrer described her role in this way: "My job as a teacher is to make sure I give everyone a fair shot, that everyone gets to play. Instead of closing doors, I want to open doors and help [students] get through them." Beth Wohlleb explained how she sees her efforts at inclusiveness as an ethical endeavor: "Kids come with a wealth of cultural knowledge that, depending on that culture, will be affirmed or not affirmed by the school, and it is my job to affirm cultures that the school does not. And one way I can do that is to get as much information about students as I can." Mary Cowhey also believed that teaching is political work, and she articulated this commitment in the following way:

> The reasons why I teach, and how the [BEM] program has contributed to how I teach and how I see myself as a teacher, is that for me being a multicultural educator is my contribution to world peace and a more just and peaceful community. And I work with the idea that through my work, if there could be even one child who is less likely to bully and more likely to defend her rights and other people's rights; less likely to follow the crowd and more likely to question the status quo; less likely to exploit and more likely to problem-solve cooperatively; more likely to look at a situation from a variety of perspectives, then I will know I have made a difference. I know from family participation and feedback and home visits that the ripples of what I do go beyond the thirty students I teach to parents and grandparents, and foster parents, and cousins, and siblings, and community people. And for me, that's why I do this.

It was clear from the interviews that these BEM teachers thought of themselves as activists. Patty Bode was inspired by an "anti-racist, anti-bias vigor." According to Patty, "Putting the social action in the forefront is what it's all about." In many cases, the teachers spoke about their out-of-school work with families and with the community at large. Patty noted that social action "unfolds" through the relationships teachers form with students and their families. Besides viewing families and students as allies, some of the teachers spoke of colleagues as political allies. Mary Cowhey, for instance, praised her coteachers and spoke about their collaboration and its contribution to her development. This was significant for her because collaborative work was something she had not done much before coming to the BEM program, in which collaboration is one of the key components. Thus, most teachers also talked about influencing other teachers' practices, school practices, and community practices. Patty Bode, for example, spoke at length about the importance of teachers in promoting whole-school change. She described two schoolwide projects centering on the education of Latino and Asian students. In both cases, teachers and families worked together to help teachers become more aware of and responsive to linguistic and cultural issues that students were facing. She spoke of the resistance that some teachers might display when asked to discuss these issues, but she concluded, "I think most teachers recognize that they need help with ESL students."

Teaching as Sociocultural Mediation

Interviews revealed that these BEM teachers thought of themselves as sociocultural mediators. They felt strongly that all teachers, regardless of whom they teach, needed to be mediators between schools and communities (Valdés, 1996). Mary Ginley, although currently teaching in a White middle- and upper-class community, had for many years taught primarily Puerto Rican Spanish-speaking children in an impoverished small city. Mary believed that the attitudes she developed there had made her a better teacher of all students. She insisted that

> all teachers need to go through some kind of multicultural education or SLA [second language acquisition] training because to try to teach without it will make you ineffective. I mean, I was a good teacher, but so much was missing. I don't think I looked through their eyes. Looking through the eyes of a seven-year-old when you're fifty-two is hard enough, but to look through the eyes of a child from an entirely different culture, who speaks an entirely different language . . . you are not going to get anywhere.

She added, "Our responsibility is to meet them where they are and take them someplace else, and have them carry who they are along with them." She gave the example of Pedro, a Puerto Rican child she had taught. She had known him from teaming with the bilingual teacher and she described him as "a leader," "animated," "alive," and "very competent." But the following year, when Pedro was placed in her monolingual class, he became a different person. He was quiet, withdrawn, and had few friends. Mary Cowhey described how she experienced a turning point with him when she brought in a children's book about a family returning to Puerto Rico. She described how, in the context of the lesson surrounding the book, "he became the expert."

Another example comes from conversations with Mary Cowhey. Mary had taken more courses in second language acquisition theory and was very knowledgeable about language issues. She spoke about "not stepping on other people's language" as she described an experience during her first year of teaching. In that class, she had a native

English speaker she described as being "very impulsive" and as always "jumping in and cutting other students off." She said, "If there was a second of silence, he would fill it." In the same class, a Puerto Rican student would raise her hand to answer, but she needed time to get her thoughts together. The native English-speaking boy would immediately interrupt her. After speaking about the situation with her students, the class took action:

> The kids generated this rule that "you can't step on someone else's words" because it messes up what they are trying to say. You really have to give them the time, the space, and the quiet so they get their idea out.

Shakira Alvarez Ferrer also spoke about the role of teachers as cultural mediators between students' home worlds and school worlds and her work with parents in helping them understand how U.S. schools work. She was emphatic about helping parents understand "the system" while pushing school personnel to explore their biases surrounding immigrant parents because she felt this kind of negotiation could not be the parents' responsibility alone. She explained, "It isn't that parents don't care or work hard, but they didn't have the knowledge of the school to provide the experiences other kids take for granted their whole life."

In another example of cultural mediation, Patty Bode described two extensive projects, including teacher workshops and all-school cultural events, in which the education of Latino and Asian (Japanese, Chinese, Taiwanese, Indian, and others) students was the focus. She explained that the real change came afterward, especially for the families:

> The families didn't want to stop having meetings, didn't want to stop coming to school. So we started having monthly meetings to talk about their kids' education. Many families wanted to be involved in the school day, reading stories, participating in art projects, and those kinds of things. And many of those relationships are still going on.

Teaching as Collaborative and Intellectual Activity in Solidarity with Others

Throughout the interviews, the BEM teachers talked about the central place of group work in the BEM program. They described how at first this aspect of the BEM program was sometimes frustrating. Mary Cowhey, for example, said that initially "all this group work was driving me nuts!" She explained that at her previous college she and her classmates had been taught about group work, but in the end, their individual work was evaluated and graded by individual professors with no feedback from other students. As time went on, however, Mary began to appreciate the importance of collaborative work:

> The thing that I came to understand from my experience at UMass and from my own classroom as a teacher was that for all the lip service paid to collaboration, the majority of elementary schoolteachers go into their individual classroom and shut their door and do their own thing. So we're telling students to collaborate, but we provide no model for what collaboration looks like.

In fact, Mary Cowhey maintained that her experience with constant collaboration in the BEM program provided the impetus for creating the collaborative, multi-age, team-teaching model her school uses to integrate bilingual/ESL students and native speakers of English in the same class, a model that had not previously existed. In commenting on a draft of this chapter, Mary wrote, "Even with my co-teachers who[m] I love, collaboration is never perfect. We all have different strengths, weaknesses, experiences, and perspectives. We push, pull, and negotiate all the time. Our collaborative work can often be messy, uneven, and somewhat aggravating, but our collective product is so much greater than what any one of us could accomplish alone."

In terms of using group work with children learning English as a second language, Mary explained, "Second language learners can get some airtime. In groups, they have the time to listen, to try out what they want to say, and to practice using new vocabulary." She gave a specific example of an inquiry-based science unit she did with her first and second graders. This project centered on students investigating several variables that might influence the motion of a pendulum (the weight of the bob, the length of the string, the height of the drop, and the color of the string). She related the story of Carlos, a second language learner who presented his group's findings at their Pendulum Exhibition; he was able to make an articulate presentation to the class (including the visiting superintendent) about his hypothesis concerning the pendulum. In his presentation, he used scientific words such as *prediction* and *variable* because he had been using these words and struggling with these concepts all week with his teammates. Mary

Cowhey's conclusion about group work was that "it is painful and glorious, but in the end there is a lot of learning that goes on in groups even when it is messy and painful and seems to be going nowhere."

Patty Bode also mentioned the impact of the group work on her thinking as a teacher. In the curriculum course she took, for example, Patty remembered everybody who had been in her group, the curriculum project each person developed, and how the projects unfolded over the course of the semester, based on the constant feedback she and others received from their groups. Beth Wohlleb also discussed the benefits of cooperative learning, which she described as central to her teaching. She had first learned about structuring group work in the BEM program, and she thought it was particularly helpful when working with learners of various strengths and abilities. Beth explained, "I think when you have kids with different skills, like a second language learner who has a lot of knowledge but may not be as adept at writing it out, in a group they can share what they know without getting bogged down." She gave the example of a student who was able to get more done in a group when the task was shared because, although he had the information, he had trouble with the writing. If she had relied on the individual worksheets he was handing in, he probably would not have passed social studies, even though he understood the content. Having the knowledge of second language issues and the ability to structure group work was an advantage to her and to her students.

For all the BEM teachers, having classes in which they interacted with widely diverse groups of graduate students was a bonus, but it could be frustrating at times. Specifically, they spoke about the value of working with other graduate students who were themselves language learners from diverse cultural backgrounds. But the diversity in BEM classes is not only cultural and linguistic. There is also diversity in terms of discipline knowledge and professional goals. This diversity was disquieting at times because it meant that teachers needed to accept a multiplicity of viewpoints with which they might not be familiar. Many teachers mentioned, however, that these experiences increased their comfort level with being an outsider, a position some had never occupied.

Beth Wohlleb also discussed how important it was to have allies who had been through the BEM program. At her first school, she looked around in vain for other teachers who shared her convictions and experiences. She explained, "It kind of felt like I had all these

things in my head, but in terms of having models, it was really hard."
Fortunately, she found Patty Bode at her next school, and now they
collaborate on numerous projects. For both of them, having someone
else who went through the program is affirming of the work they do.

Most of the teachers interviewed discussed the theory-practice
connection, which is a major characteristic of the BEM program. This
connection becomes even stronger when teachers learn to work collaboratively. Shakira Alvarez Ferrer, for example, explained that one of
the reasons she applied to the BEM program was the way it combined
an emphasis on research and theory with the "practitioner side of it."
This side of the program becomes more evident when teachers are involved in collaborative projects that engage them in both philosophical debates and concrete activities. Shakira maintained that a lot of
other programs she had looked at had the academic rigor she was seeking, but they did not focus on the preparation of teachers. She said:

> On the flip side, there were a lot of programs that were training
> teachers but weren't framing their work in a larger social or politi-
> cal way. So I was left with the idea that I can go to night school
> for six months and get an ESL certificate and not be any further
> along in my thinking, or I could sit in a classroom for two years
> and not ever actually see any kids, or I could come to UMass.

Finally, and also as a direct result of their collaborative inquiry,
the BEM teachers talked in ways that elevated the status of the profession of teaching in a manner that ran counter to the usual discourses
surrounding teachers' work and school change. These discourses are
ones that often position teachers as "the problem," as "anti-
intellectuals," or as "foot-draggers" in the process of school reform. In
contrast to this perspective, these teachers described themselves as reflective practitioners with extensive knowledge of how best to connect
theory and practice as they work toward an agenda that focuses on equity in education.

Conclusion: A Program in Progress

As we read and discussed the interviews, we became aware of a number
of tensions or contradictions between what we as faculty members in
the BEM program view as major principles and goals of the program
and some of the ways the teachers described their experiences. Because

we view our program as a work in progress, we welcomed the opportunity to look more critically at our work through the teacher interviews.

One issue that surfaced in the interviews immediately was the weak connection between the BEM program's articulation of the link between language and culture and the teachers' understanding of that link. That is, the teachers spoke eloquently about multicultural issues, but they spoke less specifically about the role of language practices within multicultural education. The exceptions were the teachers who had taken a good number of courses in bilingual and ESL education. Because most of the teachers interviewed had focused on multicultural education in their academic work, however, their course work was heavily concentrated in this area. Although all our courses address aspects of language and culture, the interviews made it clear to us that we must work more purposefully at making our understanding of language as a social practice more visible, tangible, and concrete for teachers (Fairclough, 1989, 1992; Gee, 1996).

A second issue is a structural one, namely, we have deliberately never had a list of required core courses; instead, we have encouraged teachers to think about their own academic and professional goals and what courses they need to take to reach these goals. We suggest that they take courses not just in our program, but also in other programs in the School of Education and in other departments in the university. Maintaining this flexibility is important to us because of the way we envision the program. At the same time, it has become increasingly clear that common courses and other experiences are necessary if graduates are to develop a broader and deeper understanding of issues connecting language, culture, and social justice. As a result of this thinking, we have begun to redesign courses so they better reflect our understanding of the connections between these fundamental components of our program. Moreover, we now have one course that all BEM students are required to take ("Introduction to BEM Education") to make our understanding of the connection between language, culture, and social justice in multicultural education explicit. This new title makes it clear to teachers that regardless of their eventual teaching context, they all need to give time and attention in their studies to the education of language minority students.

It also became evident through the interviews that we need to work more diligently to help our graduates develop counter-discourses about their work with language minority and other culturally dominated students. This is especially urgent given the growing strength of discourses about standardization and accountability taking hold in schools around the country. These discourses have resulted in the erosion of institutional supports that affirm both student diversity and teacher professionalism. Language minority students are especially vulnerable in this climate of standardization because their language strengths are frequently overlooked in the rush to "pass the test," which is generally in English. Teacher professionalism is challenged by accountability measures that are narrow in scope and punitive in nature. We have thought about a number of ways to address this problem, including helping our graduates develop a political base among themselves in their diverse schools and inviting graduates to speak with those new to the BEM program. However, it is clear to us that one program, no matter how well conceived or implemented, cannot challenge these negative discourses on its own. Coalition building across programs and between organizations is needed to support teachers in their work with linguistically and culturally diverse students.

In spite of the contradictions between the goals and guiding principles of the BEM program and the current context of schools and society, we know we are doing what is needed both morally and substantively to prepare effective and caring teachers of language minority students. No child loses when this is the case. When all teachers become more effective with their language minority students, when they understand the role of their identities and biographies in their teaching, when they describe their work as a political and ethical endeavor, and when they view teaching as collaborative work in solidarity with others, teachers also learn to view all their students, not just language minority students, as having talents and strengths that can help them learn.

Notes

1. "Becoming bilingual" is a phrase the BEM faculty members use to capture the process by which all students can become linguistic and cultural border-crossers (Giroux, 1992).
2. It should be noted that although these interviews were taped, transcribed, and analyzed, they do not constitute a formal study or evaluation of the BEM program.
3. The exception was Mary Cowhey who, although already certified as an elementary schoolteacher, at first thought she might like to work toward her ESL

certification while in the program. She changed her mind, however, and ended up following the noncertification route.

References

Bartolomé, L. I. (2000). Democratizing bilingualism: The role of critical teacher education. In Z. F. Beykont (Ed.), *Lifting every voice: Pedagogy and politics of bilingualism* (pp. 167–186). Cambridge, MA: Harvard Education Publishing Group.

Bakhtin, M. (1981). Discourse and the novel. In M. Holquist (Ed.), *The dialogic imagination: Four essays by M. Bakhtin* (pp. 259–422). Austin: University of Texas Press.

Bakhtin, M. (1986). *Speech genres and other late essays.* Austin: University of Texas Press.

Beykont, Z. F. (1997). *Dismantling language-based oppression in schools and youth programs.* Cambridge, MA: MIT Urban Studies and Planning.

Darling-Hammond, L. (1994). Developing professional development schools: Early lessons, challenge, and promise. In L. Darling-Hammond (Ed.), *Professional development schools: Schools for a developing profession* (pp. 1–26). New York: Teachers College Press.

Fairclough, N. (1989). *Language and power.* London: Longman.

Fairclough, N. (1992). *Discourse and social change.* Cambridge, Eng.: Polity Press.

Freire, P. (1970). *Pedagogy of the oppressed.* New York: Seabury Press.

García, E. E. (1995). Educating Mexican American students: Past treatment and recent developments in theory, research, policy, and practice. In J. A. Banks & C. A. M. Banks (Eds.), *Handbook of research on multicultural education* (pp. 372–387). New York: Macmillan.

Gebhard, M. (2000). *SLA and school restructuring: Reconceiving classroom SLA as an institutional phenomenon.* Unpublished doctoral dissertation, University of California, Berkeley.

Gee, J. (1996). *Social linguistics and literacy: Ideology in discourses.* London: Taylor & Francis.

Giroux, H. A. (1988). *Teachers as intellectuals: Toward a critical pedagogy of learning.* Granby, MA: Bergin & Garvey.

Giroux, H. A. (1992). *Border crossings: Cultural workers and the politics of education.* New York: Routledge.

González , J., & Darling-Hammond, L. (1997). *New concepts for new challenges.* McHenry, IL: Center for Applied Linguistics.

Ladson-Billings, G. (1995). Multicultural teacher education: Research, practice, and policy. In J. A. Banks & C. A. M. Banks (Eds.), *Handbook of research on multicultural education* (pp. 747–759). New York: Macmillan.

Little, J. W. (1990). The persistence of privacy: Autonomy and initiative in teachers' professional relations. *Teachers College Record, 91,* 509–536.

Lortie, D. (1975). *School teacher.* Chicago: University of Chicago Press.

Louis, K. S., & Kruse, S. (1995). *Professionalism and community.* Thousand Oaks, CA: Corwin Press.

McIntosh, P. (1988). *White privilege and male privilege: A personal account of coming to see correspondences through work in women's studies* (Working Paper No. 189). Wellesley, MA: Wellesley College Center for Research on Women.

Minami, M., & Ovando, C. J. (1995). Language issues in multicultural contexts. In J. A. Banks & C. A. M. Banks (Eds.), *Handbook of research on multicultural education* (pp. 427–444). New York: Macmillan.

Nieto, S. (2000a). Bringing bilingual education out of the basement, and other imperatives for teacher education. In Z. F. Beykont (Ed.), *Lifting every voice: Pedagogy and politics of bilingualism* (pp. 187–207). Cambridge, MA: Harvard Education Publishing Group.

Nieto, S. (2000b). Placing equity front and center: Some thoughts on transforming teacher education for a new century. *Journal of Teacher Education, 51,* 180–187.

Olsen, L. (1991). *Embracing diversity: Teachers' voices from California classrooms.* San Francisco: California Tomorrow.

Olsen, L. (1994). *The unfinished journey: Restructuring schools in a diverse society.* San Francisco: California Tomorrow.

Ovando, C. J., & Collier, V. P. (1998). *Bilingual and ESL classrooms: Teaching in multicultural contexts* (2nd ed.). New York: McGraw-Hill.

Pennycook, A. (1994). *The cultural politics of English as an international language.* London: Longman.

Pennycook, A. (1998). *English and the discourses of colonialism.* London: Routledge.

Portes, A., & Rumbaut, R. (1996). *Immigrant America.* Berkeley: University of California Press.

Thiessen, D., Bascia, N., & Goodson, I. (1996). *Making a difference about difference: The lives and careers of racial minority immigrant teachers.* Toronto: Garamond Press.

Valdés, G. (1996). *Con respecto: Bridging the distances between culturally diverse families and schools.* New York: Teachers College Press.

Willett, J., Solsken, J., & Wilson-Keenan, J. (1998). The (im)possibilities of constructing multicultural language practices in research and pedagogy. *Linguistics and Education, 10,* 165–218.

Yasin, S. (2000). More attention to language diversity needed in teacher preparation. *Briefs, 21*(11), p. 1. (Newsletter of the AACTE, Washington, DC)

About the Authors

Theresa Austin is Associate Professor in the Teacher Education and Curriculum Studies Department at the University of Massachusetts Amherst. She investigates how non-native languages and literacies are learned through schooling. She has studied bilingual socialization in Paraguay, academic literacies in Japan, and innovative foreign language curricular practices in the United States. Her recent publications include *An Interactive Approach to Content-Based Second Language Learning* (with M. Hall Haley, forthcoming), and "Social Interaction and Language Development in an FLES Classroom" in *The Development of Second and Foreign Language through Classroom Interaction* (with E. Takahashi and Y. Morimoto, edited by J. K. Hall and L. S. Verplaetse, 2000).

Lilia I. Bartolomé is Associate Professor in the Applied Linguistics Graduate Program at the University of Massachusetts Boston. Her research interests center on home/school cross-cultural language and literacy practices, oral and written classroom discourse acquisition patterns of language minority children in U.S. schools, and critical pedagogy. Her recent publications include *Dancing with Bigotry: The Poisoning of Culture* (with D. Macedo, 2000), "Democratizing Bilingualism: The Role of Critical Teacher Education" in *Lifting Every Voice: Pedagogy and Politics of Bilingualism* (edited by Z. F. Beykont, 2000), and *Misteaching of Academic Discourses* (1998).

Berta Rosa Berriz has taught in U.S. urban public schools for twenty years. She is currently a Bilingual Staff Developer in the Boston Public Schools and Adjunct Professor in the Creative Arts and Learning Program at Lesley University in Cambridge, Massachusetts. She is interested in teacher research in urban classrooms, cultural arts and bilingualism, and multicultural and antiracist education. As a teacher researcher, she has examined the role of the arts in the identity and literacy development of children in bilingual settings. She authored "Raising Children's Cultural Voices: Strategies for Developing Literacy in Two Languages" in *Lifting Every Voice: Pedagogy and Politics of Bilingualism* (edited by Z. F. Beykont, 2000).

María Estela Brisk is a Professor at the Lynch School of Education at Boston College. Her research and teaching interests include first and second language and literacy acquisition, literacy methodology, and the preparation of teachers to teach in urban schools. Her most recent books include *Literacy and Bilingualism: A Handbook for ALL Teachers* (with M. Harrington, 2000) and *Bilingual Education: From Compensatory to Quality Schooling* (1998).

Mary Dawson is a Reading Specialist at the James A. Garfield School in the Boston Public Schools. As a Reading Recovery teacher, she works mostly with early elementary grades. Her professional interests include working with bilingual students in large urban school systems, best teaching practices for literacy development in students' first and second languages, and school reform issues.

Audrey A. Friedman is Assistant Professor of Teacher Education at the Lynch School of Education at Boston College. She has also worked as a classroom teacher, researcher, teacher developer, and consultant to public schools. Her areas of professional interest include literacy development in secondary urban schools, teacher education, and reflective practice. She is author of "Using Literature-Based Inquiry to Nurture Reflective Judgment" and "Writing and Evaluation Assessments in the Content Area," both of which appeared in *English Journal* (2000), and "Making It Real" in *For the Love of Literature: Children and Books in the Elementary Classroom* (edited by J. Savage, 1998).

Patricia Gándara is Professor of Education at the University of California, Davis, and Associate Director of the University of California's Linguistic Minority Research Institute. Her current research interests center on equity and access to higher education for linguistic and other minority groups. Her latest publications include *Paving the Way to Postsecondary Education* (2001), *The Dimensions of Time and the Challenge of School Reform* (1999), and *Priming the Pump: Strategies for Increasing the Achievement of Underrepresented Minority Undergraduates* (with J. Maxwell-Jolly, 1999).

Meg Gebhard is Assistant Professor at the University of Massachusetts Amherst. Her research focuses on the development of academic literacies in multilingual/multicultural contexts, the professional development of ESL and bilingual educators, and the impact of school reform on the work of second language teachers and their students. Her publications include "The Construction of Bilingual Educators in the Context of Charter School Legislation" in *Teachers College Record* (forthcoming), and "Debates in SLA Studies: Redefining Classroom SLA as an Institutional Phenomenon" (2000) and "A Case for Professional Development Schools" (1998), both in *TESOL Quarterly*.

Walt Haney is Professor of Education at Boston College and Senior Research Associate in the Center for the Study of Testing, Evaluation, and Educational Policy (CSTEEP). He specializes in educational evaluation and assessment and educational technology. His numerous publications on testing and assessment include *The Myth of the Texas Miracle in Education* (2000) and *Less Truth Than Error? An Independent Study of the Massachusetts Teacher Tests* (with C. Fowler, A. Wheelock, D. Bebell, and N. Malec, 1999).

Millicent Hartgering is a Teacher at Frederick Douglass Charter School in the Boston Public Schools. She has worked in mainstream elementary classrooms and with students from diverse backgrounds. She specializes in reading and literacy. Her present areas of professional interest center on education in urban settings, children's first and second language literacy development, and effective pedagogical practices with second language learners.

Nancy H. Hornberger is Professor of Education and Director of Educational Linguistics at the University of Pennsylvania Graduate School of Education. She specializes in sociolinguistics, language planning, bilingualism, biliteracy, and educational policy and practice for indigenous and immigrant language minorities in the United States and internationally. Her publications include *Continua of Biliteracy: A Framework for Education in Multilingual Settings* (forthcoming), *Research Methods in Language and Education* (coedited with D. Corson, 1998), and *Indigenous Literacies in the Americas: Language Planning from the Bottom Up* (1996).

Elizabeth MacDonald teaches at James A. Garfield School in the Boston Public Schools. She has taught reading in each grade at the elementary level. She serves as a mentor for university student teachers, and her classroom has been a model for innovative teaching practices. Her professional interests include literacy, reading strategy development for low-achieving students, and leadership in urban schools.

Julie Maxwell-Jolly is a doctoral candidate at the University of California, Davis, and Coordinator of the Linguistic Minority Research Institute Policy Center. Her dissertation study focuses on teachers and mandated reform in California. Her other research interests are the preparation of quality teachers for second language learners and the effects of reform on English learners. She is author of "Factors Influencing Implementation of Mandated Policy Change: Proposition 227 in Seven Northern California School Districts" in *Bilingual Research Journal* (2000), and *Priming the Pump: Strategies for Increasing the Achievement of Underrepresented Minority Undergraduates* (with P. Gándara, 1999).

Sonia Nieto is Professor of Education at the University of Massachusetts Amherst in the Language, Literacy, and Culture program. She has been a teacher for thirty-five years, teaching students from elementary grades through graduate school. Her research focuses on multicultural education, the education of Latinos, immigrants, and other culturally and linguistically diverse students, and Puerto Rican children's literature. Her books include *Af-*

firming Diversity: The Sociopolitical Context of Multicultural Education (3rd ed., 2000), Puerto Rican Students in U.S. Schools (2000), and The Light in Their Eyes: Creating Multicultural Learning Communities (1999).

Miren Uriarte is Associate Professor at the Human Services Center of the College of Public and Community Services and Founding Director of the Mauricio Gastón Institute for Latino Community Development and Public Policy, both at the University of Massachusetts Boston. Her research focuses on the impact of public policy on the Latino community and the development of community institutions. Most recently she has studied the impact of high-stakes testing on Massachusetts Latino students. She is the author of *Latino Students and Massachusetts Public Schools* (1998) and coeditor of *Latinos, Poverty and Public Policy in Massachusetts* (with E. Melendez, 1994).

Jerri Willett is Associate Professor at the University of Massachusetts Amherst in the Language, Literacy, and Culture program. Her professional expertise is in second language learning and teaching from a sociocultural perspective. Her research interests center on the construction of multicultural practices in classrooms and communities, and the possibilities and challenges these practices present for learners who are becoming bilingual. Her publications include "Troubling Stories: Valuing Productive Tensions in Collaborating with Families" in *Language Arts* (2001), and "The (Im)possibilities of Constructing Multicultural Language Practices in Research and Pedagogy" in *Linguistics and Education* (1998), both coauthored with J. Solsken and J. Wilson-Keenan.

Lucinda Zehr is a Reading Specialist at Berkowitz Elementary School in the Boston Public Schools, where she works with English language learners in English-only classrooms. She specializes in literacy, special education, and teaching English as a Second Language. Her current professional interest centers on developing the language and literacy skills of diverse students in multilingual classroom settings.

About the Editor

Zeynep F. Beykont works as a researcher and consultant in school, museum, and community-based educational programs serving ethnic and language minority groups in the United States and internationally. Her professional interest centers on identifying language policies and programs that support the cultural, linguistic, and academic development of minority youth. She is co-author of "Against the Assimilationist Tide" in *History Lessons: Transforming Social Relations of Power in the Classroom* (with B. Johnson-Beykont; edited by J. Cummins, D. Dragonas, A. Frangoudaki, and H. Smith, in press), "Inclusiveness in Higher Education" in *Equity and Excellence in Education* (with C. Daiute, 2002), and editor of *Lifting Every Voice: Pedagogy and Politics of Bilingualism* (2000). Her forthcoming book, *Achieving Linguistic Democracy: The Role of Research*, focuses on the role of research in addressing issues of equity, access, and cultural and linguistic democracy in educational institutions.